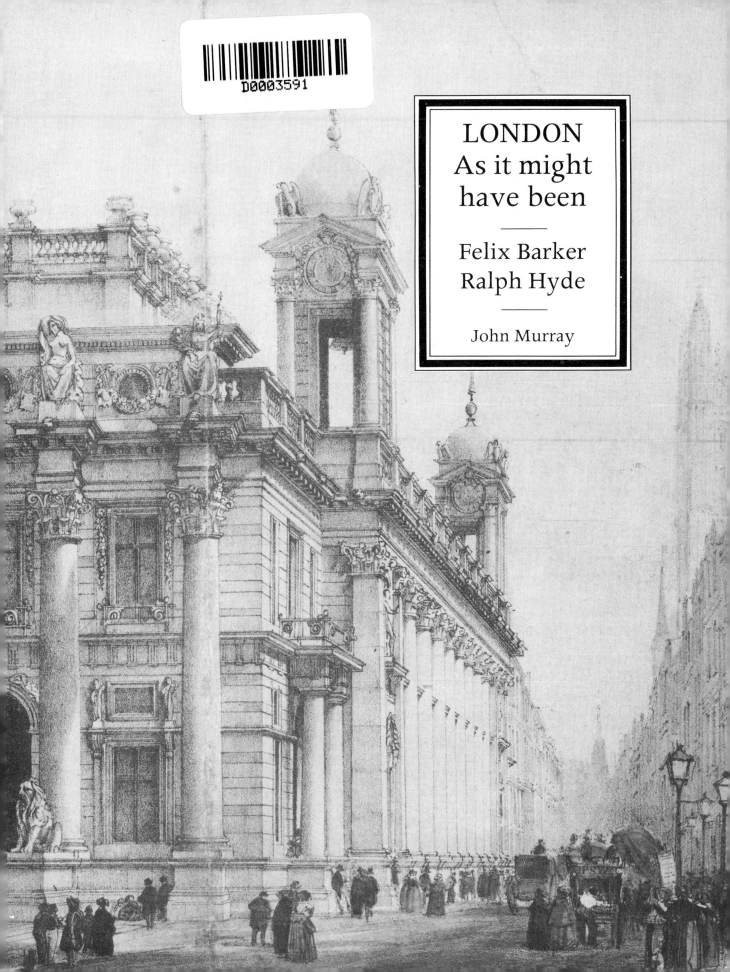

LONDON
As it might have been

Felix Barker
Ralph Hyde

John Murray

© Felix Barker and Ralph Hyde 1982

First published 1982
by John Murray (Publishers) Ltd
50 Albemarle Street, London W1X 4BD

Paperback edition 1984

Printed and bound in Great Britain by
Fletcher & Son Ltd, Norwich

British Library Cataloguing in
Publication Data
Barker, Felix
   London as it might have been
   1. City planning—England—History
   2. London (England)—City planning—History
   I. Title   II. Hyde, Ralph
   711'.4'09421   HT169.G7226

ISBN 0-7195-4131-X

Cover front: Detail of the
proposed Imperial Monumental
Halls & Tower (1904) at Westminster
(courtesy of the British Architectural
Library, RIBA, London)

Cover back: James Clephan's
proposed London Railway (courtesy
of Guildhall Library & Art Gallery)

Title-page: The ornate Graeco-
Roman design for the Royal
Exchange, submitted in
competition by C. R. Cockerell
under an assumed name. (See also
Plate 82)

Contents

Preface

WHERE on earth, we have frequently been asked, did we find all these things? It is hardly a surprising question because there are no clearly defined paths for the researcher in pursuit of what, to invent a word, might be called *inflorescentia*. Unfulfilled projects are inclined to lack chroniclers. On the whole, architectural historians tend to be more concerned with buildings that exist than those that do not.

Our safari into the little-charted jungle of follies and defeated aspirations owes a great deal to guides encountered along the way. No sooner did we tell people about our quest than they offered their own favourite contribution. Privately hoping to confound us, they would triumphantly produce some bizarre plan. 'Could you do with a lunatic asylum for Millbank?' inquired one librarian. 'You know, of course, that Seifert planned a Press Club in the shape of a quill pen,' suggested someone else. The asylum turned out to be a mare's nest, and a number of suggestions led to dead ends. But many others did not, and, faced with a deadline for our book, we have almost come to fear news about further undiscovered schemes.

To cope with this emergency we have kept open as long as possible a miscellaneous chapter, 'The Awkward Squad', into which, creeping under the wire, have been deposited such last-minute items as Adam's spectacular hall for Lincoln's Inn and the mausoleum for Sir Isaac Newton's house off Leicester Square.

Mined as it is with surprises, this is a field of research that can never hope to be definitive. So, as we go to press, we admit we still have to discover whether – as we are assured – there were once plans for a third London airport at Kidbrooke, SE3. Some tantalising drawings of a Radio City in the early 1930s Manhattan style for Hyde Park Corner await further information. As yet we have not been able to find plans for a sumptuous spa town of 1,500 houses on Shooters Hill complete with a lake and central island approached by four bridges. To whet your appetite further, and then snatch yet another tasty morsel from your lips, we have thought it best, awaiting further investigation, to leave out proposals by an Indian artist who wanted to mount cannons all round London to dispel fog and to build an Indian Centre in ornate Mongol style in Long Acre.

This does not mean that we won't welcome further discoveries which we may, perhaps, be able to offer at some future date. In the meanwhile we think we can promise adequate compensations in the pages that follow, and for providing leads, helping us to catch some rare butterflies, and giving us advice we are grateful to many people. Thanks are due to Hilary Evans (Mary Evans Picture Library), Richard Fawkes, John Fleming, Jonathan Gestetner, John Harris (RIBA Drawings Collection), Julia Holland, Malcolm Holmes

(Camden Public Library, Local History Librarian), Julian Hunt (Department of the Environment), Jill Lever (RIBA Drawings Collection), Vivien Mackay (Royal Institution of Chartered Surveyors), Priscilla Metcalf, John Phillips (Curator of Maps and Prints, Greater London Council), Joan Pollard (sometime Curator of Paintings and Drawings, Museum of London), Ian Roxburgh (Greater London Council), June Sampson, Dr Geoffrey Sneed (Science Museum), Margaret Swarbrick (Archivist, Westminster Public Library), Michael Trevallion, Julian Watson and staff (Greenwich Public Library, Local History Collection) and David Webb (Reference Librarian, Bishopsgate Institute).

We extend special thanks to John Fisher who assisted with the London As It Might Have Been exhibition at Guildhall in 1976; to James Stevens Curl for lending death photographs from his own collection; to Colin Dyer for advice on matters Freemasonic; to Dr Terry Friedman for discovering with us a London palace for the Old Pretender; to Michael Port for photographs of Parliamentary might-have-beens; to Mrs Alan R. Warwick for providing the rare picture of Beulah Spa Crescent from her late husband's collection; to Alan Hodgkiss for his plans of Whitehall Palace and railway termini; to Denise Silvester-Carr, whose historical acumen in proof-reading was almost intimidating; and above all to Peter Jackson, who was very closely involved in the early stages of this book, most cleverly concocted the montage of Whitehall Palace, and has lent pictures from his famous collection.

For putting us straight on several tricky points, we are grateful to Sir John Summerson and Miss Dorothy Stroud and their assistant, Miss Scull, at the Sir John Soane's Museum. The many people and organisations that have helped with illustrations are all, we trust, given credit at the end of the book.

Lastly, to Ruth Hyde thanks for limitless forbearance, and to Anthea Barker praise and gratitude for critically reading our manuscript and typing several sections.

FELIX BARKER   RALPH HYDE
Lindsey House, Blackheath   *Point Hill, Greenwich*

Chapter 1

Phantom Plans of the Past

DISCARDED designs and rejected plans lurk like unhappy ghosts behind every important building in London. Our streets are lined with unfulfilled good intentions. They are paved with the broken hearts of disappointed architects. Men of vision have been subject to arbitrary decisions, their schemes condemned because of suddenly veering changes of taste. Great schemes have frequently been obstructed by bureaucrats and unimaginative businessmen, with the result that we have been fobbed off with the dull and the stolid.

Also, of course, London has been spared a great deal of rubbish. Many nightmares have faded mercifully before they turned into daylight realities. Sometimes it has been a very good thing that money ran out, or some slightly unhinged genius died before he created a New Jerusalem that would have turned out a bargain-basement Babylon.

We may scorn those dusty councils that have pigeon-holed so many brave schemes; but who can doubt that they have also spared us many monstrosities? At least our skyline is not disfigured by colossal statues. A giant Britannia does not stare imperiously over London from the heights of Greenwich Park; Sir Robert Peel does not rise from the middle of the Thames at Vauxhall; nor does a French sculptor's 70-ft image of Shakespeare look down from the top of Primrose Hill. Pyramids destined for Trafalgar Square and Shooters Hill have been sent about their business. Piccadilly Circus has managed somehow to escape persistent attempts to turn it into a multi-level fairground. A Crystal Tower Bridge, an Eiffel Tower at Wembley and a Roman Colosseum at the top of Whitehall are among the follies that have enjoyed brief giddy moments of acclaim and then, having strutted their hour, are heard no more.

From public archives, private drawers and the Royal Library at Windsor we have unearthed plans for London conceived during the last four centuries. Among them are prodigious palaces and pleasure-domes, such as one wistfully studied by Charles I in prison, and another optimistically envisaged for Hyde Park by the Old Pretender while in Italian exile. Our reeling senses have had to cope with a planner so intent on rivalling Haussmann in Paris that he would have destroyed parts of fashionable and business London to create a monumental avenue from St Paul's to Hyde Park. We have been asked to travel on overhead railways and along underground streets. The London that might have been is nothing if not varied.

Sometimes, things were never built because they were never meant to be taken seriously. They were academic exercises or *capriccios* conjured by artists out of their imaginations in what one of them called 'the gay morning

1 Colonel Sir Frederick William Trench, MP, London's most persistent and eccentric amateur planner. He is portrayed working on the panorama for his 1824 Thames Quay and is surrounded by some of his other varied schemes. The bust overseeing his endeavours is almost certainly that of his patroness, the Duchess of Rutland

of youth'. In more leisurely times, and especially during the Regency and early Victorian period, these vaunting ideas were sometimes conceived by men with private means who had tame architects in tow. Some were dilettantes of taste; others not. Scattered through these pages you will find frequent references to one of these ardent amateurs, the egregious Colonel Sir Frederick William Trench, MP, (Plate 1) whom we are in danger of making an Aunt Sally. It is hard to keep a straight face (and to be truthful we have not tried very hard) when chronicling the follies of this persistent meddler.

But fantasies are the icing on the cake, finial pineapples piled on storeyed urns. They amuse, but we have to be careful that they do not obscure many sound ideas by architects genuinely dedicated to the improvement of London. Sometimes there is a touch of fanaticism about them, and none the worse for that. There is a strong case for taking their might-have-beens very seriously indeed.

Especially in the last century, when so much building was going on, and architects saw themselves as men with a divine mission, many rejected plans have a profound interest. In the Battle of the Styles — the great Victorian conflict between Classic and Gothic — choice sometimes seems very arbitrary. The wind of change in public taste would have had to alter very little, it seems, for London today to have a Classic Houses of Parliament and a Classic Law Courts. In a different context what is one to make of the puritanical idea that a building should be rejected because a design was 'dangerously artistic' or 'seductively ornamental'? Can we accept the mystical Victorian assumption that there was something 'essentially English' about Gothic? Architectural historians would enjoy a field-day if they were to study the reasons buildings were not built instead of why they were.

Inevitably there have been moments when the chronicling of so many unrealised schemes has been dispiriting. All very negative, we felt; but then we began to learn that the rejection of designs was not always wasted effort. Elements in them were often incorporated in later buildings which did materialise. The legendary theory that Gilbert Scott's rejected Foreign Office died, only to be reborn as the hotel of St Pancras Station should not be entirely ruled out, as we show. It is only natural for an architect to be reluctant to abandon a good idea. In time a plan might be adopted or adapted by an assistant or influence a research student.

A kind of immortality might be ensured by competitions even though at the time they seemed the graveyard of so much enterprise. Unsuccessful entrants sometimes published their plans privately. They also arranged for them to be publicly exhibited. In professional magazines designs were reproduced and critically discussed. Though they were never actually built, they could carry as much weight as the winning plans, sometimes even more.

Disinterring many of those long-lost, almost totally forgotten plans has been one of our main concerns in this book. They are the serious phantoms of the past which have a fascination, if not the amusement value, of the freaks and follies. They may, we hope, help people to decide if we are better off with the city we have or London as it might have been.

Chapter 2

Whitehall Pleasure-Domes

MEDIEVAL architects were responsible for some magnificent work, but seem to have done a thorough job in destroying their preliminary plans. Few records survive of buildings before the middle of the 16th century, and no unfulfilled ones that we have been able to trace. Yet obviously there must have been thousands of discarded schemes and rejected proposals to reach such perfection.

Where are the sketches that Gundulph, Bishop of Rochester, made in consultation with William of Normandy as they planned the Tower of London? It is hard to believe that so complex a building, incorporating a royal palace, chapel and stronghold all in the White Tower, could have come about without trial and error. What happened to all the drawings which Henry de Reyns, French masterbuilder from Rheims, used during the three years he and Henry III discussed decorative variations for Westminster Abbey? One hundred feet taller than any other English ecclesiastical building, it would surely have required many experimental designs.

So prodigious a builder of palaces as Henry VIII must have called for innumerable plans from his surveyors, but tentative proposals are not to be found among the records of the Office of the King's Works. The one sketchbook of a Tudor surveyor, as architects were then called, is by John Thorpe who designed a number of houses after 1570 for rich patrons. Some were planned for Kensington, and a few were whimsically laid out in the shape of the patron's initials, but whether they were actually built or not we do not know.

In Tudor times Whitehall Palace, which Cardinal Wolsey surrendered to Henry VIII, was constantly changing. In the Ashmolean Museum at Oxford there is a drawing by Antony van den Wyngaerde showing a highly elaborate version of the Privy Stairs. This design does not feature in the Flemish artist's London panorama, or any other contemporary view, and it is just possible that Wyngaerde made a prophetic sketch of a design which Queen Elizabeth decided not to carry out.

Sadly we are missing any visual evidence at all for another Tudor suggestion. When the *Golden Hind* returned from her journey round the world in 1580, the Queen was anxious that Drake's ship should be preserved as a memorial 'to all posterity'. The historian Holinshed put on record one way this might have been achieved. Why not re-erect 'the brittle bark' on the tower of St Paul's in place of the spire destroyed by lightning twenty years before? 'A knight of good account and rarely qualified' suggested this would greatly improve the unsightly stump and 'being discerned far and near might be noted and pointed at by people with these true terms: Yonder is the bark that hath sailed round the world'.

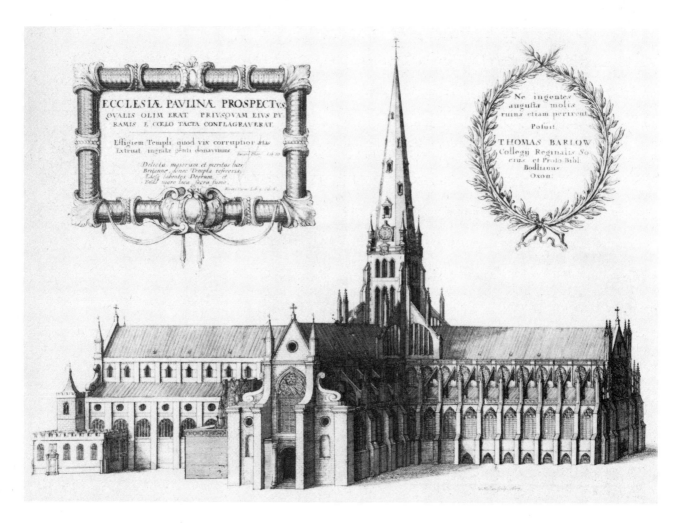

ECCLESIÆ PAVLINÆ PROSPECTvs
QVALIS OLIM ERAT PRIVSQVAM EIVS PY
RAMIS E CŒLO TACTA CONFLAGRAVERAT

Effigiem Templi quod vix corruptior ætas
Extruit ingratæ genti donavimus *Daniel Plin. Lib 10*

Delicta majorum et meritus luce
Britanne, donec Templa refeceris,
Ædesq labentes Deorum et
Fœdi nigro luce sacra fumo. Horat Carm Lib 3 od. 6.

Ne ingentes
angustæ molis
ruina etiam perirent
Posuit
THOMAS BARLOW
Collegy Reginalis So
cius et Proto Bibl.
Bodlianus
Oxon

2 *Spire and clock for old St Paul's, engraved by W. Hollar (1657)*

A more practical idea for the improvement of the cathedral was put forward early in the next century. The octagonal steeple, with a clock to the south and a number of small ornamental windows, was never executed, but appears in an engraving by Wenceslaus Hollar dedicated to the Bishop of London (Plate 2).

From the beginning of the 17th century London started to experiment far more imaginatively with architectural ideas. Detailed plans were prepared for a variety of buildings, and fortunately some of the rejected drawings are preserved. Among them are designs by Inigo Jones (Plate 3), disciple of Palladio and passionate purveyor of Italian ideas. Son of a Smithfield clothworker, and perhaps a carpenter as a young man, Jones became an artist, and until he was nearly forty was content to dazzle the Stuart Court with designs for theatrical masques. A preoccupation with buildings only followed his appointment as Surveyor to James I in 1615. He had, however, made two interesting drawings seven years earlier for buildings neither of which materialised.

The first of Inigo Jones's proposals was for the New Exchange in the Strand; the other an idea for the restoration of the main tower for St Paul's.

Prototype of the modern department store, the New Exchange was conceived by Jones as a long two-storeyed building (Plate 4). Drawn in line and with delicately applied colour, the elevation shows three towers, the central one with statues at the base of what looks like a vast candelabra. Superbly theatrical, this would have been ideal as the decorative backcloth for a masque, but Jones's patron, the Earl of Salisbury, preferred something more modest, and settled for a lower arcade and no towers. Jones's new finial for St Paul's came in the same year, 1608. Admittedly less eccentric than the *Golden Hind* sailing over London, Jones's solution was still strange for a 13th-century tower. He created a cut-out fairy-castle effect with an octagonal onion-shaped dome on the summit of which was a conical spire (Plate 5).

3 Inigo Jones (1573–1652) – Van Dyck's original drawing

4 Design for the New Exchange in the Strand by Inigo Jones (c. 1608)

5 Inigo Jones's design for the completion of the central tower, old St Paul's (c. 1608)

A visit to Italy – his second – gave Jones a chance for further study of Palladio and equipped him for his position as Surveyor-General. In 1617, two years after his appointment, he produced a far more sober, mature design for a new Court of Star Chamber. The building in Westminster Palace that housed the court was falling into disrepair, and Jones's elegant little classical building, though never built, was later to be incorporated into proposals for a royal palace (see Plate 6).

Inigo Jones's two most famous buildings, the Queen's House, Greenwich (1617) and the Banqueting House in Whitehall (started 1619) were preparations for his most spectacular scheme – a vast and stately pleasure-dome for Charles I which, had it ever been built, would have completely transformed the face of London.

In 1638, thirteen years after his accession, Charles I became greatly concerned with the idea for a new palace. He wanted to build Whitehall 'new again in a more uniform sort': so the gossip went round the town. On the scale he was envisaging, the palace would cost a fortune, but money did not seem to be a serious problem to the King in his determination to challenge the splendour of anything on the Continent. A 'very ample sum of *Money*' was available (a report went) 'toward erecting of a *Royal Palace* in his *Majesties* Court in Saint James's Park according to a *Model* drawn by *Inigo Jones* his excellent Architectour. . . .'

This was the start of a grand plan, an eternal mirage, which was constantly to fascinate the King, and was to be taken up with similar enthusiasm after the Restoration by Charles II. During the next twenty-five years ever-changing proposals inspired at least seventy drawings. They show plans spreading over vast sites, and elevations each more magnificent than the last. Endless sketches of statuary and decorative detail were prepared in the quest for an elusive ideal.

With some difficulty the considerable collection of designs can be grouped into six main schemes, and to avoid being choked by the indigestible mass of material we shall restrict ourselves to the four most important. Even so, it is no good pretending that it is easy to find the way through labyrinths which, though fascinating, are extremely complex. Four ground-plans (see p. 16) should, however, be a help.

Charles I inherited a palace at Whitehall which resembled a small town, and it was to give some dignity and form to this maze of courtyards and twisting alleyways that he invited suggestions for a new and splendid palace overlooking the Thames. The year 1638 seems, at first, a strange time in his reign to be thinking of such a building. Far from being a period of prosperous stability, this was when the King was feeling the mounting tide of opposition that was to lead to his ultimate downfall. But perhaps he saw a great palace as a reassuring symbol of survival. The divine right of kings could hardly have been more arrogantly displayed than in Inigo Jones's earliest plan of 1638 (Plate 6) for a massive rectangular edifice with a frontage of 874 ft along the Thames – about the length of the present Houses of Parliament. It went back westwards 1,152 ft into St James's Park, and just how large it would have been can be judged from our plan (Plate 7, Plan A). We must imagine modern Horse Guards Parade completely enveloped and the south-western tower of the palace on the edge of the present lake. The north-western tower would have reached the Mall just short of Duke of York's steps.

The northern wall would have passed just south of Admiralty Arch, through the Whitehall Theatre and reached its north-eastern tower where Great Scotland Yard joins Northumberland Avenue. The river-front façade, running east and parallel with Whitehall, encompasses the greater part of the area occupied by the block of modern Government offices.

The old Tudor sprawl was disciplined into a symmetrically proportioned classical building with a large square central courtyard surrounded by ten other courts. A main entrance was on the river and through another the visitor passed into an open circular courtyard and so through the Great Hall into the Grand Court. Here, on the left, was the Council Chamber which so closely resembled Jones's abandoned Star Chamber that it is clear that he was determined not to waste a good piece of design. On the far (west) side of the Grand Court was the Royal Chapel, domed and cruciform in shape. Immediately behind the Chapel were the Royal Apartments, each with its separate court, facing out onto the park. While the main formal approach at

the front of the palace was by water (Plate 8), at the back the gateway was for coaches. Coming in from St James's Park visitors passed through a highly ornamented entrance with male and female statues in place of columns. The Royal Apartments were set behind a delicate façade in contrast to the severe monumental appearance of the Palace from the Thames.

In 1638 when Jones was perfecting his plans there was no parallel to this building in England. Charles I would have been provided with a palace through which he could walk more proudly than Philip IV in the Escorial outside Madrid, which was only half the size. He could have outmatched Louis XIV with a Grand Courtyard twice the dimensions of the Cour du Louvre. The circular vestibule could be compared with the Roman baths built for the Emperor Caracalla.

Why, then, was the grand design never realised? The morally dismissive 18th-century explanation that it could not be put into execution because of 'ye iniquity of ye Time' is hardly satisfactory. One practical difficulty was Whitehall – that is the thoroughfare. The proposed palace lay directly in the

6 The Royal Palace, designed by Inigo Jones in 1638, as it would look in the middle of modern Whitehall. The exact position is fixed by Jones's Banqueting House (marked by arrow) in the south-east side of the central courtyard. This montage, which imposes Fourdrinier's engraving (1727) on an aerial photo, slightly falsifies the perspective and proportions; Northumberland Avenue would not be encroached on (see map, p. 16). Modern details include Nelson's Column, Admiralty Arch and Cockspur Street in the foreground; in the distance, the Houses of Parliament, Westminster Bridge and County Hall

15

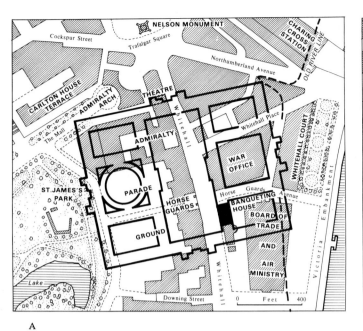

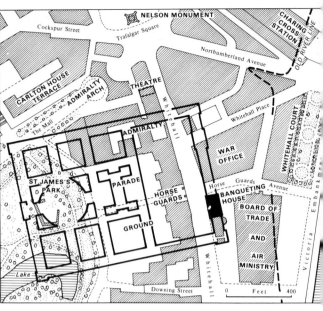

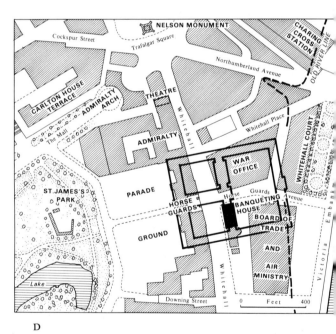

7 *The four main plans for Whitehall Palace imposed on a modern map: (A) c. 1638; (B) 1647/8; (C) 1661; (D) 1665. The Banqueting House remains the constant feature of all the designs*

line of the main street from Charing Cross to Westminster. The street, if not diverted, would have run north to south straight through the Grand Courtyard, a problem which had only been indifferently solved in Tudor times by a connecting palace passageway over the Holbein Gate.

This difficulty may well have influenced Jones or John Webb when a second plan for Whitehall Palace was submitted by one of them – more probably it was Webb – in about 1647 (Plate 7 Plan B). Webb was a pupil of Jones, related to him by birth and marriage, and their collaboration was so close that distinguishing between their work is sometimes difficult. This second design was for a building of about the same size, but it took in more of St James's Park because it was set back roughly 300 yds from the river. This would still impede the traffic in Whitehall, but instead of a complete barrier it would be possible to re-align the street to pass between palace and river.

In this second scheme the inside of the palace is considerably changed. The visitor entered (presumably from the new riverside road, though this is not shown on the plan) straight into a large forecourt. The mass of domestic and state apartments grouped round the circular vestibule were confined to the west of the palace overlooking the park. An inscription on this plan by Webb says it was 'taken' (i.e. accepted) by the King, and this is particularly interesting when we remember the date – 1647. By this year the Civil War was lost to the Roundheads and Charles I was a prisoner. But so invincible was his self-confidence that even in captivity he was thinking about a new palace. Webb, a loyal Royalist, was summoned to show him re-sited and redesigned schemes while he was confined at Hampton Court and Carisbrooke Castle.

The King's execution brought a halt to plans which lasted through the Interregnum. But they were quickly revived after the Restoration. As Jones's former deputy, Webb was the obvious man to carry on the work. Following in the tradition of his master, he brought the same style to the new designs. Only the scale was changed.

Charles II was granted an income of £1,200,000 by the country, so there would seem to have been ample money available. Even so, Webb's 1661 proposals (see Plate 7 Plan C) were far more modest than those of the previous reign. The size was reduced by about a third.

Like the plan accepted by Charles I, the Restoration palace was set back from the river to allow a road to the east. But the building was entirely reoriented. Instead of being sited on an east–west axis, the main entrance faced north towards Charing Cross. An impressive turreted gateway led into a columned courtyard. The Royal Apartments were now on the south overlooking the Privy Gardens.

This was an altogether practical and pleasant scheme, but evidently Charles II had his own ideas. John Evelyn described how in 1663 he was in the Privy Gallery at Whitehall when the King told him to follow him to one of the windows and asked him for a sheet of paper and crayon. 'I presented him with both,' says Evelyn, 'and then laying it on the window-stool he with his own hands design'd to me the plot for the future building of White-hall, together with the rooms of state and other particulars.'

8 *Charles I's Whitehall Palace as it would have looked from the garden terrace of old Somerset House. This little-known mid-18th-century view, preserved in the Royal Library at Windsor, is the visionary concept of the topographical artist, Thomas Sandby (1721–98). The ghostly figures in the unfinished foreground are probably by his brother, Paul Sandby (1725–1809)*

The diarist was impressed by the King who, he said, 'had an extraordinary talent becoming a magnificent prince'; but he does not specify the design. It may have been a freehand variation on Webb's 1661 plan or on the lines of an even smaller palace the architect prepared some time before 1665 (see Plate 7 Plan D). With a 564-ft river-frontage and a depth of 695 ft (just straddling Whitehall), this version consisted of a main rectangular courtyard on the riverside and two square courtyards for the Royal Apartments to the west.

Nothing came of this fourth scheme. Apart from the street difficulty and the cost, there was the question of uprooting courtiers and officials, to say nothing of mistresses, in the 2,000 rooms of the existing sprawl. There must also have been the vexed problem of how to integrate the Banqueting House with any surrounding and adjoining buildings. With its perfect proportions, delicate detail and Rubens ceiling, Inigo Jones's building was a gem that shone brilliantly on its own. To make it part of another complex would be very difficult.

So successful is the Banqueting House that it is quite a shock to find in the architect's sketchbook that originally he had different ideas for the façade. A 1619 drawing shows that we might have had a building in Whitehall with a triangular pediment over the three central bays and two sculptural figures supporting a central medallion. The pediment and other features resemble those in his shelved, smaller Star Chamber of two years before.

It seems quite possible that even when he was first designing the Banqueting House Jones had in mind that one day it would be part of a greater whole. It features in practically every suggested palace scheme. In an alternative version of the 1638 plan (not shown here) the Banqueting House

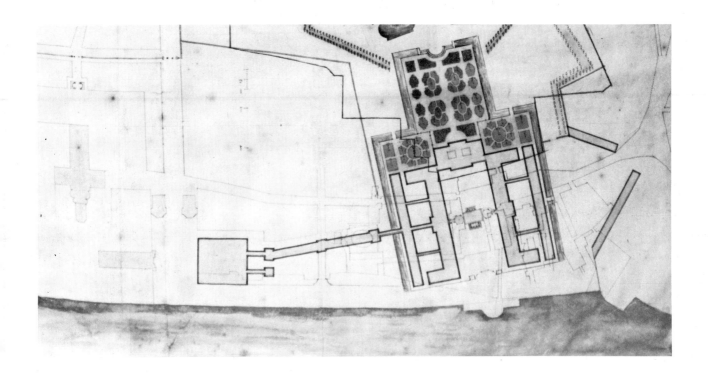

9 Wren's plan (c. 1694) for Whitehall Palace linked to a Parliament House by a long, arcaded corridor (see also Ch. 9, p. 95)

is slotted neatly into a corner of the main courtyard; in the 1647 plan (B) it is to the left of the river-front entrance (with a replica to the right for symmetry's sake); in the 1661 plan (C) it could be a feature of the east side; and in the 1665 plan (D) the Banqueting House overlooks the main courtyard. It is shaded in on each of the plans.

Naturally Inigo Jones would want to retain the building, and, although Charles I was executed there, Charles II had a lifetime affection for the Banqueting House, designed when he was in his teens and the place where he had been triumphantly received on his return to London in 1660. 'King Charles 2nd was unwilling to comply with some designs for the rebuilding of Whitehall,' states the antiquary George Vertue, 'because they proposed to pull this [the Banqueting House] down.' Jones's masterpiece appears to have been both an attraction and an impediment in plans to create Whitehall Palace.

Proposals did not quite end with the setting aside of Webb's 1665 plan. Two reigns later there was a revival of the idea after two fires destroyed the old palace and changed Whitehall into a topographical expression. About 1694, three years after the first and lesser fire, Christopher Wren, ever the versatile opportunist, produced his scheme (Plate 9). His main plan shows a resemblance to Greenwich Hospital which he was designing about the same time: that is, it consists mainly of two flanking wings which stretch down to the Thames. At half their length they are joined by a transverse block. This block was the Banqueting House, once again making its presence felt, and given increased importance by domed towers at each end. With a forecourt open to the water, the effect from the Thames can be imagined if we visualise

Greenwich as it would be today were the Queen's House brought forward into the middle of the complex.

Wren was unable to resist an 'improvement' to the Banqueting House. This took the form of a massive portico with four Corinthian columns, 100 ft high, imposed on Inigo Jones's façade, all right in their way but destroying the original simplicity (Plate 10). The Royal Apartments lay behind the Banqueting House joining the west end of the wings. The small size of Wren's palace allowed room for a formal parterre garden (on the site of Horse Guards Parade) which stretched down to the long canal in St James's Park. Because this ornamental water went off at an angle, Wren added a second, shorter canal to balance it. To the south, and joined to the palace by a gallery, 500 ft long, was a new Parliament House (see p. 95).

King William commissioned Christopher Wren, his Surveyor-General, to prepare the designs, which suggests that there must have been a pressing urgency for a Council Chamber and lodging for court officials dispossessed by the fire. But this monumental palace in Baroque style aroused insufficient enthusiasm in the Dutch King. He and Queen Mary were happy to remain in the seclusion of a modest mansion in Kensington Gardens. Wren had to accept the King's excuse that to live close to the river would be bad for his asthma, and so the last, and possibly finest plan for a Whitehall Palace was abandoned.

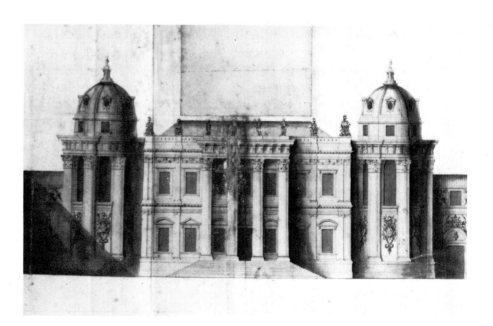

10 Wren's 'improvement' to the Banqueting House, with columns and flanking domes

Chapter 3

The Reluctant Phoenix

THIRTY years before Wren sketched the last of the Whitehall Palace plans for King William a far more terrible disaster than the two local Whitehall fires had struck London. In the Great Fire of 1666 seven-eighths of the City was destroyed and there was an urgent need for new ideas. The five September days which reduced so many fine buildings to charred ruins had the same effect as a war or a time that sees the breaking of a nation.

Men began to reassess the things they had so long taken for granted and were now no more. Did they want to go back to the old styles, rebuild the City as it had been, or take the unique chance of improving on the past? Despite a sentimental regard for the old and much innate conservatism, this period was a watershed for new ideas. Many remarkable schemes emerged from the smoke and rubble.

With the City virtually laid waste, the most natural thing was to consider whether an entirely new ground-plan was desirable. This was immediately taken up by Christopher Wren. Then in his mid-thirties, Wren was very far from being a working architect. He was still more concerned with astronomy and natural philosophy; architecture had become an added intellectual diversion only six years earlier. After clambering over the smouldering ruins, and within a week of the Fire coming under control, Wren presented Charles II with a plan for a new City.

Wren's basic idea was that the winding streets and old courtyards that had existed almost unchanged since medieval times should be replaced by monumental avenues. Only just back from Paris, where he had spent eight months studying classical buildings and formal layouts, he proposed that the avenues and streets should radiate from circular piazzas (Plate 11).

In his plan the main avenue ran virtually in a straight line from Aldgate to Fleet Street, passing through a great circus in the centre of which stood a rebuilt Royal Exchange. A second great avenue ran straight from the Tower along a realigned Cannon Street to converge with the other one at St Paul's. This more southerly avenue bisected two other large piazzas, one with six streets radiating symmetrically from it. The Fleet Street piazza (400 yds west of modern Ludgate Circus) had eight symmetrically set streets radiating from its centre. With other streets set out in a grid pattern or making diagonal intersections, Wren hoped to provide the City with a plan in which (as his son put it) 'Deformity and Inconvenience of the Old Town was remedied by the enlarging of the streets and lanes and carrying them as near parallel to one another as might be; avoiding if compatible with great Conveniences, all acute Angles; by seating all the parochial Chirches conspicuous and insular; by forming the most publick Places into large Piazzas . . . by uniting the Halls of the twelve chief Companies into one regular Square annexed to the Guildhall; by making a commodious Key on the whole Bank of the River from Blackfriars to the Tower . . .'

All this was very fine indeed, but decisions arrived at after so hasty a survey were bound to have faults. The most serious drawback to Wren's scheme was an inaccurate ground-plan. Its great virtue was in providing an entirely new concept. But though a boost to the morale of a City shattered by the disaster, the plan was not the great panacea that it has sometimes been considered. The idea that a great opportunity was missed appeals to Wren's more ardent supporters, and this is allied to the popular belief that his

11 The City as it would have looked from the air had Wren's plan been adopted. The central bridge over the Fleet River in the foreground links Fleet Street with an avenue which, after bisecting at St Paul's, goes right, in a straight line to Aldgate, and, left, to the Royal Exchange. The Exchange is in the centre of the largest of several piazzas all with symmetrically radiating streets. A wide quay with individual warehouses runs along the waterfront. The view is not contemporary: it appeared in the Builder *(1875)*

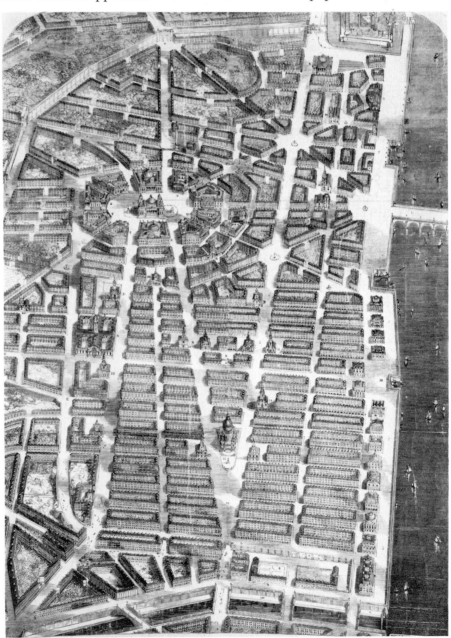

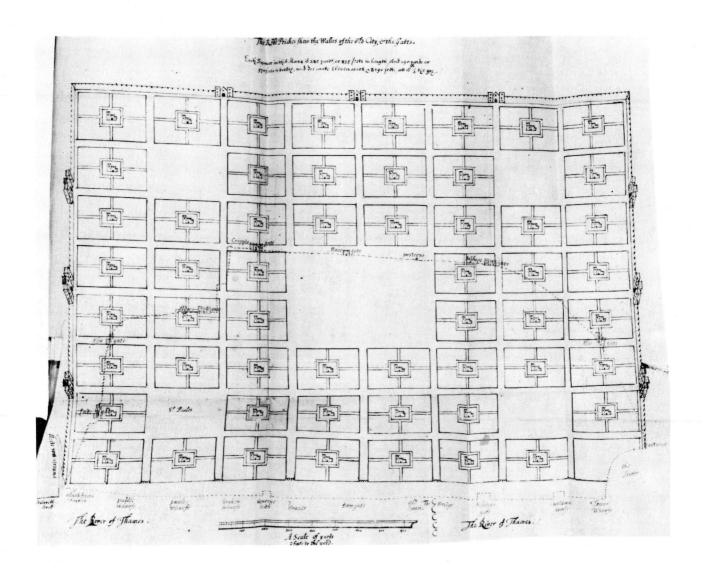

master-scheme was frustrated by philistine and greedy property-owners.

Modern research shows that the plan was impracticable on several accounts and at no time seriously entertained or accepted by King or Parliament. The accusation that the plan was 'unhappily defeated by faction' (perpetuated by Wren's son in *Parentalia*) is now known to be false. Probably the scheme was never taken over-seriously by Wren himself; it was simply a visionary idea full of ingenious conceits to beguile King and Court. There is no record that it was ever considered as a practical basis for rebuilding.

John Evelyn kept the thing in proportion when he wrote: 'Everybody brings in his plans,' and cheerfully admitted that when he put in his idea two days later, 'Dr Wren had got a start on me.' Travelling in person from Sayes Court, Deptford, Evelyn presented his plan to the King who after dinner talked it over with him for nearly an hour in the Queen's bed-chamber. Charles was interested in the similarities between Evelyn's scheme and

12 *The formal gridiron plan which would have transformed the City into 55 rectangular 'squares' of identical size. Each square was a separate parish with a church at its centre. The large open space was for the Guildhall. St Paul's was to have been in one of the four smaller open squares. This post-Fire plan was by the Somerset cartographer Richard Newcourt*

23

13 The Monument: one of several variations suggested before Wren's present design of the flaming urn (inset) was adopted. Hawksmoor's engraving shows the Doric column surmounted by a 15-ft statue of Charles II in Roman costume

Wren's, and suggested various alterations. Everyone was fired by a heady enthusiasm for what the diarist called a 'glorious Phoenix'; but, as was to be discovered, the phoenix rose reluctantly from the cinders.

In their schemes Evelyn and Wren wanted to clear London Bridge of houses, and built an open semicircular piazza at the north end of the bridge, but otherwise they are only superficially alike. Evelyn wanted twelve interconnecting squares and piazzas, five of them on a line along the river front. His most revolutionary piece of resiting was to bring the Royal Exchange down from the centre of the City to one of his Thames-side piazzas (where Cannon Street Station is today). A straight east-to-west thoroughfare cut its way for a mile and a half from 'King Charles Gate' (in the London Wall, south of Aldgate) to Temple Bar where there was a piazza with eight radiating roads like Wren's.

Another feature of Evelyn's plans was a series of 'spacious openings' each featuring some building landmark and all set at 'proper distances'. This was a further attempt to transform the medieval city into a London with a continental appearance. A week after the King saw Evelyn's scheme, the Common Council were shown the ideas of Robert Hooke, who imposed a system of grid roads with a geometric precision that might be expected from a Reader of Mathematics at Gresham College. Of the plan by another City surveyor, Peter Mills, the only thing known is that it is said not to have been as good as Hooke's.

An opportunist army officer, Captain Valentine Knight, also proposed a wild scheme. Hoping to get the ear of the King he suggested an idea that would bring the Crown a big revenue: this was a canal, 30 yds wide, making a circle within the City from the Fleet to Billingsgate, and, presumably, it would have brought in money from tax imposed on the landing of goods at the large number of docksides. The outcome of this suggestion was hardly what the Captain had hoped. He was promptly arrested on the orders of the King, and put into prison, there to reflect on Charles's angry assertion that he would never 'benefit by so public a calamity'.

Most revolutionary of all the post-Fire plans was the brainchild of Richard Newcourt, a 17th-century cartographer who, working in Somerset, was uninhibited by proximity to the problem. We do not know what happened to his scheme at the time; it was only partly published in 1806; and remained virtually unknown until 1939 when the accompanying ground-plans were reproduced for the first time (Plate 12). Newcourt envisaged 'great expatiation and enlargement' which, in effect, meant extending the City limits more than one-third of a mile to the north. Containing his new City within a rectangle, Newcourt rebuilt the London Wall (on the west) from Blackfriars due north to Percival Street, Finsbury, and (east) from the Tower to the end of Old Street, Shoreditch. The straight east–west northern side of the wall lay 660 yds north of Aldersgate.

But the walls were only the frame for the picture. Within this rectangle seven equidistant streets ran from north to south and the same number from east to west. Each street was 80 ft wide (say the width of the modern Pall Mall). This meant that the new City was divided into fifty-five parishes, each a rectangle of identical size (285 yds × 190 yds), each bisected by four streets (24 ft wide) and each with a 'square' in the centre containing its own parish church and surrounding churchyard.

The only variations permitted on this vast gridiron pattern were four open spaces (the same size as the parishes) placed in an exact symmetrical

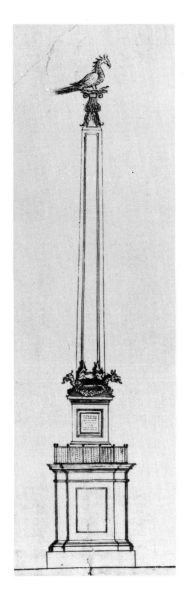

14 The Monument: Wren's earlier design with a large symbolic phoenix was discarded as too difficult to understand

formation, one-parish-in from the four corners. In the centre was an even larger open space (four parishes in size) to accommodate Guildhall which stood in splendid isolation. The open space to the south-west saved Newcourt the embarrassment of having to demolish St Paul's.

No ancient Roman or modern American city is so rigidly formal. In place of a 17th-century London with winding, odorous lanes and fire-prone houses, the architect gives us a brave new city, a clinical view of the future. The unnatural, formalised pattern chills the heart, and where Wren, Evelyn and others were peddlers of dreams, one senses that Newcourt possessed an intense fanaticism. What other sort of man would proclaim that the building of a house was more important than the choosing of a wife, because a wife 'is of but short continuance' but à house is in existence for 'generations to come'? There is a touch of religious fervour, too, in his aspirations for 'a noble city ... whose builder and maker is God' and his belief that God himself is 'the great architect of Heaven and Earth'. Richard Newcourt was the first of many frustrated idealists who failed to make their mark on London.

While the City was being rebuilt after the Fire, piecemeal and on more haphazard lines, it was decided that a monument should be erected 'to preserve the memory of this dreadful visitation'. But by a curious inversion of values the spot chosen was not at the place where the Great Fire ended, but where it started. A site near Pudding Lane, Billingsgate, was preferred to Cock Lane, West Smithfield. Wren was given the job of designing the Monument.

The Monument, 202 ft high, which is the present landmark, is not the one it might have been. Several alternative suggestions were proposed by Wren before the flaming gilded urn above the fluted Doric column was decided on. The architect first showed his designs to the King and then submitted them with his and the King's comments to the City. One of these, which we can judge from an engraving by Nicholas Hawksmoor, places a statue of Charles II, 15 ft tall, on top of the column (Plate 13). Wren liked this and so did the King, who would have been depicted in Roman costume with laurel wreath and baton. But it appears to have been discarded as too expensive.

Wren's earliest idea was for a pillar surmounted by a large phoenix (Plate 14), but on second thoughts he shelved it as 'not easily understood at that height', because its outspread wings would be dangerous in a high wind, and because this was also too costly. Another design had 'flames' made out of brass bursting through loopholes in the sides of the pillar – a practical device to conceal the small windows that lit the circular interior staircase. The King told Wren that he thought a large ball of metal gilt would be most agreeable because people would see it at a great distance. In the end, however, the flaming urn, popularly known as the 'Blaze', was adopted.

Chapter 4

Experiments to the Glory of God

DURING restoration work on St Paul's early in the 1970s the dome was obscured by a web of scaffolding and so resembled an architectural sketch that someone was provoked to say he wished Wren would rub out his pencil marks. He did not know the number of actual lines the architect had sketched in and then erased during the constant changes that were made during the forty-three years of the cathedral's evolution. Today St Paul's looks so immutable on Ludgate Hill that we get the impression of a single, carefully premeditated design. But this is misleading. The building might well have turned out very differently from the one we know.

No less than four widely varying designs were proposed and drawn by Wren. As late as 1702 – that is twenty-seven years after the foundation stone was laid – prophetic and quite inaccurate engravings were on sale of a St Paul's that never materialised. Wren only made his final decision about the ultimate appearance of the dome sometime between 1703 and 1706 when the work had four more years to go.

Modern St Paul's is not, as is sometimes assumed, Wren's solution to the problem of rebuilding *after* the Great Fire. For many years before the old Gothic cathedral was burnt out the building had been a cause for worry. The foundations were cracked, the upper walls of the nave out of true, and the main tower reduced to a stump ever since the spire had been struck by lightning in Elizabeth's reign. The Queen ordered the Lord Mayor and Archbishop of Canterbury to levy a tax, and she herself made an initial contribution of £666 to the restoration fund. Responsibility for the work fell on John Revell whose reaction seems to have been somewhat flippant. On New Year's Day 1562 he gave the Queen a present of a marzipan model of St Paul's with a new steeple. This ceremonial confection led to something more practical – a drawing thought to have been made in the same year by William Cole, a master painter-stainer. Cole's drawing still exists and was the basis of Hollar's 17th-century engraving referred to earlier (p. 12) which shows the new spire that was never built.

The next solution for the truncated tower came as we have seen from Inigo Jones, and twenty-four years later in 1634 when he was Surveyor-General, Jones drew a new west front for the cathedral. Modelled on the Gesu church in Rome, the façade had triple doors, pilasters, scroll brackets, and figures standing like sentries in alcoves under the flanking towers. This was the first tentative move to change the Gothic St Paul's into a classical one. It was abandoned in favour of another façade by Jones with a portico of Corinthian

15 Wren's 'Pineapple' dome for old St Paul's

16 Wren's 'Nightmare' design

columns, a feature paid for by Charles I out of his own purse. This was destroyed in the Great Fire.

A general repair fund of over £100,000, raised by Charles I, was confiscated during the Commonwealth when St Paul's, contemptuously treated as a symbol of Popery, had cavalry mounts stabled under the arches. Scaffolding shoring up the central tower was removed by a Roundhead colonel and sold to make up his arrears of pay. As a result, the roof fell in and the south transept became a ruin. The whole building's critical condition led the Dean, Dr William Sancroft, to write to Wren, then a professor of astronomy at Oxford. This was in the spring of 1666 when Wren, who had not yet designed a building, was just back from six months abroad. In Paris he had met Bernini, the leading exponent of Italian Baroque, had been greatly excited by the Louvre and Fontainebleau, and had made so many drawings that he had, as he put it, 'all France in Paper'. Wren surveyed the dilapidated cathedral, and then back at Wadham College, Oxford, set about making designs which were greatly influenced by all he had seen on the Continent.

The plan for St Paul's which Wren unrolled for the Royal Commissioners as they walked round the building one August day in 1666 was revolutionary by all the English architectural standards of the times. He proposed a most unusual feature. A large dome was to be built on piers at the 'crossing' of the cathedral instead of a spire. (Plate 15.) There were other classical features, and the whole design was clearly influenced by Bramante's dome for St Peter's in Rome and by churches such as the Val-de-Grace which Wren had so recently seen in Paris.

The strangest feature of all was an elongated pineapple, 68 ft high, which appeared to be growing out of a basket perched on the top of the dome. Pineapples had only recently been brought to England from Barbados and presented to the King, and Wren was the first to see their possibilities as a decorative finial. This touch of fantasy ensured that his earliest plan would always be known as the 'Pineapple Design'. It was temporarily banished from everyone's mind by the Great Fire which broke out six days later.

Nearly four years were to go by before the second of Wren's four plans for St Paul's appeared. In the period of numbed uncertainty that followed the

17 A 1930s sketch of St Paul's Cathedral as it would have looked had it been built to Wren's 'Great Model' design. The artist was H. L. G. Pilkington

devastation of the Fire major projects had to give way to emergency measures. Simply as a temporary compromise the wrecked tower was demolished and just the old nave retained. Then in the summer of 1668 following the collapse of some masonry, the Dean wrote to Wren and invited him to prepare 'with all speed' and disregarding costs a plan that would be 'handsome and notable and suitable'. Demolition of the walls still standing required a team of thirty labourers with a battering ram, and while they were engaged on this dangerous work, Wren set up an office to the south of the site. A single drawing and the fragment of a small wooden model are all that have survived of Wren's first post-Fire design which was ready for the King's approval in 1670. It does not seem to have been widely admired, and Wren appears to have prepared it simply as an interim scheme to be replaced by the far more important 'Great Model' plan three years after that.

The Great Model was one of several designs submitted to King Charles, who ordered that a large-scale wooden model should be made of this one which he especially liked. A carpenter and twelve assistant joiners worked on the model, which cost £500 and still survives in the Trophy Room at St Paul's.

A first glance does not suggest anything radically different from the final design of the cathedral. The momentary illusion that the Great Model design is very like the present building is created by an apparently realistic view made in the 1930s by H.L.G. Pilkington (Plate 17). With buses and modern traffic in the foreground there is the quite spurious impression that this is the St Paul's of today. In fact, it is different in practically every detail. The dome is different; the portico with eight huge Corinthian columns is quite unlike the double-tiered portico that we have now with flanking towers; the small dome seen behind the portico does not exist; and there is no curved wing such as Wren conceived (and Pilkington depicts) for the south transept.

It is only when we take a closer look at the Great Model design in conjunction with a ground-plan that we learn how much more revolutionary this scheme was than its predecessor, and far more radical than the plan finally adopted. This is not simply because it was classical rather than Gothic and had a dome instead of a spire. By 1673 that battle for change had been won. The Great Model cut right across ecclesiastical tradition by assuming the shape of a Greek Cross with four equal arms. The accepted idea for all cathedrals in the west at this time was that, simulating the Christian Cross, they should have a long nave (the lower upright part of the crucifix) leading to the choir and high altar (the upper part) with two transepts branching out at right angles (the crosspiece to which Christ's hands were nailed).

Wren's third design, with only a slightly extended section towards the west door, provided no ritual approach by a long nave to the High Altar. The 'crossing' became the absolute centre of the cathedral over which was the vast dome supported on eight piers. This was the shape François Mansart had planned for his unrealised chapel at St Denis (which must have been known to Wren from his Paris visit) and, coming closer to home, it had much in common with a design John Webb had made for a Greek Cross church. This, another never-realised conception, was one in a series of 'idealistic' churches, which Wren probably saw after Webb's death, and may well have influenced him.

The Great Model was Wren's favourite scheme, and his son insists that it pleased 'Persons of Distinction, skill'd in Antiquity and Architecture'. But the clergy did not like the design. Where was the choir in which daily services would be held? Where was the nave for larger Sunday congregations? An Anglican cathedral was being abandoned for something reminiscent of a pagan temple. Though granted a Royal Commission under the Privy Seal, the Great Model was abandoned on the insistence of the Dean and Chapter. Wren petitioned the King in person. The architect is said to have had tears in his eyes, but he pleaded in vain.

Faced once again with preparing a new design, the architect took his bruised feelings into hiding and worked on his next plan in secret, resolved 'not publickly to expose his Drawings'. The dome remained a constant feature, but there was no alternative but to go back to a plan which, though the ornamental detail was classical, would be basically Gothic with choir transepts and long nave and aisles. Although he was Surveyor-General, Wren had no unchallenged right to the commission. He had to bow to his ecclesiastical clients. So he went ahead with his carefully guarded plans, and in May 1675 had the satisfaction of being granted a Royal Warrant by the King who wrote that 'among divers designs which have been presented to Us, We have particularly pitched upon [this one] . . . because We found it very artificial, proper and useful . . .'

In the usage of the times the word artificial means ingenious; but in the modern sense, too, there is something very artificial, not to say bizarre, about the 'Warrant Design' which has become known as the 'Nightmare Design' because of the accretions on top of the dome (Plate 16). Out of the long flat-topped roof emerges a broad dome decapitated like an egg with, above that, a drum flanked by pilasters and scrolls. The next layer has a modest dome or cupola. Then comes the dominating and most uncomfortable feature of the whole apparition. Out of the dome springs a spire looking as inappropriate as the horn on the forehead of a unicorn. Shaped like a minaret, this spire can only be regarded as an ironic concession to the Gothic style, a folly which Wren's apologists try to pass off as a deliberate hoax. He may even have hoped that it would be rejected out of hand, and interest in his favourite design revived.

Whatever the motive, he started this plan, and for the next eight years this was the St Paul's which London had every reason to expect. But Wren had no intention of being restricted by his original drawings. There were many variations on the dome, and one of them is seen in the panorama published by William Morgan in 1682 (Plate 18). Like many topographical artists, Morgan had to anticipate the completed building. On the basis of 'ye best information we could get' when going to press, St Paul's was given three domes one above the other, each diminishing in size and resting on three drums also getting smaller as they went upwards. This pyramid was surmounted by a small spire.

By this time other modifications were being made. The length of the nave

Highgate   St. James Clerkenwell   St. Pauls Cathedrall

The Dukes Theater   Dorset Staires   New Canal   Black Friers Staires   Pauls Wharfe

*18 In his 1682 panorama
William Morgan showed a tiered,
three-domed St Paul's, a design
which Wren is not known to have
envisaged and certainly never
pursued*

was reduced from five bays to three so balancing it with the choir. At the
same time the transepts were slightly increased in length. With these stealthy
changes Wren was getting back more and more to the conception of his
beloved Great Model.

He also had in mind a secular idea which, had they known, would surely
have outraged the Dean and Chapter. He planned to convert part of the
cathedral into an observatory by installing a giant telescope in the south-
west tower. The Royal Society had been presented with the telescope so that
the mathematician James Hodgson could make observations of the stars, and
as a fellow-astronomer, Wren was keen to help. When the Monument was
found unsuitable to accommodate it, an ideal alternative seemed to be the
hollow in the great circular staircase he had designed for one of St Paul's two
towers. The scheme never got very far because the telescope was 123 ft long
and the staircase only 93 ft high. To have it emerging from the top of the
tower would hardly have been seemly. The disappointed architect looked
around for another shorter instrument, but was unable to obtain one.

As far as the dome was concerned, William Morgan's prophetic view
proved wholly inaccurate. By 1702 this main feature had been changed yet
again, and an engraving by Simon Greblin shows a dome that could be
mistaken for the one actually built. In the last six years before the dome was
completed, Wren was to change his mind twice more. His main alteration was
to place a large, far more important dome on a circular drum surrounded by
Corinthian columns and to abandon the small spire (shown by Morgan) in
favour of a modest finial.

The final variation on earlier drawings came with the removal of the small windows between the vertical ribbing of the dome which can be seen on the Greblin engraving. With these eliminated we have the St Paul's we know today. No other building in London can have changed so often on the preliminary drawing board and during actual construction, or switched to alternative possibilities so late in the day.

In October 1710 when the last stone had to be placed on the lantern, Wren sent his son to the top of the dome to carry out this final ceremony for him. His thirty-six years' work on St Paul's was finished, and at seventy-eight, he might well have been thought entitled to a rest. But fatigue, if he felt any, was only temporary. Saint Paul's completed, he turned his attention to St Peter's, the minster in the west.

Since 1698 Wren had been Fabric Surveyor of Westminster Abbey, and he pronounced the condition of the stonework 'crazy', a favourite word of his. But replacing decayed masonry and other piecemeal repairs did not satisfy him. In 1713, then over eighty and indefatigable, he wrote to the Dean of Westminster: 'The West front is very requisite to be finished because the two Towers are not of equal height ... the great West-window is also feeble ... The original Intention was plainly to have a Steeple ...'

So began a further attempt to change the face of London we know by the addition of a spire to the Abbey. Though it never came about, the idea exercised not only Wren, but his assistant William Dickinson, and after him Nicholas Hawksmoor, who had worked closely with Wren on various schemes for nearly twenty years.

At the end of his letter to Dean Atterbury, Wren said he had prepared drawings for the spire and tower as he thought the original architect had envisaged them and 'without modern Mixtures to show my own Inventions'. A glance at the outside of the Abbey as it remains to this day shows the reason for Wren's concern. We can see, as he did, that the medieval builders never finished their work. At the 'crossing' the central tower is cut off only a few feet above the ridge of the roof. This truncated look contrasts with the impressive central towers and tall spires of nearly every cathedral in the country. Wren was anxious to give the Abbey comparable grandeur.

As we can see from his drawings, however, he didn't quite fulfil his promise about not incorporating his own ideas. He raised the central tower, and his personal hallmark is seen in the ribbed cupola embellished with acorn and pineapple devices. The actual draughtsman is William Dickinson, but as his assistant and deputy, he would have been working under Wren's authority. The architect was clearly very serious about his idea of a centre spire which he thought would give the Abbey 'a proper grace'. He had a model made, 6 ft high, in oak with pearwood columns to show the Dean and Chapter how it would look (Plate 19). There are also two or more contemporary engravings which depict Westminster Abbey with a spire and carry the legend 'as designed by Sir Christopher Wren' (Plate 20).

Neither cupola nor spire was ever built, of course, and it next fell to Hawksmoor to devise ideas for the completion of the Abbey. He can hardly be said to have covered himself in glory with his main scheme prepared after

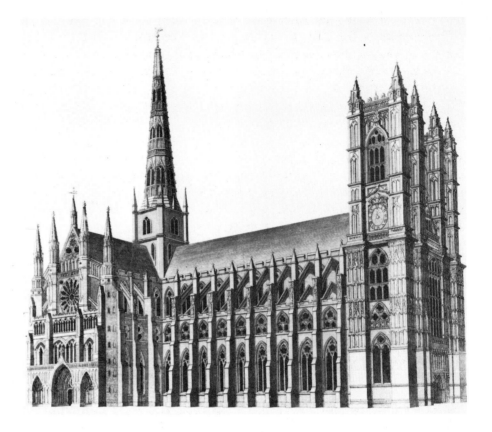

20 A spire for Westminster Abbey attributed to Wren and drawn by Nicholas Hawksmoor's successor, John James, at the Abbey. Fourdrinier's engraving, published in 1737, features Hawksmoor's new towers, begun in 1734, in position on the West Front

19 Wren's model for a centre spire for Westminster Abbey made in 1715. Recently restored after damage, the model is in the keeping of the Dean and Chapter

Wren's death and when he succeeded him as Surveyor-General in 1723. He planned to encase the entire building in what, for want of a more precise term, has been called a 'Gothic Tuscan' shell. A curiously mosque-like look is given to the Abbey by a greatly broadened central tower crowned by an ogee-shaped dome. Nothing further was heard of this extraordinary vision.

Hawksmoor's main contribution to the Abbey was the actual building of the west towers in 1734, but ideas for altering the outside did not stop there. Wren had really started something. A mid-18th-century painting provides a realistic and persuasive view of the north side with two spires rising from the west towers. On the central tower is a tall, impressive cupola. So full of life is the scene and so detailed the painting that this attractive possibility really appears to exist (Plate 21).

The notion of a spire for Westminster was resurrected in the 19th century by Charles Barry, the architect responsible for designing the neighbouring Houses of Parliament. We can spot it in the Abbey section of Barry's comprehensive scheme for Whitehall development (see p. 112). Perhaps the Established Church sensed competition from a rival ecclesiastical building. The English and Welsh Catholic hierarchy was restored by Pope Pius IX in September 1850, and within a few weeks of Bishop Wiseman's appointment as Cardinal Archbishop of Westminster it was learned that Roman Catholics were in treaty for a piece of land in Victoria Street then under construction. A few hundred yards from the Abbey, it was rumoured, would arise a magnificent cathedral dedicated to St Patrick.

Incensed at English Catholics presuming to reorganise themselves as they felt fit, Protestant England saw this Romish cathedral as another threat of subversion. With considerable relief *Art Weekly* reported later: 'The boast of an intention to build a new and splendid Roman Catholic Cathedral in Westminster is fortunately at an end: the [Victoria Street] Commissioners have declined to grant land for the purpose.'

Despite this setback £16,000 was contributed by Catholic faithful and a site purchased immediately to the south of Victoria Street in Carlisle Place alongside Westminster Bridewell prison. Priests were dispatched abroad to raise money, and various schemes advanced. Some favoured a basilica; others a reproduction of Monreale Cathedral in Sicily; and yet others a slightly shrunken replica of St Peter's in Rome.

Cardinal Manning who succeeded Wiseman in 1865 could only with difficulty be persuaded to turn his mind to the building of a costly cathedral. When finally he did so in 1867, he somewhat arbitrarily appointed a fellow convert and relation by marriage, Henry Clutton, as the architect. There were inevitable charges of nepotism and favouritism. Manning remained adamant, but to relieve Protestant apprehensions that London might have to accept a cathedral 'designed in the Italian or Roman style' the Cardinal decreed a building in the familiar English Gothic style.

21 Westminster Abbey with spires and small dome. The painting by Pietro Fabris shows Hawksmoor's towers but with imaginary spires added. The prebendary buildings (centre) existed until 1740. Just to the left of the tree is the Gate House Prison

22 Sir Tatton Sykes: a 'Spy' cartoon in Vanity Fair *(1879)*

When Clutton's designs were made public (Plate 23), the *Morning Post* heaved a sigh of relief. 'Good taste,' readers were informed, 'has prevailed over all foreign influences.' What escaped the journalist's attention – perhaps Manning's too – was that Clutton's building resembled such continental cathedrals as Cologne, Amiens, Rouen and Notre Dame in Paris. With its flèche and large windows it was essentially 13th-century French Gothic, not English at all. There were two towers, three portals and twenty-five side chapels. Protestants also noted with concern that the cathedral was not only as long as Westminster Abbey but higher and broader.

To build the nave and side chapels alone £80,000 were needed. Royal and distinguished Catholics abroad including the Emperor and Empress of Austria, as well as English Catholics, forwarded contributions. The *Builder* commented darkly: 'Rome sends its quota of gold and silver in aid of the work.' On the day the foundation stone was laid Manning diplomatically caused a diversion by holding an anti-drink demonstration on the site.

The money collected during the 1870s was far less than was needed, and Manning refused to sanction building until adequate funds were guaranteed. Unwisely he declared that the cathedral would take a century to complete. While public interest waned, the cathedral saga took a new turn in the form of a strange counter-proposal.

In 1882 Sir Tatton Sykes of Sledmore (Plate 22) visited Vienna. This eccentric Yorkshire sportsman, with a loathing of flowers and a passion for wearing several overcoats simultaneously, saw the recently completed Votivkirche and was greatly impressed. The great building was 300 ft long with twin towers crowned with spires and with an ambulatory bristling with radiating chapels. A Votivkirche, Sir Tatton decided, was precisely what was needed in the tiny village of Sledmore. He therefore approached the architect, Baron Heinrich Ferstel, who expressed himself happy to oblige with a duplicate.

When news of this proposal reached Cardinal Manning he got in touch with Sir Tatton and suggested that perhaps the cathedral should be built at Westminster rather than in the East Riding where it would at the most benefit three or four Catholic families. The logic of this seems to have appealed to Sir Tatton for he wrote to say that he was prepared to agree and offered £25,000 annually or £295,000 on his death. His one stipulation was that the designer should be Ferstel and not Manning's architect designate, Henry Clutton. Manning happily accepted the offer. He was weary of the long-standing problem of providing his diocese with a cathedral. Brushing aside the plans of an incredulous Clutton, he purchased the ground of the redundant Westminster Bridewell as a site. Everything was set when, at this critical juncture, Ferstel died. His son, who might have continued with the work, declined the commission. It was the end of the Victoria Votivkirche.

Neither Manning nor Clutton lived to see the final solution which was put in hand by Henry Vaughan when he succeeded Manning in 1892. Vaughan estimated that he probably had only ten years to live and was resolved to see the cathedral completed before his death. Recalling the earlier warning that Clutton's building would take a century, he therefore decided to reject

Gothic elaboration. John Francis Bentley, who was appointed architect, soon concocted a Latinised Byzantine edifice. A more alien Christian style for London could hardly be imagined, but building went forward quickly and it was consecrated in 1903.

Criticism was inevitable. As the great campanile rose high above Victoria Street (and well above the height of Westminster Abbey) the cathedral was denounced by some as a manifestation of Vaughan's megalomania. There were misgivings about its appearance. Baron Corvo (Frederick Rolfe) described it as a 'pea-soup and streaky-bacon coloured caricature of an electric-light station'. But after the storms and despite the jibes, the cathedral has become part of the accepted London scene and has won a place in the hearts of English Catholics for whom it is a spiritual centre.

23 Henry Clutton's proposed Westminster Cathedral

24 *View through Thomas
Sandby's Bridge of Magnificence
near Somerset House, from west
to east. A carriage passes across
the bridge from south to north and
a fashionable crowd in the central
ornamental building have a view
down-river of St Paul's*

Chapter 5

Crossing the River

25 (A) Reynolds's portrait of Sir William Chambers (1723–96), who conceived a romantic Blackfriars Bridge

MOST London bridges clearly assert that they are practical feats of engineering, not works of art. Except for the girder-Gothic splendour of Tower Bridge, any hint of monumental grandeur is generally repressed. Beauty is invariably sacrificed to utility. All of which is strange, because over the last 200 years there has been no lack of ingenious and elaborate proposals.

Old London Bridge, that prodigious flowering of the medieval imagination, was a wonder of the world but unfortunately did not set a precedent. Until the middle of the 18th century it was the only bridge that London possessed, and to this day there are only six vehicle and pedestrian bridges between the Pool and Westminster. This compares with a bridge every 580 yds across the Seine in Paris, a difference that outraged a Victorian City Councilman who pointed out that instead of a miserly six bridges London, in proportion to its population, deserved at least forty-four.

There has been a constant demand for new bridges and an intermittent need to replace old ones. London Bridge (completed early in the 1300s) has been rebuilt twice, in 1831 and 1973; Westminster Bridge (1750) was rebuilt in 1860; Blackfriars (1769) rebuilt 1869; Southwark (1819) rebuilt 1921; Waterloo (1817) rebuilt 1939; and Tower Bridge (1894) has frequently been threatened with replacement. There was plenty to exercise the imagination of 19th-century engineers and architects, and they came up with some rich, often extraordinary ideas.

25 (B) Raeburn's portrait of Thomas Telford (1757–1834), engineer of a single-span, cast-iron London Bridge

Perhaps some were too ingenious. Would the bridge that took vehicles up 80 ft by hydraulic lift have been popular, or just have frightened the horses? That moving bridge running on rails fixed to the bed of the Thames was not perhaps the ideal answer. And was the man who at the height of the Blitz suggested a Tower Bridge encased in glass to be taken entirely seriously? We will deal with them all in more detail later, but just as an interim thought it seems sad that these flights of imagination were waived aside along with many other inspired ideas by Standing Committees which granted their originators little more than token murmurs of appreciation.

London's second bridge, built at Westminster in 1750, could hardly have been more conventional. It was the design of a naturalised Swiss, Charles Labelye, and since his bridge partially subsided even before it was opened, it cannot be regarded as a total triumph. Protests were raised by Labelye's rivals who rushed forward with alternative suggestions. Batty Langley, an eccentric and not ill-named architectural theorist, advocated fewer arches, and at his house in Soho he prepared a pamphlet castigating 'the Swiss pretender'.

25 (C) Self-portrait of George Dance (1741–1825), who wanted not one London Bridge but two

39

Hawksmoor was all for piers built on little boat-shaped islands. Another proposal which would have given Westminster Bridge a decidedly different look impressed the Bridge Commissioners but was finally rejected. This was a structure devised by James King of St Martin's Lane to be made entirely in timber. Mr King, it should be noted, was a carpenter.

Ten years later the City, still solely dependent on a decaying London Bridge, decided to build an alternative at Blackfriars. A competition was held for Pitt's Bridge, as it was to be called, but was renamed simply Blackfriars Bridge when the Prime Minister's star declined in the 1760s. There were sixty-nine entrants and the winner was Robert Mylne, the 27-year-old Scot who had arrived in London after a tour of Italy only the year before. Greatly daring, he defied the weighty opposition of Dr Johnson by setting his bridge on elliptical rather than round-headed arches. This was a break with tradition, but not nearly so radical as the proposal submitted by William Chambers (Plate 25A).

Chambers, the future architect of Somerset House, conceived Blackfriars Bridge in a romantic, historical style. A surviving print shows one short section consisting of a loggia of Corinthian columns and with statues adorning the piers between the arches. This would have been a remarkable structure for the Thames, even though Chambers's Blackfriars Bridge would

26 Sir John Soane's Corinthian Triumphal Bridge would have linked Lambeth and Westminster approximately where present-day Lambeth Bridge crosses the river. The artist, J. M. Gandy, shows Westminster Bridge and the Abbey in the background

have been a very modest affair compared with the Triumphal Bridges, Bridges of Magnificence and Monumental Bridges then fermenting in the minds of many French and Italian designers. Deemed impractical or else too romantic by the competition assessors, its rejection was inevitable.

Triumphal Bridges had first appeared a decade or so earlier in Italy inspired by Piranesi and by Palladio, whose reconstruction of an ancient Roman bridge was a direct source for Chambers in his Blackfriars design. Elaborate and fantastic, these bridges enjoyed a vogue when, improvised in papier mâché, they were built abroad by students for festivals and public entertainments. They were fine as temporary structures blessed by Italian sunshine. But it was a big step to think of them converted into Portland stone and resisting the tides of the Thames. London weather frowns on outdoor conceits.

But stern practicality was not to deter impressionable students. In London the first intimation of these classical delights was received by those attending lectures delivered by Thomas Sandby at Somerset House. Little realising the fire he was starting, Sandby, Professor of Architecture at the Royal Academy, illustrated his talks with a Bridge of Magnificence he had devised a few years earlier (Plate 24). Later it was to cause a stir at the 1781 Academy exhibition.

Sandby's proposed bridge across the Thames was at Somerset House on the line of the future Waterloo Bridge. An artist-designer closely involved with the aristocracy and affected by the romantic movement, he incorporated just about every imaginable architectural ornament. A colonnade of Doric arches stretches from one end to the other. Domed wings at each end contain apartments. Fashionable crowds could promenade in the ornamental building resembling an Italian *galleria* built over the central arch of the bridge.

The heady effect that this kind of fantasy had on Sandby's pupils is seen in the work of John Soane, on whom the bridge made a great impression. Soane was then twenty-three and not yet launched on a career when in 1776 he designed a Triumphal Bridge of his own. This won him the Royal Academy Schools' Gold Medal and a travelling scholarship to Italy. Soane's additions to his teacher's design included curved wings and double flanking pavilions at either end, each with a dome. Sandby's central *galleria* was elaborate enough, but Soane went one better with a grandiose 'pantheon' adorned with statues. He envisaged his bridge at Westminster as a Grand Entrance to London, which can be construed as the classicist's answer to Gothic London Bridge. Many years later he was to incorporate this vision, conceived as he put it 'in the gay morning of youth', in his view of a classical House of Parliament entitled 'Design for a Senate House' (Plate 70).

Soane drew six versions of this fanciful bridge, and when, following Sandby, he became a professor at the Academy, creating variations was a popular exercise among *his* students. The tradition did not stop there. As Sandby inspired Soane, so Soane inspired a subsequent Gold Medallist, J. M. Gandy, who was a draughtsman in his office. Gandy was himself a romantic visionary infatuated with the classical style, but could not afford to indulge in frivolity. In an endless struggle to support a wife and nine children, he was

forced to accept a great deal of hack work. This included making elaborate watercolours of Soane's drawings, of which the bird's-eye view of a Corinthian Bridge between Lambeth and Westminster is an example (Plate 26).

The 19th century drew in the reins on extravagant caprice. Crossing the Thames could no longer be imagined in terms of classical elegance. There was an immediate call for practical solutions because London Bridge was in a very bad way. Further patching was no longer possible. The whole bridge had to be rebuilt, and the question arose about the bridge now needed.

This challenge inspired two outstanding ideas, one by an engineer, the other by an architect. The first was suggested by Thomas Telford (Plate 25B) whose advice was sought in 1800. Telford, who had come from Scotland to London to try his fortune, was very much a man of the Industrial Revolution with a growing reputation. He thought in terms of iron rather than Portland stone. He had built a single-arch bridge, 130 ft long, over the Severn two years earlier, and now proposed a bridge of revolutionary design also with a single arch to span the 600 ft of the Thames. Its curve would give ships' masts a 65-ft clearance at high water.

Startlingly modern though the bridge was, Telford allowed some concessions to tradition. 'I would make the outside Rib in the Gothic manner,' he stated in his report, 'on account of the lightness and elegance of the forms.' As Thomas Malton's aquatint shows (Plate 28) the 6,500 tons of iron constructed as a single span was to be part of general improvements to the Port of London which included new warehouses along the City waterfront. Some people ridiculed Telford's bridge at first, but when the

27 George Dance's double London Bridge. Large vessels, for the first time since the building of old London Bridge, would have been able to sail upstream beyond the Pool of London. Conceived shortly after the Battle of the Nile, the project contains several Egyptian design-features. The obelisk on the Surrey side was intended for a suggested National Monument

28 Thomas Telford's elegant, 600-ft-span, cast-iron London Bridge – pronounced entirely practical. Thomas Malton's large tinted aquatint of it was still selling well 10 years after publication

43

drawing and plan appeared in 1800 they won approval from George III, the Prince of Wales and other influential people such as the author of *The Age of Reason*, Tom Paine, who called it 'a bold stretch', and whose Anglo-American enthusiasm helped to banish doubts about structural feasibility. 'A bridge on Telford's system', he declared, 'could as well be thrown across the Atlantic.'

Eminent engineers concurred, and work seems to have been actually started. But Telford's bridge never got beyond work on the banks for reasons which become clear from a scrutiny of Malton's print. Obviously the bridge had to be negotiable by ships at high tide, and this needed considerable headroom. This could only be partly achieved by the curve of the arch, which if too steep would create an impossible gradient for vehicles. So to reach the required height a road approach was built at a high level alongside the river, with a gently sloping ramp up to the bridge. This road and ramp can be seen beyond and to the right-hand side of the arch. Road and ramp stand on a colonnade of dignified design, but the cost of building this, together with the acquisition of all the warehouses along Upper Thames Street, would have been prohibitive. The access rather than the iron bridge was the fatal snag.

The second proposal was published in the same year, 1800, by the City architect, George Dance, the younger (Plate 25c). It was one of the most ambitious schemes ever suggested, and probably takes the prize as the most dazzling of all London's unfulfilled dreams. It is hard to say whether Dance or William Daniell, the artist who depicts it, is more responsible for the wonderfully persuasive effect.

The scene before us (Plate 27), observed as if from a balloon tethered over Southwark Bridge, transforms London into Rome or Paris, the Thames into the Seine or Tiber. Dance had studied in Italy, and a hippodrome like the Circus Maximus is the inspiration for the crescent-shaped piazzas which provide approaches of monumental grandeur. In their centre is a reminder of the Place de la Concorde. Wren's Monument to the Great Fire, rescued from a destroyed Fish Street, provides Dance with his northern axial feature, while to the south of the river an obelisk commemorates British naval victories.

Not one bridge but two are required both for imposing effect and practicality. One hundred yards apart, and parallel with each other, each bridge has a drawbridge. One or the other can be raised to let through a ship while traffic is diverted to the alternative route. On both sides of the river curving flights of stairs go down to the water's edge.

Joseph Farington, the diarist and close friend of Dance, who saw the drawings at the architect's Gower Street house in June 1800, noted that the design had been approved by a Committee of the House of Commons and that at least two peers were 'warm for it'. But the warmth did not extend to meeting costs likely to be about £100,000, or reconciling various conflicting interests. The vital records are lost, so that we are left in tantalising ignorance of what killed so suddenly the magnificent plan that would have transformed London. The suspicion is that the scheme was sacrificed to private development by merchants who owned warehouses likely to have been affected. Though the bridges were theoretically favoured by the City their erection would have involved the merchants in moving the Legal Quays and a consequent loss of revenue. Why did Dance not protest when London Bridge was shelved? His public silence suggests that he never seriously expected that his fantasy would ever be built.

Traffic congestion is not exclusively a modern malady. From the middle of the 19th century and even earlier London Bridge was so often clogged with carts, carriages and animals being driven to the slaughter houses that there was an urgent need for an alternative bridge a little further down river. The constant difficulty was to devise a bridge that would allow tall-masted ships to come alongside the Legal Quays in the Upper Pool. This problem was to exercise designers and the usual quota of crack-brained inventors until Tower Bridge became a reality right at the end of the century.

A proposal for a bridge just east of the Tower appeared as early as 1824. The design, patented by a Royal Naval captain, Samuel Brown, eight years earlier, was revolutionary. A wide elevated roadway more than 1,000 yds long would be carried 80 ft high across the Thames on a bridge using iron chains between four stone piers. More than twenty years before Brunel's smaller but comparable Hungerford footbridge at Charing Cross, Captain Brown and James Walker, a civil engineer, issued their prospectus for 'St Catherine's Bridge of Suspension' with an engraving which showed an extremely graceful silhouette. The road, often higher than adjoining houses, went from the Minories, above Little Tower Hill, parallel with the east side of the Tower moat, across the river (requiring only two widely spaced piers) and ended in Russell Street (now Tanner Street), Bermondsey. The promoters produced statistics to show that tolls were likely to yield over £100 a day and that investors could expect ten per cent on their outlay. But even though the

29 Tunnel entrance to a 'sub-riverian arcade' on the bed of the Thames, suggested by John Keith as an alternative to Tower Bridge

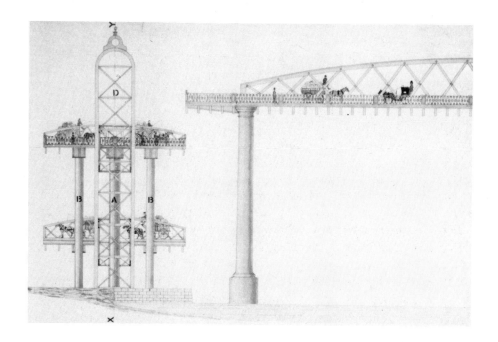

30 High-Level Tower Bridge with hydraulic lifts raises vehicles 80 ft above the river

45

31 Like Dance's London Bridge, Frederic Barnett's 'duplex' Low-Level Tower Bridge would have allowed 'uninterrupted continuity of vehicular and general traffic'

design was outstanding, and the suspension bridge described by a magazine as a 'stupendous undertaking', nothing came of it, and nearly half a century elapsed before weird alternatives were put forward.

New impetus came from a Bill in 1872 seeking Parliamentary authority to build what was termed a 'tower bridge', and at once the Bridge House Estates Committee, the body responsible for all the City's bridges, was inundated with extraordinary ideas. Among them were schemes that dispensed with a bridge altogether. These included a tunnel (a 'sub-riverian arcade') (Plate 29) and a raised deck above water-level running on stilts along rails which were laid on the riverbed. There was a floating chain bridge and the Paddle Wheel Ferry Bridge.

Most fanciful of the actual structures was the High-Level Bridge (Plate 30) with hydraulic lifts at each end. Drawings show horses, carts and a hansom cab being carried 80 ft up in the lift and crossing the river on a horizontal metal bridge. The designer, Sidengham Duer, claimed it would carry 250 carriages each way in an hour. His critics countered by saying 'it would require very much to induce the carrier and travelling public to entrust themselves to the hydraulic lifts instead of making use of their own and horses' feet'.

By far the most persuasive of the early plans was the 'duplex' Low-Level Bridge (Plate 31) which really does seem to solve the shipping problem and is not nearly as odd as it looks. To prevent any stoppage of traffic the 'duplex' divided, as the name suggests, into two carriageways in the centre of the bridge. A two-way loop was thus provided, each with a swing-bridge crossing. When a ship needed to pass, the up or downstream bridge swung back and traffic was diverted to the alternative route and other bridge. Once

32 One of a pair of prints that were issued to show how Horace Jones's Tower Bridge — his original design — would appear open and closed

the ship was in the middle basin the traffic would be re-routed to the other causeway and the second bridge opened to let the ship out.

Perhaps this dock-like engineering solution patented by Frederic Barnett was not dignified enough for the City because it was soon swamped by enthusiasm for the designs of the City's own architect, Horace Jones. His grand concept was mechanical but aesthetically more to Victorian taste. Jones, designer of Guildhall Library and Smithfield Market, proposed a bascule bridge with an arched span between feudal Gothic towers (Plate 32). The bascules would lift on chains like the drawbridge of a Crusader castle. A major-general with the title of Surveyor-General of Fortifications commended the way this 'tower bridge' blended with the Tower of London to which it was going to be so near. At the same time, and doubtless concerned with defending London against a second Armada, the general demanded that the bridge should be armed with cannons. The siting of artillery perhaps proved too difficult, for guns were abandoned.

Because the curved superstructure of the double drawbridge would not open enough to provide ships with a wide passage, Jones's original idea had to be modified. An engineer, Sir John Wolfe Barry, was called in, and together they devised a way of eliminating the semicircular arch in favour of a bridge in which the bascules would be raised not by chains but by internal hydraulic machinery. There was also a high-level footbridge with two lifts in each tower to carry pedestrians up and down, a facility discontinued after 1909 and some suicide attempts. Jones, knighted in 1886, died the following year when hardly more than the foundations were laid. When finished in 1894 the main features preserved from Jones's Tower Bridge were the Gothic towers with their pointed corner turrets, though these were now far taller,

and the ornamental cladding for the steel skeleton more spectacular.

Tower Bridge is the most elaborate of London's bridges, but it would have been certainly challenged by Waterloo Palace Bridge had that ornate glass and iron structure ever been built. On the foundations of Rennie's 1817 bridge the Waterloo Palace Company proposed a superstructure reminiscent of a seaside pier. There was to be a roadway for traffic, but above it, supported on a colonnade, were two Winter Garden Promenades. Filled with semi-tropical trees, these enclosed walks led to the Concert Hall over the central span of the bridge. The hall was necessarily somewhat narrow, but was a spirited design with sixteen circular stained-glass windows and two pairs of onion-shaped domes. A stairway from street level took the music-lover or tree-fancier into a Pavilion built at either end. Obviously inspired by the Crystal Palace, but offering no very clear idea of its practical purpose, this brainchild of an architect, Frank Lang, was proposed in 1861, but was never heard of again.

Only mid-19th-century railway mania can account for the building of the iron bridge that still exists over the river at Charing Cross. The satisfaction of bringing trains right into the West End blinded Parliament to the discordant effect of a strictly utilitarian structure in so prominent a position. Down came Brunel's delicate Hungerford footbridge. Ignored was the expert opinion that what London really needed here was a road bridge. A design suggested by Sir Charles Barry was forgotten. Started in 1859, the new railway bridge was a *fait accompli* before people began to protest that an 'artistic atrocity' had arisen in their midst. It took even longer before an influential group of politicians and architects writing in the *Observer* in 1916 were to condemn it in these terms: 'The site is aesthetically one of London's greatest assets, and it is a really monstrous thing that the finest point in the river ... should be occupied by this ugly railway bridge.' *Punch* satirised its retention with a cartoon showing a demoniac Spirit of Ugliness proclaiming, 'You're my masterpiece.'

Attempts were made in the 1890s and during the next twenty years to persuade the South Eastern Railway Company to pull back their terminus from the Strand to the south side of the river. The company always made a show of being amenable, and even prepared some plans. But their added proviso that the cost would have to be borne by the Government or the LCC effectively prevented any change. Several private architects produced panoramas showing how fine a road bridge would look if only the railway could be replaced.

The first really impressive design was made by T. E. Collcutt, famous for his Imperial Institute in South Kensington as well as being the architect of the Savoy Hotel and Palace Theatre. Shown at the Academy in 1906 (Plate 33), it was a decade or so ahead of alternative designs, a great many of which appeared in the mid-1920s. With Old London Bridge and the Ponte Vecchio as his inspiration, Collcutt spanned the river with a bridge which had fifty shops on each side sheltered behind a classical colonnade. Views up and down the river were obtained through columns in the centre. The main axis was from Trafalgar Square along Northumberland Avenue in a straight line with Waterloo Station, which was rebuilt to serve as a double terminus. Collcutt had a theory that if property on the south side of the Thames were to be developed, pedestrians crossing the river must have protection from the weather, which was an additional reason for his covered pavements.

The death of Edward VII gave fresh impetus to the constantly reopened subject of a new Charing Cross Bridge which, said a writer to *The Times*, should be called after the late King. Captain George S. C. Swinton, clearly a royalist of no small enthusiasm, reminded the readers that the King had loved 'a splendid London', and conjured up the wonderful vision that would confront all visitors from abroad as they arrived at a new Waterloo Station. 'Everyone knows the value of an entry and of a first impression,' he wrote. 'Would it not be something to arrange that all newcomers, as London bursts upon them, should exclaim, "How fine!" and then when they know that the bridge is called by King Edward's name, "How worthy!"'

Five years later with Britain at war, Swinton came back to his theme of a new bridge, but had changed the direction of his attack. He now suggested that it should be a Memorial to Our War Dead. The great battles fought and won, old comrades would meet at a new station alongside Waterloo which should be named Verdun. 'It is autumn and smoke clouds have encouraged a brilliant sunset,' Swinton wrote lyrically, and in the gathering dusk the Frenchman would greet the square outside Verdun Station as 'another Place de la Concorde'. Together the friends from Flanders pass through Allied Gate at the southern end of the bridge, and at the bridge's centre pause to admire statues to three men: 'King Edward who gave us our alliance; Lord Roberts who stirred our best blood; Lord Kitchener who raised our armies.' On the further shore is the monumental Britain's Gate, a shrine on which 'as long as our race survives its children's children will read the names of all who served our cause'.

In the same vein of highly charged patriotism a Tower of Victory was proposed in July 1919, on the site of a demolished Charing Cross Station. This monument, 235 ft tall, was to contain colossal statues of Liberty, Retribution, Peace and Victory. At the top of the tower a belvedere, reached by lifts, would command fine views of the river and the Embankment, transformed into an Avenue of Victory lined with statuary depicting incidents in the Great War.

This macabre idea never materialised, but the plan for a Victory Bridge was revived in 1926 and was elaborated a year later into a War Memorial Bridge of Empire, with provision for twelve great heroes (four of them on horseback) to be set in commanding positions. Both faded in the more practical plans published at the same time by a Royal Commission appointed to consider cross-river traffic.

Artists might banish Hungerford Railway Bridge, but the hated thing was still there, and this led to the idea of a double-purpose bridge. Sir Edwin Lutyens, then at the height of his neo-Georgian fame, was brought in to advise on the desirability of a double-decker road and railway bridge at Charing Cross. There would be six railway tracks on the existing lower level with above them a road for traffic, 60 ft wide. This meant the demolition of the station and hotel which were to be rebuilt immediately to the east from Villiers Street to Buckingham Street. As well as a new road and rail bridge, a scheme in 1929 included a block of buildings above the main traffic concourse containing small flats, restaurant and roof garden. Designed for 'city workers of very moderate means who now have to travel to and from some distant suburb', this appealed to the Ministry of Transport already seriously worried about the increase in commuter traffic.

Had the double-decker Charing Cross Bridge been built Rennie's Waterloo Bridge might have been saved because with an extra bridge there would not have been the same need to widen the existing one. But a plan, however good, could not have been raised at a worse moment. It was 1931, unemployment stood at 2,500,000, and the Labour Government had been forced into a coalition. So when Herbert Morrison, the Minister of Transport, told the LCC that the Government's 75 per cent grant could not be renewed there was little argument. The Depression ruled out any question of a £12,500,000 bridge. Instead of traffic relief at Charing Cross, Waterloo Bridge was rebuilt to take six lines of vehicles.

For ninety years the most persistent phantom haunting the Thames was the shadowy constantly re-emerging St Paul's Bridge. The idea of a bridge over the river from Southwark to a point opposite St Paul's was first raised by a City Councilman in 1851, and the ghost was finally laid only in 1941. As

*34 St Paul's Bridge by Albert
Richardson in 1914 cuts through
warehouses backing onto Upper
Thames Street with a street that
passes the east end of St Paul's to
join Cheapside*

well as showing how inadequate werc our bridges compared with Paris,
Francis Bennoch pointed an outraged finger in the direction of Lyons. That
city had nineteen bridges to serve a population of 350,000. By this token
London should have 132! Bennoch's idea, modest by comparison, was that
the City should build at least one new bridge just to the east of the cathedral.
The cost would be only £100,000.

His idea gained support from a Parliamentary committee which three years
later reported that the existing bridges were insufficient and favoured a
bridge that would link Aldersgate with the south of the river and at the same
time open up a fine approach to St Paul's. By then Bennoch had extended his
scheme to incorporate a railway to bring the Continental mails across the

51

Thames and then by tunnel directly to the Post Office – 'one of the grandest designs that ever was conceived,' he declared with no undue modesty.

But it was to be another half-century before St Paul's Bridge, floating insubstantially on the edge of London's imagination, again awakened real interest. In 1911 an Act of Parliament permitted its construction, and this brought out into the open the reason why there had been so long a delay. The siting of the bridge was the cause of dissension. One faction, mostly architects and others with an eye for design, wanted it to cross the river immediately opposite St Paul's. A wide road on a line with the dome leading up to the doorway in the south transept would, they asserted, provide a vista from the bridge that would show Wren's building in all its glory. Some idea of what this view would have been like may be gained from looking up the newly created pedestrian walk, Peter's Hill, from Queen Victoria Street. Opponents pointed out that this would mean a road that simply came to a dead end. Anyway, Wren had never intended the side elevation to be looked at from any great distance. A great building, insisted the opposition, needs no monumental approach. Look at the Parthenon!

For practical reasons this latter argument had the support of the Common Council and the LCC. The City wanted the bridge to provide a north–south link from Aldersgate to Southwark, and the LCC, dedicated to the expansion of the new electric trams, saw St Paul's Bridge as ideal for a service between the Angel, Islington, and the Elephant and Castle.

With the conflict still unresolved, a competition was launched in 1914 and was won by G. Washington Browne with a massive bridge which had twin pedestrian stairways on Bankside, sentinel pylons and a flamboyant winged goddess driving a two-horsed chariot. The best idea of how St Paul's Bridge would have looked, if sited to the east of the cathedral, is provided by Albert Richardson's design (Plate 34). Since the results of the competition were announced exactly a month before the outbreak of the Great War a further postponement was guaranteed. By 1920 costs had trebled, and with the buying up of property £7,500,000 might well have been needed. Also conventional fears were raised about danger to the Cathedral's fabric from traffic vibration.

In November 1921 a seemingly premature newspaper story reported that plans for St Paul's Bridge were almost complete, but this was instantly denied by the chairman of the Bridge House Estates Committee who said there was 'no intention of proceeding with the work just now.' Five years later a Royal Commission advocated that the plan should be abandoned in favour of a high-level road bridge between Southwark Street and Holborn Viaduct; in 1937 a Highway Survey suggested that the project should 'be allowed to lapse'; and then in 1941 planners looking towards the City's post-war reconstruction, waved aside the whole idea with the dismissive, seemingly bored comment: 'We would find it difficult to revive the St Paul's Bridge proposal.' This drove the final stake into the heart of the corpse.

Of all the unfulfilled ideas for London's bridges none would appear more extraordinary, not to say perverse, than the idea for Tower Bridge solemnly proposed towards the end of 1943. Vast areas of London lay in ruins after the

Blitz; the city was nightly on the alert for German bombing; and every window was pasted over for fear of flying glass. This was the moment when the architect to the National Provincial Bank chose to suggest a Crystal Tower Bridge. As his drawing shows (Plate 35) W. F. C. Holden envisaged a bridge almost totally encased in glass. At a time when people were creeping nightly into deep shelters, Mr Holden had in mind a Tower Bridge cunningly converted to incorporate large airy offices (200,000 sq ft of them) with large sunny windows.

The architect not merely submitted his proposals, but had the aplomb to follow them up with a meeting over lunch when he explained his ideas to the Bridge House Estates Committee. He was able to show that there was method in his madness. He was thinking, of course, not of the present but the future. The Tower of London had received several direct hits, and Tower Bridge might well be the next casualty. After the war why spend money on repair and restoration? Why continually repaint the enormous structure? Why not surround it in glass?

The Bridge House Estates Committee took his point, but suggested mildly that they would have to wait for 'more favourable circumstances'. Holden bided his time, and in May 1945 – the month the war ended – heard that his proposed all-glass structure was being considered by consultant engineers. Their report probably was not very favourable. The Crystal Tower Bridge joined the noble company of eccentrics and discarded ideas.

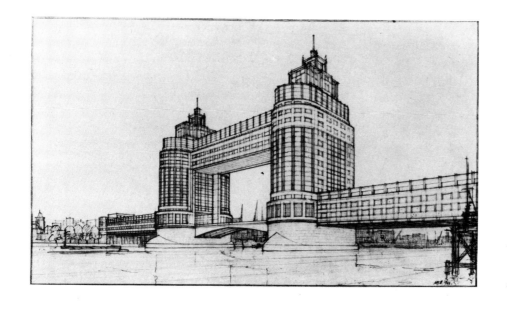

35 Encased in glass a crystal Tower Bridge was conceived by W. F. C. Holden during the bombing of London in 1943

36 Palace for 'James III' to be built in Hyde Park following a successful Jacobite uprising. A great avenue would link it to Hampstead. Louis XIV's royal pavilion at Marly served as its model. It was after staying at Marly that Lord Mar, leader of the 1714 uprising and amateur architect, resolved to design a palace for the Old Pretender

37 Detail from John Gwynn's plan of London with proposed improvements, including two royal palaces. The principal palace in Hyde Park was to be raised on an artificially constructed mound 20 ft high. Other Gwynn improvements included embankments north and south of the river, and London streets generally were to be laid out with far more regularity

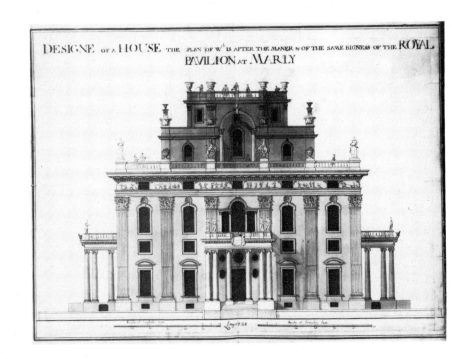

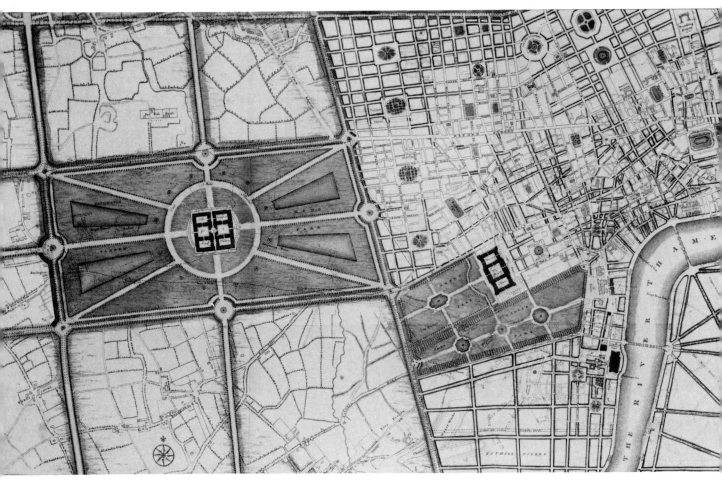

Chapter 6

Palaces in the Air

WHEN the sprawling warren of buildings which made up Whitehall Palace was burnt down at the end of the 17th century, it was no great architectural catastrophe. A foreign visitor described the palace as 'a heap of houses erected at divers times and of different models'. The careless Dutch laundry girl who caused the main fire could almost be said to have done the monarchy a favour. Now, surely, something impressive would have to be built in its place.

In fact, there followed more than a century during which the Royal Family led a restless existence, settling briefly in several houses, none of which completely suited them. The chance of building a great riverside palace had been missed, and for William and Mary, Queen Anne, and the early Hanoverians, the alternatives were makeshift.

There were, however, several theoretical exercises. Among castles, or rather palaces, built in the air in the early part of the 18th century was one for Whitehall – the plan is now lost – by Johann Bodt, a Huguenot employed by William III as a military engineer. Two Florentine dilettanti designers also produced drawings, and the idea of one of them, Alessandro Galilei, was probably too extreme. He sited his building in the middle of St James's Park, with a colossal gateway facing Pall Mall, a plan which also involved the demolition of St James's Palace. George I declined even to see the drawings, and, his hopes dashed, Galilei returned to Italy.

Three other 18th-century designers, John Talman, William Vardy and William Stukeley, heeded the much-travelled Earl of Shaftesbury when, early in George I's reign, he pronounced that the creation of a royal palace – 'a noble subject' – was an architectural challenge to the nation. That there was no palace of sufficient splendour for the monarchy seems to have upset the country far more than it did the Crown.

William Stukeley was the most unlikely of all the planners. He had not even the vaguest pretensions to being an architect. Noted antiquary, Druid enthusiast, and eccentric rector of St George-the-Martyr, Queen's Square, Stukeley 'invented' a royal palace, as he put it, and the place he 'pitched upon' in 1749 was St James's Park. The 'open, dry wholesome situation', a few hundred yards north-west of where Buckingham Palace stands today, used the rise of Constitution Hill to provide views over London as far as Shooters Hill and Highgate. 'There is not such another spot on the globe for the purpose,' he pronounced.

For the most unexpected of all plans for a royal palace at this time we have to leave London for Italy. Though George I might have shown scant interest in a home, a man with his eye on the English throne was far more concerned.

In exile, James Stuart, the Old Pretender (Plate 38), warmed his hands in contemplation of a London palace which he hoped he might eventually occupy.

This vicarious pleasure took place at Urbino, south-east of Florence, a mountain fortress where the Pope had offered asylum to James Stuart after the crushed Jacobite rising of 1715. Among his entourage was John Erskine, 11th Earl of Mar, who had been head of the Pretender's forces at the defeat at Sheriffmuir. He did not like Urbino any more than did his master.

'Our distance here is cruel,' wrote Mar, 'and the place we are in is a damnable one.' The consolation he shared with James Stuart, who styled himself James III, was the planning of a palace to be used after a next – successful – uprising. At Urbino Mar began to prepare a series of very detailed architectural drawings of royal palaces for James as well as plans for radical improvements to London generally. These he continued to embellish long after he had lost confidence in the Pretender and had parted company with him.

The sources of our knowledge of these London schemes are the Mar-Kellie Collection of architectural drawings in the Scottish Record Office and an anonymous manuscript volume, entitled *Description of the Designs for a new Royal Palace for the King of Great Britain in London*, dated 1726, in Westminster Public Library. The significance of these dispersed Mar documents and the link between them has previously escaped notice.

The principal palace, to replace Whitehall, was to be built on the site of Buckingham House, and the Duke of Buckingham moved to a new building nearby. A second palace was to be built in Hyde Park (Plate 36). This would have closely resembled a chateau called Marly just to the west of Paris.

The lake in St James's Park, then called 'The Canal', would be supplemented by two new canals stretching south and west to the Thames – these enabling the King to sail through the park to wherever he wished. The buildings between the Admiralty and the Cockpit Theatre were to be demolished, and so, in the heart of the City, were those between the Royal Exchange and the river. This would create an uninterrupted view westward across the royal palace and serve as a permanent reminder to the citizens of the King's presence.

Mar's wide-embracing plans had a parallel in those of John Gwynn forty years later. Gwynn, who came from Worcester, was said to have been a carpenter until, in his late forties, he became an architect 'by industrious study'. He was to prove a rare visionary. Not only a royal palace features in his prophetic *London and Westminster Improved* published in 1766; Gwynn urged that the map of London should be considered as a whole and future activity controlled by a general plan. Quays along both sides of the Thames (described in Chapter 8) were part of his imaginative overall scheme.

Gwynn's 'improvements' allowed for two royal palaces, the smaller one on the north side of Green Park. Incorporating St James's Palace at the southern end, and with a frontage along St James's Street almost up to Piccadilly, the northern wing would have been where the Ritz and Arlington Street now stand. Since a palace on a slope would hardly be dignified, Gwynn's idea was to raise the southern end nearly level with Piccadilly with a terrace from which the King could review his troops.

Even more impressive was to be Gwynn's other palace right in the centre of Hyde Park, raised on an artificial mound 20 ft high. With no buildings permitted between the palace and the Thames, Gwynn predicted this would make 'the finest scene in the universe', and 'from its detached position would not be affected by the smoke from the town which is the utter enemy to stone'. Built round six large courtyards and a smaller central one, the palace would have been on the site of the present Ranger's House and police station.

As Gwynn's map (Plate 37) shows, diagonal avenues splay out to the corners of the park from a surrounding completely circular road one mile in circumference. A comprehensive symmetry is achieved by building a new road on the south side from Hyde Park Corner in a straight line to the junction of Prince's Gardens and Exhibition Road. Since this would mean that Knightsbridge, Kensington Gore and much of Kensington Road would be swallowed up in the royal park the road would hardly have been popular.

Despite all these suggestions it was not until well into the next century that there was any serious talk about a central new palace for London. There seemed no real need. Saint James's was always available when George III, leaving rustic pursuits, came up to town from Kew or Windsor. Then in 1762 the King purchased Buckingham House from the Duke of Buckingham's heirs. Enlarged, and with a few alterations carried out by William Chambers, 'Buck House' made a modest, adequate home for the royal family's occasional visits.

Even after his accession in 1820 George IV showed himself in no hurry for anything more ambitious. Ideas remained in the melting pot for about five years, during which time various architects came up with rival plans, and a great noise was made by an Irish Colonel Frederick William Trench MP. In the year after he launched his Thames Quay scheme (see Chapter 8), this irrepressible busybody declared that the time was ripe, if not scandalously overdue, for the King to have a home in Hyde Park 'second to no Palace in the world'. The elaborate plan which he published in 1825 was prepared by the brothers Benjamin and Philip Wyatt, who had been his collaborators on the Thames Quay. Though his ideas were quite unsolicited, Trench managed to convey the impression that they were almost divinely conceived.

With a characteristic blast of rhetoric, Trench contemptuously dismissed 'narrow tradesman-like views', avowing himself 'an advocate for the *splendour* and magnificence of the crown'. He could name 'fifty noblemen much better lodged than their Sovereign' and thought this 'highly discreditable to the country ...' With his opening salvo – a letter in the *Morning Post* – Trench declared that the conditions surrounding Buckingham House were too deplorable to contemplate. A nearby steam-engine, a great smoking brewery, a main sewer running 'close under his Majesty's window', a basement liable to flood – these made it sheer folly to attempt any improvement of the existing 'damp, dark and unwholesome' building.

Buckingham House duly annihilated, Trench marched in and raised his

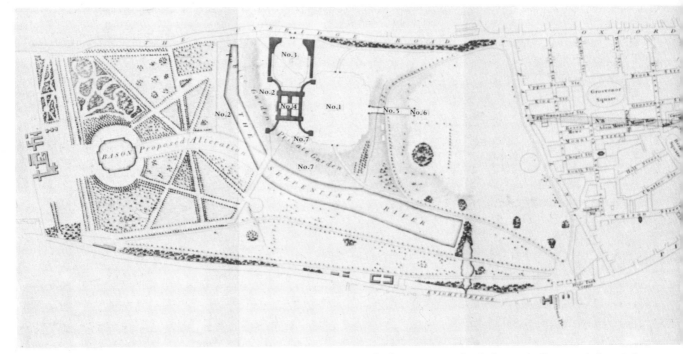

39 Lt-Colonel Trench's two-mile-long triumphal way leading from St Paul's Cathedral to a new royal 'metropolitan residence' in Hyde Park. Key to palace area: (1) grand entrance courtyard, 1,100 ft × 1,000 ft; (2) palace garden of 14 acres; (3) stable court with accommodation for 40 carriages and 150 horses; (4) the palace itself; (5) grand terrace of approach; (6) triumphal arch; (7) 15 acres of private garden for the King. 'The lungs of the metropolis', Trench believed, would be considerably benefited by the change

standard elsewhere. He and the Wyatts had been influenced by John Gwynn's scheme, but instead of putting their palace right in the middle of Hyde Park, they sited it further north alongside the Bayswater (then the Uxbridge) Road. But Trench was not satisfied with simply proposing a vast palace to be built at the cost of £800,000. He wanted a monumental approach. Nothing less than an avenue, two miles long and 200 ft wide, stretching in a straight line from St Paul's.

Philip Wyatt's plan for this astonishing thoroughfare (Plate 39) shows it cutting a swathe right through some of the most important legal, commercial and residential districts of London. Starting from St Paul's, the road makes its lethal progress through the Temple, narrowly missing St Bride's but successfully demolishing the Temple Church and St Clement Danes. Two royal theatres – Drury Lane and Covent Garden – are threatened in the journey of destruction through Covent Garden and Golden Square. Trench only nicks the north-east corner of Berkeley Square (but enough to destroy the home of the celebrated beauty Lady Jersey) and manages to steer a course south of Grosvenor Square to bring his monumental avenue out in Park Lane at the junction of Grosvenor Street. Even Trench referred to the idea as 'the vision of a splendid impossibility'.

Breaking cover, and leaving injured Mayfair, the splendid impossibility then makes its way across the north side of Hyde Park, and, passing under a National Triumphal Arch, reaches the Grand Entrance Court of the Palace. We do not know exactly what the palace would have looked like. 'I will abstain from giving it to the public at the present,' wrote Trench, perhaps shrewdly keeping a big gun in reserve. But he describes the building as 500 ft square with the main block linked by crescent-shaped corridors to four flanking corner pavilions. He chose a knoll north of the Serpentine.

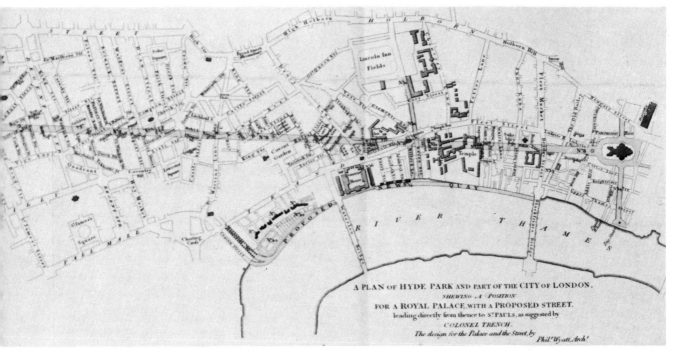

A PLAN OF HYDE PARK AND PART OF THE CITY OF LONDON,
SHEWING A POSITION
FOR A ROYAL PALACE, WITH A PROPOSED STREET,
leading directly from thence to S.T PAULS, as suggested by
COLONEL TRENCH.
The design for the Palace and the Street, by
Phil.P Wyatt, Arch.t

Trench immediately set about his customary policy of trying to influence the influential. In October 1825 he showed his plan to a houseparty at the Duke of Wellington's country seat, Stratfield Saye, and in her journal the Duke's close friend, Mrs Arbuthnot, records the reaction:

It is the worst plan of a house I ever saw, & quite colossal, for he proposes a statue gallery 500 feet long, a drawing room 190, & other rooms in proportion. It is the most ridiculous plan I ever saw for, added to it, is the idea of a street *200 feet wide* extending from the end of Hyde Park opposite the New Palace to St. Paul's!! The King and the Duke of York are madly eager for the plan; but the former says he supposes his d———d Ministers won't allow it. Mr Arbuthnot was very angry with Col. Trench, for he said it was too bad anybody shd go & get the King's ear & set him against everything that is being done for him. Col. Trench has persuaded him that Buckingham House will always be a damp hole unfit for him to live in ... All the rest of us laughed at Col. Trench & his plans; we advised him to put his palace in Kensington Gardens & not to touch the 'lungs of the people of England', as the newspapers call the parks; and we reminded him that his new street wd just go over Lady Jersey's house who wd make the town much too hot to hold him. He said she might go and live at her Shop in Fleet Street [Child's Bank].

While Trench was trying to hatch his scorned plan, the two dominating architects of George IV's reign, Soane and Nash, were also hard at work. In fact, Soane's first idea for a royal palace dated back many years to the time when he was a young architectural student of the Royal Academy Schools. His earliest design was an elaborate conceit drawn in 1779 during his time in Rome on a travelling scholarship.

Aged twenty-six, and receptive to all the stimulating influences he encountered, Soane (Plate 40) had visited the palace-fortress at Caprarola near Rome built for the Farnese family. This provided him with his outline,

and on Vignola's design he imposed details borrowed from ruins of the Palatine palaces, Hadrian's Villa at Tivoli and the Palace of Diocletian at Split. The central domed building drew its inspiration from the Pantheon. To this declared endeavour 'to combine magnificence with utility and intricacy with variety and novelty', Soane gave the title of 'Palace for the Sovereign'. Many years later J. M. Gandy, who made so many elaborate watercolours of Soane's buildings, did a painting which shows just one corner of the vast triangular building (Plate 41). Rows of crouching lions guard every approach. Unicorns sit sentinel by the steps, and high above the forest of Corinthian columns are mermaids, goddesses and mounted horsemen.

The rumour that George IV was toying with the idea of rebuilding Buckingham House sent Soane rummaging back for his old Roman design. Latterly he contended that this palace was always destined for Hyde Park Corner, and if this is so it shows astonishing foresight. It would seem more likely that the youthful *jeu d'esprit* was made without a particular place in mind, and then, some forty years later, when he needed a London setting to interest the King, Soane chose the Hyde Park Corner site and for the engraving cunningly inserted St Paul's and Westminster Abbey into the background.

The London details emphasise the incongruity of the vast Roman edifice and, obviously recognising this, Soane in 1820 designed another palace, sumptuous but on less extravagant lines. With massive buildings on three sides of an open forecourt leading up to a great portico, the palace is reminiscent of Blenheim. He still favoured the same position at the apex of

40 Sir John Soane (1753–1837), painted when he was in Rome aged 26 by C. W. Hunneman

41 Soane's 'Palace for the Sovereign', painted by J. M. Gandy. The architect used a profusion of columns to give elegant disguise to the fact that the building had several floors

the triangular-shaped grounds of Buckingham House. The entrance, at the top of Constitution Hill, is through a triumphal arch, while the main aspect overlooking the garden to the south-east commands a panorama of London slightly obscured by rain and a fog cloud. To ensure that the full impact would not be lost on the King, Soane once again employed Gandy to paint a romantic view for the 1824 Royal Academy (Plate 42).

As official architect responsible for several royal buildings including Buckingham House, Soane had reason to expect that if a new palace were to be built – or an old one rejuvenated – he would be given the commission. But his expectations received a nasty jolt in the summer. The Surveyor-General requested him to hand over any plans of Buckingham House that his department might possess. This was the writing on the wall, and Soane's fears were confirmed in July when he heard that George IV, hesitant about committing himself to a new palace, had asked John Nash, Surveyor-General and his favourite architect, to convert Buckingham House into a grand private residence for him.

Soane must have known that his chances were small if Nash were available. Nash, a friend of the King, had been nursing a number of ideas for a royal residence since the start of the century. These had included alterations to Carlton House which George IV, then Prince of Wales, had taken over

42 Palace designed for George IV by Sir John Soane. The site was to be Green Park at Hyde Park Corner. The triumphal arch anticipates the one actually erected close by in 1825

43 Two designs for Carlton House by John Nash (1752–1835): (A) his remodelled classical facade as seen looking down Lower Regent Street

when he came of age. Nash had produced a magnificent classical design for Carlton House with a dome, impressive central portico, pointed towers and a wide colonnaded façade. The view (Plate 43A) is looking down Lower Regent Street where the remodelled building stands at the end of a widened Waterloo Place. When this failed to satisfy the royal whim, Nash, with the ease of a skilled conjuror, pulled an alternative from his portfolio – a Gothic building (Plate 43B) with twin towers as it would have looked from St James's. But it was still no good. At this time the Prince could not concentrate his mind on any single building and certainly did not want to dwell on anything as weighty as a palace.

For years the Prince had been led on a merry architectural dance by Nash and had responded by being aggravatingly dilatory in settling on anything. There was, for instance, the attractive idea of a summer pavilion in Marylebone. At the southern end of Regent Street Carlton House was the Regent's official residence; for the northern extremity of a 'Magnificent Thoroughfare' Regent's Park was to be created. As a feature of this garden city for the nobility Nash planned a royal villa. It is an altogether very mysterious building.

In the first plan for the new park, which appeared in 1809, this mini-palace for the Prince is quite clearly shown. Two years later a ground-plan (Plate 44) marks a large building with two wings forming an open square which faced east toward Cumberland Terrace just west of the Broad Walk and a narrow stretch of artificial water. But no drawing of the *Guinguette*, as it is referred to, has come to light, and there is no mention of it in Nash's papers. It continued

to appear several times subsequently, but in later revised plans for Regent's Park this summer pavilion has completely disappeared. It remains one of the most tantalising of London's might-have-beens.

When he became King in 1820 George IV was at last compelled to focus his wandering thoughts on the question of a palace. Rebuilding Carlton House or Buckingham House held little appeal for him, and now Nash didn't favour alterations either. The architect was for a new palace which (like the Gwynn, Trench and Soane buildings) would stand higher up in Green Park in a line with Pall Mall. This was once discussed in the presence of Lord Farnborough, an adviser to the royal family on palace decoration, and produced a good-natured rebuke from the King. 'I tell Nash, before you, at his peril ever to advise me to build a Palace', he warned. 'I am too old to build a palace.'

The King remained true to his resolve. He procrastinated for a few more years and then in 1825 finally ordered Nash to remodel Buckingham House for which he said he had a sentimental attachment. It was a job the architect did not at all relish, and also meant the end to any faint hopes Soane might still have had that his palace at Hyde Park Corner might be adopted.

George IV was never to take up residence in this partly converted building; William IV disliked and never occupied the place; and Queen Victoria, the first sovereign to make Buckingham Palace the royal home, required further radical changes.

Colonel Trench thrived, of course, on all the troubles that bedevilled Nash's conversion. The soaring costs, the allegations of the architect's unauthorised expenditure, and criticisms of the appearance and facilities

(B) the Prince Regent's residence transformed into a 'collegiate Gothic' palace, seen from St James's Park. Carlton House was in such a bad state in the 1820s that the upper rooms had to be propped up whenever large numbers assembled in them

were more ammunition for another barrage of invective. How manifestly right he had been! Hadn't he warned the nation? He rose in the House of Commons in 1831 to scare Parliament with the news that the whole basement of the palace was under water. This was a complete fabrication, and certainly seemed an odd reason for his advocating that the building should be turned into a National Picture Gallery. As a slightly more appropriate alternative use he suggested a laundry for half-pay officers.

Even when Queen Victoria was happily installed with her family, Trench felt obliged to return to the attack, and in 1846 began writing in scathing terms about the 'gloomy, inconvenient and unwholesome' Palace in Pimlico. Reports of a new front did not cheer him up in the least. A closed courtyard would render the place only more dismal and unhealthy. Mounting his old hobby-horse for a last gallant charge, the Colonel again proposed to Parliament that a palace should be built in Hyde Park. 'I do earnestly hope', he wrote, 'that no false Pride or false Economy will condemn Her Majesty and Her lovely Children to remain in such an objectionable Locality.'

But remain they did. To provide more accommodation and State rooms a completely new east front was added by Edward Blore in 1847. Nash's forecourt became an enclosed courtyard, and all vestiges of his work were hidden behind this heavy, ornamental façade. In its turn this was replaced by the present unobtrusive classical front in 1913. From Inigo Jones to Soane architects had striven mightily to create a far grander royal palace for London, but all their efforts came to nothing, and now Buckingham Palace has become so firmly established as a symbol of monarchy that it seems likely to resist any replacement.

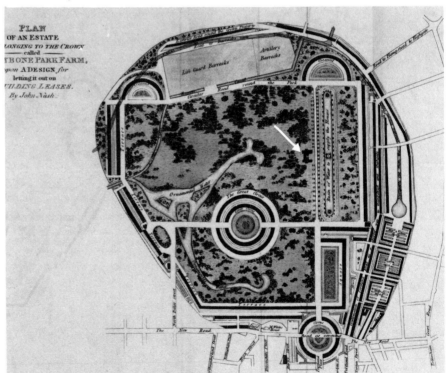

44 One of the suggested layouts for Regent's Park, formerly Marybone Park Farm (1811). Nash's 'Guinguette' (royal villa) is indicated by an arrow

Chapter 7

Monuments to Genius

BECAUSE of the comfortable assumption that they will always be there, we rarely spare more than a glance at familiar landmarks such as Nelson's Column, Eros and the Albert Memorial. We pass by them with raised hat or a shudder according to taste. That they were once violently abused like so many other London monuments is forgotten; virtually unknown is the fact that they might easily be very different from what is now there. If tomorrow we suddenly found them gone, our consternation would be nothing compared to our reaction to what could easily be in their place.

Our perambulation of London's unrealised memorials, statues, pyramids, triumphal arches and obelisks starts in Trafalgar Square. In 1818 when the idea of a monument to Lord Nelson was first discussed, but no site proposed, the space at the top of Whitehall, which was to become the square, was largely occupied by the royal stables called the King's Mews. Eight years later the mews and a number of 'vile houses' were demolished as part of a scheme by Nash to provide a prospect up Whitehall to the new National Gallery. Clearly the area in front of the gallery needed to be laid out, and the most romantic of various suggested schemes was by the neoclassical architect John Goldicutt the year before his death (Plate 45). An elaborate monument of William IV is backed by a square in which trees largely obscure the building. This was named Trafalgar Square in memory of the naval victory and to the 'Sailor King' with no idea at this stage of a monument to Nelson.

An initialled letter in *The Times* in 1837 suggested that this would be an ideal place for such a memorial. He had already been given a pillar in Dublin and a column in Great Yarmouth, but was still without an outdoor monument in London. The letter triggered off ideas for what was called a 'Nelson Testimonial'.

The English, it has been said, will laugh at everything except cricket and Nelson, and so sacrosanct is he that it takes a clear eye to see that there is something pretty preposterous about that tiny figure on top of a 170-ft Corinthian column. As for Edwin Landseer's four bronze lions, should they not, it was once suggested, be fitted with gramophones so that they roared intermittently? The designer of the chosen memorial was William Railton, an ecclesiastical architect with a talent for economical parsonages, whose contemporaries had no inhibitions about voicing criticism. They immediately pointed out that the column was disproportionately tall to the statue, that the proper function of a column is to support heavy roofs not tiny figures, and that Nelson's Column spoilt the Whitehall vista.

There had been no lack of alternatives. A committee chaired by the Duke

45 *Trafalgar Square, according to John Goldicutt's layout. At the centre of the naval monument stands not Nelson but William IV, the Sailor King. The 'Pepperpot' scheme building peeps down the Strand*

of Wellington and including Sir Robert Peel had 120 designs and forty models from which to choose. They were infinitely varied. Nelson stood, sat, lolled. He balanced precariously on a dome; had his feet uncomfortably entangled in an anchor; bestrode a globe. Goddesses, marine and terrestrial, raised their arms in his praise and held aloft wreaths of victory. Lions crouched, prows of ships jutted, Britannia was in frequent and majestic attendance.

One design ignored Nelson completely in favour of a towering trident, 89 ft high, which the *Art-Union* decided 'from any distance ... would be nothing more than a large toasting fork'. Another absent-minded column simply had two dolphins on top of it. More ambitiously, Thomas Hopper, a teetotaller dedicated to water, provided a great fountain as a central feature of a naval temple to play at anniversaries of Nelson's birth and his three battles. More symbolically Timothy Butler included the figure of a seaman stripped for action 'representing an unshrinking front and unquailing heart with which England has ever met her enemies'. John Goldicutt, a tireless but frequently vanquished competitor, poised a 13-ft Nelson, 'hero of an hundred battles', on a globe of the world which was 30 ft in diameter and naturally showed Britain uppermost.

Goldicutt was unstinting. He surrounded the globe with allegorical figures – among them were Fame, Neptune, Victory and Britannia – and also with a small lake ('a permanent sheet of water which the adjacent mains may supply'). The bronze or granite globe was to be polished to resist smoke and atmosphere, and have a hollowed-out chamber 'to contain the busts of illustrious persons distinguished for their acts of valour and where thousands who visit the great metropolis may be admitted to inspect the same. . . .' We can see what it would have looked like from a view (Plate 46) from the portico of the National Gallery during some military soirée.

Water played a part in the scheme of an anonymous 'Architect of Middlesex' who wanted to show the spoils and trophies of victory 'brought on the Admiral's ship to the capital of the British empire'. To accommodate this sculptural pageant Trafalgar Square was to be transformed into a port in which the *Victory* was moored (a large stone model one assumes: the architect is none too clear) with a huge statue of Nelson in the centre of the deck.

Another plan which would have been an exhibition rather than a monument was the Nelson Cenotaph by John Britton. As an antiquary Britton favoured a British Naval Museum, an octagonal Gothic building (Plate 47), resembling the Chapter House of Westminster Abbey. There would be a library, galleries for naval objects, a residence for a curator, and rooms for janitors who, Britton thought, should be 'naval men who had served their country, but who from wounds or other causes may be unfitted for active service'. From the spire on Trafalgar Day a lantern, illuminated by a gas jet behind coloured lenses, would flash out all over London.

At least three designers proposed temples. Among several vast statues was one by William Pitts of Nelson 'overlooking the city which his judgment and valour have preserved'. Moral example was the aim of Henry Cass whose Memorial of Achievement was 'calculated to excite at a glance in the thoughtless idler or hurrying man of business, the desire by a life like Nelson's, active and honourable, to win honours like his from a grateful country . . .' Time had clearly erased from the mind of Mr Cass any unfortunate memories of Emma Hamilton.

The memorial by R. G. Wetten with a languid Nelson contemplating three mermaids apparently playing water-polo (Plate 49) is representative of many

47 *A Gothic cenotaph for Nelson proposed for Trafalgar Square*

46 *John Goldicutt's later proposal as seen from behind the columns of the National Gallery. Nelson stands precariously on a gigantic globe supported by sculptured figures*

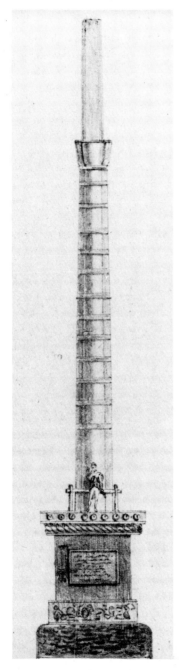

48 Nelson standing at the base of a mast was one surprisingly informal idea

medium-sized, middle-of-the-square suggestions. Certainly the most modest and original was sent in by a designer simply signing himself M.M. He describes himself as a layman, and apologises for his presumption, but creates a simple effect with a mast in place of a column (Plate 48). Even more disarmingly, instead of putting a statue of Nelson on the top of his 112-ft mast, he brings him down to the base. A figure in repose, Nelson stands there, seemingly leaning against a wooden spar, in human rather than godly relation to visitors.

Before we leave Trafalgar Square two other earlier proposals deserve a mention. There would certainly have been no room for Nelson if in 1815 Colonel Trench had been permitted the memorial he wanted to erect there to naval and military victories over France. Pyramids were much in the public mind in the two decades following the Egyptian campaign against Bonaparte, and inspired Trench, the unflagging champion of lost causes. His pyramid (Plate 50) was to be not less than the height of St Paul's – 364 ft – and with a base of the same dimensions it would have almost completely covered the old King's Mews. Each year of the war was to be symbolised by a tier, and on all twenty-two of them would be friezes commemorating deeds of arms. The Duke of York allowed his Pall Mall house to be used for an exhibition of the design by Philip and Matthew Cotes Wyatt, but the pyramid, like all Trench's grandiose schemes, was doomed to oblivion.

Nelson's other potential rival was nothing less than the Roman Colosseum. John Goldicutt, following his antiquarian leanings, proposed it for the square in 1832. But the London Amphitheatre was not to celebrate victories. Nor was it for gladiatorial contests or chariot races. No cages were to be provided for wild beasts. The architect's intention was peaceful and humanitarian – a building 'to concentrate the Scientific Bodies of the Metropolis and to provide suitable accommodation to the encouragement of Infant Societies'. In his view (Plate 51) the portico of St Martin-in-the-Fields is on the left, the Royal College of Physicians, right, and old Northumberland House in the distance. In addition to scientific societies the London Amphitheatre was to be large enough to house the Royal Academy, Royal Society of Literature, Geological Society, Astronomical Society and many others.

Goldicutt's Colosseum was an inflated version of a much smaller, oblong building that Nash had proposed six years earlier for a Royal Academy to form a central feature of the anticipated square. As this had been turned

50 Colonel Trench's pyramid was designed by Philip and Matthew Cotes Wyatt to serve both as a naval and military monument. As tall as St Paul's, it would have cost £1 million, which Trench considered 'an expense not burthensome to the nation'

51 *Proposed Roman Colosseum*
for Trafalgar Square (1832)

down at the time, it is hard to imagine how Goldicutt could have imagined —
if he did — that his mighty Colosseum stood any chance.

If we now move down Whitehall, and pass through the gateway on the
right onto Horse Guards Parade we are on the site of one of the innumerable
monuments suggested, like Trench's pyramid, to mark victory over the
French. Proposed by Soane in 1828 the Monopteral Temple was as unusual as
its name (Plate 52). Squat, with a shallow dome and three entrances
supported on short Doric columns, the temple was not simply a victory
monument: it was to enshrine the Duke of York who had died the previous
year. Before Benjamin Wyatt's Duke of York's Column was decided on,
several designers were casting around for ways to commemorate George III's
second son who was Commander-in-Chief at Waterloo. Soane displayed him
with Field-Marshal's baton extended on top of the dome.

Nine far-from-functional caryatides decorate the temple along with twelve
urns and a large number of lions so dismal that they could never be called a
pride. On either side of the entrances are the temple's most curious features:
rearing cavalry mounts are challenged by kneeling soldiers with raised
bayonets. Unfortunately the infantrymen, who, since they wear shakos, are
presumably the hated French, look far more gallant than the English
horsemen. Along with a fulsome letter in his own hand to George IV this
infelicitous affair by Soane seems to have been a last-minute addition to his
1828 version of *Public Improvements* for the presentation volume at Windsor.

For real memorial problems we cross the park to the top of Constitution
Hill where Wellington was involved in battles as gruelling as any in his
campaigns. At Hyde Park Corner we find the Iron Duke very modestly
immortalised on a horse. To have achieved a memorial anyway comparable to

Nelson's, Wellington would probably have needed to die at Waterloo. Not that the nation was ungrateful: but a living war leader cannot quite arouse the same pitch of patriotic fervour as a dead hero.

One of the earliest ideas to mark Wellington's 'ever glorious victory at Waterloo' (as the inscription would have read) was a Triumphal Arch beside Apsley House. This heavy, ornate affair (Plate 53) by Robert Wetten in 1828 makes us grateful that instead we have the delicate Decimus Burton screen and gateway at the entrance to Hyde Park. The arch was discarded as was

52 *Sir John Soane's Temple of Victory on Horse Guards Parade. As well as celebrating the defeat of the French it was to serve as a mausoleum for the Duke of York, whose statue is on the dome*

53 *Robert Wetten's triumphal arch at Hyde Park Corner to commemorate the Battle of Waterloo was to be placed astride Piccadilly. Visitors arriving in London from the west would be obliged to pass beneath it*

another Waterloo monument of the same decade, a bridge which the visionary John Martin proposed for the Marylebone Road. Martin's 1820 drawing (Plate 54) shows the public climbing up and over a very steep flight of steps between Portland Place and Regent's Park under a statue of Wellington who is poised on the tallest of the truncated marble gun barrels.

The greatest controversy over a Wellington memorial raged in 1846 when there was a determination to honour him at Hyde Park Corner even though he was still very much alive. The Duke had the strange experience of coming out on his balcony at Apsley House to watch a colossal equestrian statue of himself being erected. Weighing forty tons and 27 ft tall, the statue required twenty-nine dray horses to bring it to the top of Constitution Hill and giant cranes to lift it onto the triumphal Wellington Arch.

The statue was yet another idea by Colonel Trench that misfired, and can only be called a might-have-been in so far as it might still be part of the London scene, but isn't. Trench once again involved the Wyatts – the sculptor Matthew Cotes Wyatt, on this occasion assisted by his son James, also a sculptor. Their figure of the Duke on his horse, Copenhagen, at Waterloo immediately came in for a hail of criticism. 'The grossest outrage on the public taste which has ever disgraced Her Majesty's Reign,' a writer to

54 John Martin's design for a National Monument to commemorate Waterloo. His triumphal arch would have been built across Marylebone Road (then the New Road) at the north end of Portland Place. Holy Trinity Church (now the SPCK headquarters) can be seen through the archway

The Times called it. *Punch* described the giant horse as a *night-mare*, but it wasn't a mare, and for anatomical reasons is said to have so shocked Queen Victoria as she viewed it from below that she required its removal. In 1884 the statue was taken down, banished into rural exile in a clump of trees outside Aldershot, and replaced by the small existing statue of the Duke.

A mile further west we come to London's most abused memorial and one which the prescient Prince Albert dreaded. When a monument to him was suggested after the 1851 Exhibition he had written: 'I can say, with perfect absence of humbug, that I would much rather not be made the prominent feature of such a monument ... If (as is very likely) it became an artistic monstrosity, like so many monuments, it would upset my equanimity to be permanently ridiculed and laughed at in effigy.'

No one could save Albert from this prophetic fate when he died in 1861. Several of the principal designers of the day immediately went into top gear, and one of their first ideas was a 150-ft obelisk on the site of the Great Exhibition. An appropriate, but wildly impracticable thought would have been to turn the Crystal Palace on its end (Plate 55) so that it became a 1000-ft Crystal Tower. In fact, this was not a memorial suggestion but a way of getting rid of the building which, by Albert's death, had already been removed to Sydenham.

Queen Victoria did not care for the obelisk idea, and in the May following Albert's death seven architects were asked for their advice – as individuals not competitors. But, even if politely called a 'submission of proposals', a competition inevitably took place. Finally nine designers were involved, among them Sydney Smirke, the brothers Charles and Edward Barry, James Pennethorne, and Matthew Digby Wyatt (cousin of the sculptor of the ill-fated Wellington statue).

Before the choice fell on George Gilbert Scott's enormously elaborate structure, the Queen had a varied collection of designs from which to choose. At first she did not fancy Gilbert Scott's memorial which reminded her too much of Kemp's monument to Sir Walter Scott in Edinburgh. Some others she found too mausoleum-like. Her early preference was for the statue by Philip Hardwick. Hardwick was one of the few designers who left the figure of Albert completely uncovered to the sky, and not overshadowed by elaborate superstructure (Plate 56A). Raised above a terraced garden, the approach to the standing figure was past a fountain pool and three different flights of stairs. Albert was closely surrounded by female beauties whom we may safely assume to be the Muses.

The enclosed feeling which Victoria disliked is produced by the memorial of T. E. Donaldson who at sixty-seven was the oldest competitor. This back view (Plate 56B) is interesting because it shows his idea for an Albert Hall, also not built, with a columned portico in Kensington Gore. Though the Queen was undecided, Lord Palmerston was, as usual, emphatic. The former Prime Minister thought all the designers were frittering away the main idea in 'a Multitude of complicated Details'. He wanted an open Grecian temple with a statue of the Prince 'simple and concentrated'. But for once Palmerston was not to get his way, and Gilbert Scott (whom he had bullied

55 A solution to the problem of what to do with the Crystal Palace at the end of the 1851 Exhibition without taking up too much space in Hyde Park. An architect, C. Burton, proposed standing it on its end to form a 1,000-ft tower

73

74

c

56 Prince Albert exposed and concealed. (A) (Facing, top) Uncovered to the sky, the statue for the Albert Memorial was at the summit of three flights of steps; (B) (Facing, bottom) T. E. Donaldson's proposed Albert Memorial (viewed from the back and showing his idea for the Albert Hall) was among those rejected by Queen Victoria as being 'too enclosed'

(C) To preserve the spirit of the Crystal Palace, which Prince Albert had done so much to encourage, John Wills in 1877 proposed to enshrine the statue in a huge glasshouse, with tropical plants growing in conservatory wings

over the style for the Foreign Office) was the Queen's eventual choice. Once he had lowered the spire so that the Albert Memorial was 148 ft tall instead of a proposed 185 ft, she acclaimed the effect 'really magnificent'.

After Victoria's decision was made, two other men came up with revolutionary ideas. A Liberal MP, A. S. Ayrton, did not want a memorial at all. Instead he advocated an Albert University to be built on a site which would be provided by pulling down St James's Palace. The other suggestion was also not exactly practical, but could be regarded as suitable for Albert as the guiding spirit of the Crystal Palace. John Wills wanted to enclose the entire memorial in a huge glass house, 340 ft high, with flanking winter gardens (Plate 56c). Mr Wills, florist and horticulturist, was not perhaps impartial. Like Paxton, he was also a builder of conservatories.

Our next place of call is Primrose Hill, always fatally attractive to designers. During the 19th century it was the suggested site for a sepulchral pyramid (see p. 144) and for a casino and botanical gardens. Shakespeare was also to have stood there. In 1854 the hill, recently laid out as a public open space, was selected by a French sculptor, M. Chardigny, for an enormous statue of the poet. The exact size is uncertain, but since it was to be bigger than the statue of San Carlo Borromeo on Lake Maggiore it would have been more than 70 ft tall.

The sculptor proposed to cast the figure in ten sections in France for transport to London where it would easily be screwed together. The *Revue des Beaux Arts* hoped that British pride would not take umbrage if France, 'inventive and prodigal by nature' gave Britain 'a statue of the Olympian Shakespeare'. Perhaps umbrage was taken. For the only outdoor statue of the poet London had to wait until 1874 when a modest-sized Shakespeare was placed in Leicester Square.

The French proposal for a colossal statue of Shakespeare on Primrose Hill was revived in 1864 by John Leighton, FSA, inventor of the startlingly

57 A colossal statue of Britannia, 230 ft high, which John Flaxman (1755–1826) proposed for Greenwich Hill in 1799. On approximately the same spot a modest-sized statue of General Wolfe stands today

original scheme for hexagonal London (p. 208). This was the tercentenary year of Shakespeare's birth, and, in celebration, Leighton and a committee proposed not only a statue but a road through Regent's Park. Called Prince of Wales Avenue, it would have started at Park Crescent, cut through the centre of the park, and have passed close under the statue raised on the summit of the hill 207 ft above the Thames.

On the other side of the Thames two high points were chosen for monuments, both proposed in 1799. Shooters Hill in Kent was to be crowned by a pyramid, the notion of William Capon, son of a Norwich portrait painter who had worked as a scenic designer and had built a theatre at Ranelagh. His 250-ft high repository for the records of the famous to be built in Aberdeen granite is seen in the background to the artist's posthumous portrait (Plate 58). This national monument was to be a museum, have rooms for archives, and display statues of naval and military leaders – Marlborough, Nelson, Howe and Wellington among them – erected on pedestals in a circular temple. Outside staircases sloped to the apex of Capon's pyramid which could be ascended for magnificent views of London. On the very top Britannia bestowed the Crown of Reward on victorious heroes.

Britannia was a popular symbol in 1799 – Britain was still cheering the previous year's victory of the Nile – and as well as on Shooters Hill was a candidate for Greenwich Park. She was to take her triumphant stand overlooking the Thames just to the east of the Royal Observatory. Her figure, 230 ft tall, would tower above the Queen's House and be framed by Wren's domes on the Naval Hospital.

This Britannia was conceived by the sculptor John Flaxman who, under the patronage of the future William IV, published another drawing engraved by William Blake (Plate 57) in his pamphlet *Letter to the Committee for Raising the Naval Pillar or Monument*. Above a plinth carrying the inscription, 'Britannia by Divine Providence Triumphant', the huge statue stands holding a spear and with a shield, no longer urgently needed, by her side. The British Lion peers round her skirts, faithful watchdog concerned to get an accolade or at least a bone.

Flaxman, who, in 1799, was already famous for his classical friezes, chose Greenwich Hill because it afforded 'a sublimity of prospect not equalled in any other place' and his Britannia would be visible from London and from ships coming into the Estuary. For his inspiration he took Athena in the Parthenon, for size the Colossus of Rhodes, and his idea of Britannia Triumphant as his model for the Genius of the Empire. 'It is a work,' he wrote, 'intended to last as long as the Trajan Column, the Amphitheatre or the Pyramids of Egypt. . . .'

Far from lasting, Flaxman's Britannia never began. She joins the legion of lost souls, sunk almost completely without trace, and with nothing to explain their demise. The Naval Pillar or Monument scheme seems to have merged with the Gallery of Honour or Naval Pantheon project for which the Royal Academy invited designs. Both were probably incorporated in the later Patriotic Fund Committee, and all were continually throwing up unfulfilled proposals for national aggrandisement. John Opie produced a Gallery of National Honour in 1800 to the glory of naval achievement and 'national excellence', and a similar Gallery of Honour may also have been the idea behind a grotesque octagonal tower designed by William Wilkinson of Nottingham. He presented a painting of his 'National Mausoleum' to the Prince Regent in 1814. Whatever its exact purpose, Greenwich Park again had a narrow escape for this was the planned position for this horrendous Gothic folly.

In our return across the Thames we pass yet another of these naval monuments, a huge bronze statue of Nelson rising out of the centre of the river between Waterloo and Westminster Bridges on a massive base, the brainchild of Sir William Hillary in 1825, and akin to another mid-Thames statue to Sir Robert Peel, who, supported by splayed metal stilts, was to stand high and in front of Westminster or Vauxhall Bridges.

58 William Capon with his proposed pyramid for Shooters Hill

At Smithfield and on the Embankment we encounter two very diverse obelisks, one never built, the other erected in a different place from the spot originally suggested. In 1745, the year of the Jacobite rising and of a planned London invasion by the Catholic Prince Charles Edward Stuart, the Young Pretender, an ardent but unnamed Protestant backed 'by several gentlemen of his sentiments' proposed an anti-Catholic monument in the square where the Protestants had suffered in the Marian persecution. This pedestal-shaped obelisk was topped with the figure of Victory triumphant over Popery. An engraving of the intended warning appeared in the *Gentleman's Magazine*, where it was reported that the inscription on the base would read: 'To the perpetual memory of the cruel triumphs of popery, and to instruct Protestants of what may again be expected, if the British crown should ever be placed on a Popish head. . . .' The monument was never built. Culloden made it unnecessary.

The other obelisk, Cleopatra's Needle, had a chequered career before it was finally erected in its present position on the Embankment in 1878. Fifty-nine years after it had been presented to Britain by the Turkish ruler of Egypt to mark the defeat of Napoleon, London was far from anxious to receive the gift. An almost xenophobic dislike for an object so weird and alien seemed to possess people. 'Fatally suggestive of a factory chimney' was the jeer.

The real problem was where to put it. The Adelphi steps were decided on only after several other places had been considered and much mystical nonsense talked about choosing a site of the right 'moral fitness'. Parliament Square was morally fit; the British Museum forecourt somehow was not. Cleopatra's Needle could now stand in place of Queen Anne in front of St Paul's; among urns and fountains in St James's Park; by Greenwich Hospital (associations with Nelson and the Nile); and on a purpose-built island in the middle of the Round Pond in Kensington Gardens.

Parliament Square was the site most hoped for by John Dixon, the engineer responsible for transporting the obelisk from Egypt, but this was opposed by Charles Barry, the younger, who saw it as an alien infringement on his father's building. In a bid to overcome opposition, Dixon had a full-sized replica of Cleopatra's Needle built in wood, painted, and put up near the statue of Palmerston (Plate 59). Gilbert Scott and Edmund Street, the Law Courts architect, supported Dixon, and we might well have Cleopatra's Needle not where it is but in Parliament Square had directors of the Metropolitan Railway not issued an ominous warning that vibrations from the trains might bring 180 tons of granite crashing down onto their line.

Most of the monuments considered on this perambulation are inclined to make us grateful to have been spared them. So it is a welcome corrective to make our last place of call Piccadilly Circus to look at a statue which as well as being widely loved is far superior to all rival ideas for monuments to replace it. If a number of civic dignitaries had been given their way, Lord Shaftesbury, the social reformer after whom Shaftesbury Avenue was named, would have been commemorated by a conventional likeness. Instead of Eros poised on a fountain, a bearded man in a frock coat would stand on a severe pedestal.

In the face of every sort of criticism, the sculptor Alfred Gilbert set his face against what he called 'coat and trouser' memorial statuary. Working secretly to avoid advance opposition, he produced a statue which did not show Shaftesbury the man but symbolised the love and the speed with which his charity flowed to help the needy. It was an inspired conception constructed in aluminium for lightness. Eros is not only London's most original memorial; it is almost certainly far better than any alternative would have been.

60 The Thames Quay, devised by Colonel Trench in 1825 with help from Benjamin D. Wyatt, Philip W. Wyatt and John Rennie. Details from T. M. Bayne's panorama showing a section of the quay from Waterloo to the Temple with (left) the Adelphi-style terrace, which was later scrapped. Outraged that their view of the river would be obscured, the Benchers of the Temple opposed and helped to kill the project

Chapter 8

The Thames Quay

LONDON ignored the opportunity created by the Great Fire to tidy up its ramshackle waterfront. Five days of conflagration left the riverside from the Tower to the Temple a devastated wilderness with hardly a building standing. This was the obvious moment not only for new commercial buildings but for joining all the wharves together to make a unified quay. In their post-Fire schemes Wren, Newcourt and Knight all envisaged the construction of grand new quays that would have rivalled those of any Continental capital.

The City Corporation favoured a broad, paved quay, 80 ft wide, lined with well-constructed warehouses, and with landing facilities for goods and passengers. The Rebuilding Act of 1670 settled for a more modest affair only 40 ft wide. It directed that buildings erected within this strip since the Fire should be demolished immediately. Unfortunately the City was far too busy rebuilding its destroyed centre to be over-concerned about what was happening along the river. After eight months Wren felt obliged to complain to King Charles that the riverside was still cluttered with irregular buildings, mountains of coal, boarded sheds and dung heaps. The King threatened 'utmost penalties', and royal threats seem temporarily to have been effective. An impressive 'New Key' is shown on the large-scale survey of the City of London by Ogilby and Morgan completed in 1676. But it did not survive

long. Makeshift sheds were soon re-erected, and then stealthily replaced by more permanent brick structures.

By 1746, when London's next large-scale survey was made by the émigré mapmaker John Rocque, encroachments had become so widespread that scarcely any remnants of the Restoration quay survived. Yet the need for a continuous quay along the waterfront remained, and with the growth of trade became even more necessary. In 1766 John Gwynn in his imaginative *London and Westminster Improved* proposed quays on each side of the river, each 120 ft wide with 60 ft reserved for loading or landing cargoes. Running along north and south banks, they connected Westminster, Blackfriars, and London Bridges – and a fourth bridge to be named St George's. Gwynn prophetically visualised this new bridge exactly where Rennie's Waterloo Bridge was started forty years later.

Both quays were to be lined with elegant houses and warehouses with large courtyards, and Gwynn shows the quays running the whole length of both banks, but he is imprecise about how far they would extend. This seems strange until we remember that in the 18th century there was none of the present-day concern about roads for fast-moving *through* traffic. Gwynn's quays were highways only incidentally; his main concern was the creating of a monumental effect in the centre of London. The proposal remained a dream, but in common with Gwynn's other dreams, it served to inspire visionaries of the following century.

61 Colonel Trench, MP, knighted in 1832, promoted General in 1854 (see also Plate 1)

Not surprisingly John Nash was the next to consider the necessity of a Thames quay, and incorporated it into his overall scheme for improving the western area of the metropolis. Nash's plan was for a single quay extending down the river from bridge to bridge. It would stand on columns or arches on the line of low water, concealing the mud but allowing the water to flow beneath, and barges to land their cargoes. An interesting feature of the design was the opening up of a vista from St Paul's 'to the very shores of the Thames' in a manner 'beyond measure magnificent'. Preliminary designs for the quay were drawn, but set aside while Nash concentrated all his energies on the development of Regent Street and Regent's Park.

Nash evidently regarded his quay plans very seriously. He showed them, he says, to most of his friends, and apparently to people in high places. Regrettably his drawings have not survived, and our knowledge of them is limited to the descriptions in the pages of the periodical *John Bull* by Nash and a writer who was privileged to see them.

One acquaintance of Nash who did not see the plans, but drew up curiously similar ones of his own was Colonel Trench (Plate 61), the Irish Protestant and Tory MP for Cambridge, of whose previous exploits we have already heard. He had got nowhere with his pyramid for Trafalgar Square in 1815, and in 1825 was to be ridiculed for his royal palace in Hyde Park with its two-mile avenue approach from St Paul's. Undeterred by the former setback, Trench in the previous summer had startled London with his most ambitious plan of all. It set everyone talking about the man who until then was little known to the general public.

Born in 1775 at Ballinakill in Ireland, Frederick William Trench spent most of his first forty years in mundane military duties. His appearances in the House of Commons were desultory, and he was not much heard of there until the doldrums after the Napoleonic War. The diarist Greville called him 'that impudent Irish pretender' without saying pretender to what, and other memoirs record his fleeting appearances in fashionable drawing-rooms.

All the while, Trench, who was something of a dandy, had been cultivating people in society and the arts, and it was in the Arlington Street house of the Duke and Duchess of Rutland that he first found support for his Thames Quay. Some years before, the Duke had sponsored him for a Parliamentary seat. Now nearing fifty, and still retaining the dandy's touch, Trench launched his plan in a highly original manner. He borrowed the state barge of the Merchant Taylors Company, and took an influential party of noblemen and gentlemen out into the Thames in July 1824.

At a strategic point between Charing Cross and Waterloo Bridge Trench unfolded his plan to an audience that included the Duke and Duchess of Rutland; the Earl of Rosslyn, Chancellor of the Exchequer; Lord Palmerston; the Marquess of Londonderry; and the Lord Mayor, Alderman Sir Matthew Wood. The expedition took the form of a meeting, at which the Duke of York, brother to the King, was the chairman.

Trench explained that the banks of the river which they could now see would be transformed by the construction of a beautiful promenade and carriage road, 80 ft wide, and supported on arches (Plate 60). The Quay would, in effect, be a new street for London and had been designed for him by the brothers Philip and Benjamin Wyatt with engineering advice given by John Rennie. Ultimately it would provide a new line of communication from Scotland Yard in the west to Rennie's new London Bridge in the east, on which construction had just started. But initially it would run from the bottom of Craven Street, which would be the link with the Strand, out onto a curving pier, and so, interconnecting with Waterloo Bridge, as far as Blackfriars.

With footpaths, rows of trees and lamps, and a carriage road, the Quay, very much in the style of a Paris boulevard, would be a pleasant place for a Sunday stroll. It would also relieve the intolerable traffic congestion in the Strand. Lining the quay just to the west of Waterloo Bridge would be an Adelphi-style terrace of houses and handsome fountains which, by harnessing the tides, would throw *jets-d'eau* 50 ft into the air.

The fountains and other ornamental ideas, said Trench, had been the suggestion of the Duchess of Rutland (Plate 62) whom he was delighted to see with them today. The Duchess was sitting in the barge immediately on the right of the Duke of York, and their proximity was not accidental. It was one of the social intrigues which were inseparable from Trench's campaign. The association of the Duke of York and the wife of the 5th Duke of Rutland was an open secret. Though he was over sixty, he was much enamoured of the Duchess who, now in her mid-forties, had once been a great beauty. The Duchess's drawing-room was Trench's foothold in society, and her liaison brought him into the orbit of the royal family – both invaluable to his hopes for the success of his scheme. Later in his speech, and after another

62 *Elizabeth, Duchess of Rutland, the Regency beauty with a taste for the arts, who lent her influence to help Trench's Thames Quay proposal. After successfully transforming Belvoir Castle and its estate, she set about replanning parts of London. She produced designs for an entrance at Hyde Park Corner, embellishments for the parks, a grand royal palace, and also York House, whose owner, the Duke, was her admirer*

compliment to the Duchess, he played a diplomatic card. He announced his intention of placing a large equestrian statue in the centre of the Quay. He was sure he would have everyone's agreement that this must be a statue of His Majesty King George IV.

The meeting expressed its approval, and a committee of thirty-seven members was appointed to investigate practicability. Colonel Trench could feel well pleased with the day's work. On the committee of the Quay Company (launched soon afterwards) the list of supporters was augmented by Prince Leopold of Belgium, three dukes (including Wellington), one marquis, three earls, two viscounts, three lesser peers, the Attorney-General, nineteen MPs and several members of the City Corporation.

The whole scheme seemed opportune. 'The Nation is at Peace, the Prices of Labour and Materials are moderate, Capital is plentiful,' said Trench in his company prospectus. The contrast between the beauty of Paris and London's shabby appearance could only be galling to the English, especially after the defeat of Napoleon. The Thames Quay was the right plan in the right place at the right time, or so it seemed.

But not to everyone. One week after the meeting on the river, *John Bull* accused Trench of having plagiarised John Nash's quay drawings. Nash was disturbed by the implications, and on his return from a visit abroad absolved Trench from any blame. He wrote to Trench from his home at Cowes: 'I shall have as much pleasure as yourself in seeing the River Thames and its beautiful bridges made to contribute to the magnificence of the metropolis, instead of being shut out from public view. ... If my plans to effect that purpose can be of any use to you, who have so laudably taken up the subject, they are very much at your service.'

More serious criticism came from people who would be affected by the Quay. The plan was denounced by the Duke of Norfolk and the Duke of Northumberland (both with great riverside properties), by the Benchers of the Temple (determined not to have the view of the river from their gardens cut off) and by shopkeepers in the Strand (among them Richard Twining, the tea merchant near Temple Bar) who were afraid the new road would by-pass and ruin them.

'Who would think of promenading along the channel of a great hazy, ague-giving river in any case?' asked a writer to *The Times*. Would not the narrowing of the river inundate the lower south bank and navigation be impeded? 'Colonel Trench may be a very good soldier, but he does not seem to know much about water affairs,' observed a Member of Parliament with a house on the river who drew an anguished picture of himself prematurely entombed by the Quay. At Christmas that year the controversial topic was ridiculed on the London stage in a pantomime.

An oddly divided debate followed the Bill's presentation in the Commons in the following March. At one moment Trench heard himself being congratulated; the next jeered at as a dreamer 'infatuated with his own project'. John Cam Hobhouse, friend of Byron and MP for Westminster, thought the Quay was 'calculated to beautify the Metropolis', but he opposed it. Another Member called the Quay 'a splendid improvement' but also opposed it since it might spoil the view of the river enjoyed by the Prime Minister, Lord Liverpool. But despite the weight of argument against the Quay, when the House divided eighty-five Members voted for the motion, forty-five against.

Before detailed scrutiny of the plans took place, Trench modified them. First he scrapped his Adelphi-style terrace. Although this building gave the Quay a monumental grandeur, it would have eclipsed the actual Adelphi as well as obstructing the view from about 300 houses. He also decided to dispense with the proposed harbour, behind the Quay near Hungerford Market, which was to have been used by barges for unloading goods on the existing riverbank. Its opponents foresaw that this would quickly become a 'dirty, offensive, useless pond', a 'magazine of miasma', a 'preserve for pestilence'.

The Wyatts went back to their drawing board, Trench *retrenched* (this pun was much overworked by his critics in the newspapers), and an alternative arrangement was arrived at. The area behind the Quay would be filled in, and a new market built on the ground created. To visualise the plan we have only to imagine Hungerford Market pulled down and replaced by the harbour and market occupying the same area as the present-day Victoria Embankment Gardens. The line of his Quay would have been roughly where the Embankment river wall is today.

An attractive street was to link the Strand with the Quay and unload between the arches. But even with these modifications the Quay came under fire. Within ten days a protest committee of wharf proprietors and riverside property owners called a meeting at the Crown and Anchor, Arundel Street. 'Alarm and dismay' was voiced and an objection put in a petition to Parliament in April 1825. The profits of the wharves amounting to more than £32,000 a year would be cut to £8,000. Strand shopkeepers complained they would lose nearly £70,000 a year. 'Pauperism' would be increased by the deterioration of the area, and the Government's revenue would fall.

Sensing that it would be politic to let the storm die down, Trench announced that he did not propose to press the Thames Quay Bill until the next session. But in the autumn, just when the campaign for the Quay should have been revived, the Duchess of Rutland died suddenly. Her husband was inconsolable and the Duke of York shattered. It was not a good moment to reopen talks about a scheme on which they had worked together and which held such recent memories. What Trench hoped would be only a postponement turned out to be the end. There was more newspaper controversy. Magnificent lithographs showing the Quay with and without the terrace were printed and circulated. Trench even published a *Collection of Papers Relating to the Thames Quay with Hints for Some Further Improvements in the Metropolis* with a dedication to the Duke of Rutland in which he sang the praises of the 'lamented duchess'. With remarkable fairness this volume voiced all the arguments for, as well as against the Quay. But all Trench's objectivity led to nothing.

A further blow had come in the same year, 1827, with the death of the Duke of York. As he was staying with the Duke of Rutland at Arlington Place at the time of his death, the old liaison with the Duchess would appear to have left no lingering ill will. But the two deaths meant that Trench lost first his most decorative and then his most eminent patron. Benjamin Wyatt alone benefited. He started designs for the Duke of York's Column, the memorial to be built on the site of Carlton House.

A good soldier does not hang about on the field of defeat. Trench made a tactical withdrawal pursued by the mild spray of grapeshot in the form of a poem in which the writer amiably remarked:

> Yet I like thee, pleasant Tr———;
> Though the sages of the Bench
> Would not give a single stiver
> For thy bridge *along* the river;
> Though the dames of Billingsgate
> Swore to duck thee soon or late;
> Though the guardians of the mud
> Would have swamp'd thee, ebb or flood . . .

For the pleasant Colonel further flights of fancy lay ahead. There were now also official duties. Almost as a consolation prize, it seems, the King appointed him his aide-de-camp, and Wellington made him his Ordnance Storekeeper. In the Parliamentary phrase, the Thames Quay Bill was 'ordered to lie on the table', and on the table it remained.

The idea of a quay was not instantly forgotten. In September 1829, a certain 'G.M.' (full name not disclosed) placed a lengthy description of an economy quay in the advertisement columns of the *Literary Gazette*. His quay would consist of a line of flat-bottomed ships – galleys, merchantmen, frigates, or even men-of-war of the largest size – not floating but fixed and resting on the foreshore, their bows and sterns in a line with the tide. Iron bridges, handsomely cast, would link them, and a highway, 16 ft wide with flanking pavements, would run along the top of the vessels. The upper parts of the ships would be let out to businessmen and invalids (the latter benefiting somehow from the fresh air always to be found on board ship) and the lower parts would be converted into warehouses.

For a few years after this, property owners enjoyed the fruits of their victory. They continued to operate their wharves in a state of commercial confusion untroubled by tiresome reformers. At each low tide great mudbanks were revealed, made increasingly more putrid and offensive by sewage drained into the river by the ever-growing population of London. Then in 1832 a new prophet appeared on the banks of the Thames. A landscape painter in love with history, John Martin (Plate 63), brought a touch of extravagant artistry to a practical plan. There were no takers.

Martin had come to London early in the century from Northumberland, and quickly made his name with a series of vast canvases in a romantic tradition. He specialised in scenes of wild grandeur in which classical palaces were poised on mountain peaks under thunderous skies. They were extremely popular. But even as the puny figures in these awesome surroundings defy the elements and seem intent on escaping from dark cavern or deep ravine, so Martin wanted to extend his interests beyond the confines of painting. In the age of Brunel and Stephenson, he felt frustrated at being an artist.

IIis aspiration to be an engineer and practical man led him away from painting and towards the problem of an expanding London and such mundane matters as the supply of fresh water, disposal of sewage, and the pollution of the Thames. Plans for sewers and water conduits grew into a preoccupation, and in 1827 he published a treatise on bringing pure water to London from the River Colne. This was illustrated in his best romantic manner with imaginative views of ornamental waters into which crystal streams cascaded on their limpid way from Hertfordshire valley to city tap.

Martin's life became devoted to engineering and the problem of supplying water and disposing of sewage. This led him to plan a Quay not unlike Trench's. Haunted by the nightmare of 'the excrementitious matter from nearly a million and a half human beings', he devised a scheme for two closed serwers, one on the north side of the river from Millbank to the Regent's canal. From here sewage would be carried by train to open fields of Essex for the use of agriculturists or sprayed in liquid form over Surrey.

Lest all this should seem obnoxious to sensitive nostrils, these Grand Sewers, as Martin dignified them, would be incorporated in even grander Quays along which would be magnificent buildings. Wharves would be replaced by colonnaded promenades for the public baths that were to contribute to the 'health and cleanliness of the working classes'. His imagination gave all this the splendour of ancient Carthage.

In the *Report of Select Committees on Metropolitan Improvements*, published in 1838, is a drawing by Martin which shows the Quay, probably at the Tower (Plate 64). It is a beguiling, not to say dazzling prospect. There are covered promenades on three levels, each tier supported on rows of

63 John Martin (1789–1854), melodramatic history painter and visionary planner

64 John Martin's three-level Quay, Grand Sewer and – for romantic flavour – Egyptian barges

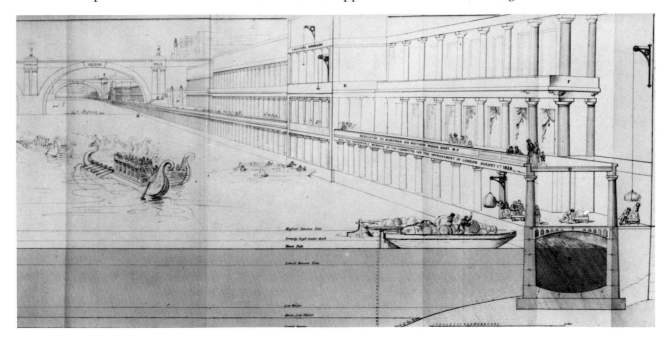

65 *A biblical fantasy entitled*
Pandemonium *by John Martin*
appears to incorporate the artist's
ideas for a Thames Embankment
with ghostly Houses of Parliament
in the background

Tuscan columns, and the middle tier on which the public stroll is backed
with alcoves which, if we can believe our eyes, are draped in tasselled
curtains. Below, at water-level, honest London stevedores load sacks into
sturdy Thames barges, but further out in the river there are twelve-oared
Egyptian galleys fit for Cleopatra. The Nile is further suggested by the bridge
on which are inscribed Nelson's Egyptian battle honours. Lest we should
forget the sterner function of the Quay a cut-off section under the bottom tier
shows the Grand Sewer that is to carry London's waste to distant fields.

A committee set up by the Institute of British Architects with Faraday and
Turner among its members studied Martin's plans, and declared the artist to
be a genius. His plan they found 'completely effectual' and – a little
surprising this – also 'simple'. Unexpected support came from the Italian-
born Dr Augustus Granville who welcomed the Quay 'from a medico-
political point of view' because it would provide walking exercise for the
working classes. Lack of this exercise, the doctor explained, 'produces in the
same class of people a melancholy and morose disposition and a spirit of
dissatisfaction increased by the want of domestic attraction and impaired
health'. This hurries them to drunkenness. Martin must have been pleased to
hear that, apart from anything else, his Quay was going to improve public
health, cheer people up, quell incipient revolution, provide a substitute for

ugly houses (or plain wives), and serve as a remedy for alcoholism.

The committee declared the Quay cheap at £1,500,000; Trench conceded it superior to his own; and the *Architectural Magazine* described it as 'grand and sublime'. This was endorsed by forty-four MPs, eighteen Fellows of the Royal Society, and six Royal Academicians. The Archbishop of Canterbury bestowed his blessing; but after one brief afternoon's sitting in 1844, the Royal Commission on Metropolitan Improvements rejected the scheme on the grounds that it was 'unequal' to other plans, and the value of manure 'unproved'. Private water companies with vested interests in pumping from the river were delighted, and assured Londoners that they need have no fears of pollution because God had provided 'special organs to prevent one being poisoned by water'.

Even before this Martin was admitting: 'I feel myself a ruined, crushed man, I shall sink now.' He had run through the small fortune earned by paintings and had reached the point of bankruptcy. Faced with the breakup of home and family and the debtors' prison, his sanity began to waver, and during sleepless nights his mind went feverishly over his failed plans. Even admiring friends feared to visit him because of his monotonous litany of how he had been swindled and ruined.

Fortunately the artist in him reasserted itself. Martin went back to painting, and slowly his finances improved. To this period of recovery in the 1840s belongs his most dramatic vision of London under the title of *Pandemonium* (Plate 65) based ostensibly on *Paradise Lost*. He shows us a view across the river at a range of buildings that resembles grandiose Houses of Parliament in the classical style and the Victoria Tower looming up mistily in the background darkness. Gas lamps illuminate a promenade built on a colonnade just like his Quay. In the foreground – as it were on the Lambeth shore – stands a figure with upraised arms who could be Satan, Joshua, Moses or perhaps John Martin himself, a shield for protection against his critics, a spear for attack, his wild hair symbolic of his state of mind. Like Prospero, he appears to be working his magic, subduing the turbulent waters of opposition, and conjuring up his mighty vision of London.

In 1841 Trench – now Major-General Sir Frederick Trench – came back into battle. Disentangling himself from other strange schemes (which included annual gifts to Queen Victoria of ornately bound bibles), he now had a new idea. The irrepressible innovator had caught the prevailing Railway Mania.

An open letter to Viscount Duncannon, First Commissioner of Woods and Forests, was couched in all his customary enthusiastic terms:

The Plan I now propose will bring Grandeur and Beauty into daily and hourly Observation, and no one will deny that a Railroad running from London Bridge to Hungerford Bridge (which may be passed over in Four Minutes) will be a great Accommodation to the Public, and I think it will be admitted that such a Colonnade as I now propose to you, affording a Walk of One Mile and Three Quarters in Length and sheltered from the Sun and Rain, will be a feature of Utility amid Magnificence not to be equalled in any Capital in Europe.

66 *Trench's Thames-side elevated railway (1841), a modified version of his earlier proposed Thames Quay. Trains would run on wooden rails above; pedestrians, protected from sun and rain, would promenade beneath. The electric telegraph employed for the signals on the line would also be made available to carry orders from the Admiralty*

Trains would be drawn along the colonnade not by steam-engines but by a power-driven cable to which carriages would be attached. The rails were to be of wood ('so that there will be no more noise than when a Carriage passes over a Wooden Pavement'!); the termini were at Hungerford Market and London Bridge; the journey far faster than horse-bus or steamer; and the fare between $4\frac{1}{2}$d and 6d.

A lithograph published with the proposal stressed the unobtrusive elegance of the scheme (Plate 66). Trench remembered that fifteen years earlier his Quay had been rejected partly because 'some Persons of Rank residing on the banks of the River were opposed to it'. So now he emphasised that his elevated railway would adversely affect no one. In the print St Paul's and Temple Gardens are shown as a misty, tranquil background to the slim delicate colonnade. Two couples leaning on 'a chaste and simple balustrade' gaze at a placid river on which a boatman is punting. As for the railway carriages, they are as graceful as a Regency coach.

Aided by Mr George Bidder, 'once known as the celebrated calculating boy', Trench had worked out dazzling prospects for investors – an annual profit of £1,000,000 a year, and a surplus over twenty-five years of a further £1,000,000 for the added attraction of an ornamental fountain and monumental approach to St Paul's. But the figures were wildly optimistic. They presupposed four carriages running each way carrying 100 passengers for twelve trips an hour, twelve hours a day for 365 days of the year. The financial fallibility did not escape the Chancellor of the Exchequer. When Trench's new plan came up in the House he suggested that the Hon. and Gallant Member should withdraw his motion in his own interests, and bring it forward at some future time.

For Trench that phrase must have had a familiar ring of doom. Now sixty-five, the old fight seemed to have gone out of him. He withdrew his motion and his elevated railway was not heard of again. But the seeds of the idea continued to sprout, and five years later visitors to the Royal Academy were confronted with a magnificent panorama for an embankment between Blackfriars Bridge and Southwark Bridge.

This was a painting by Thomas Allom (Plate 67), an architect who shared some of Martin's sense of grandeur, but saw the Quay on a more human scale. A rigid classical monotony was relieved by terraces, private houses and shops in a variety of styles and of differing heights. Allom appears to have done away with New Bridge Street in favour of a curved approach to St Paul's passing just to the west of St Andrew by the Wardrobe and prophetically taking the line of the modern Blackfriars Bridge Underpass.

As a painting Allom's conception was accounted 'quite marvellous' by the critics, but there was some carping that the architecture was 'made up of just the same showy fronts as are now in vogue in the new trading streets'. This was unlikely to have upset Allom, who, as far as we know, was concerned simply with producing an attractive *capriccio*.

The next person to pursue the idea had more serious intentions. He was W. H. Smith, now remembered chiefly as the founder of railway bookstalls.

67 A Thames Embankment as envisaged by the architect-artist, Thomas Allom in 1846. 'Pleasant but visionary' was Art Union's *opinion*

In 1851, the year of the Great Exhibition, Smith obtained exclusive rights for all bookstalls on the London and North-Western stations. A strict Methodist, he took them partly to prevent the sale of what he called 'cheap French novels of the shadiest class'. We may be sure these novels were quickly eased out of the way by Smith's own pamphlet, *LONDON not as it is but AS IT SHOULD BE* (price 6d).

Smith outlined a plan for an embankment on the north side of the river from Wapping to Westminster, and on the south from Rotherhithe to Lambeth Palace. The 'Esplanade and Terraced Highway' embodied Martin's earlier ideas for sewers, and also had underground culverts to carry gas and water. Like Trench, Smith wanted a railway as part of his plan, but instead of elevating it, he took the line underground thus envisaging the future District Line. A touch of fantasy is provided by a crude illustration in the pamphlet which brings the National Gallery (opened in Trafalgar Square thirteen years earlier) onto the new Embankment. A subsidiary benefit was to be the reclamation of 'pernicious and malignant' mudbanks that had contributed to the cholera epidemics of the previous few years.

The interesting thing about W. H. Smith's scheme is that it foreshadowed almost exactly the Victoria Embankment, really important decisions about which were taken in the early 1860s. On 9 March 1861, 'parties desirous of submitting plans for embanking the river Thames' were instructed to do so in an advertisement in *The Times*. Fifty-nine schemes arrived to be examined

68 A causeway of buildings down the river, reminiscent of the Île de la Cité in Paris, was a scheme by H. R. Newton in 1861. It would include Government offices, Law Courts, a new addition to Somerset House and some private buildings

by the Thames Bank Commissioners, and their proposers were called in one by one and grilled by the Commissioners.

Messrs Hukins & Co. described an embankment that would stretch not just from Blackfriars to Westminster Palace but all the way to Kew, and a Mr Marshall Talbot called – prophetically – for the Thames to be dammed at Woolwich. A Mr Edward Finch proposed nothing less than 'a new Bed for the River between Deptford and Vauxhall retaining the present River as a Fresh water lake'. William Bardwell, tame architect of Peter Rigby Wason who featured in the Houses of Parliament controversies (see p. 98), now called for a new channel to be dredged down the Thames for steamboats, the resulting ballast to be used for constructing a viaduct.

The most amazing scheme of all was that of Harry Robert Newton (Plate 68). Newton, who exhibited at the Royal Academy and described himself as an architect, had already made one or two forays into the territory of peculiar ideas. Now he surpassed himself. His proposal was that two great causeways should be erected, not across the Thames, or adjacent to its banks, but actually down the river – that is, within the river itself.

The advantage of this 'simple scheme' (as Newton claimed it to be) was that it would furnish the new roads London needed while at the same time creating an 'estate'. By this he meant that the causeways would serve as sites and the roads themselves would thus eventually pass through tunnels ('apertures') of magnificent buildings. These buildings would include in

their full Gothic glory the Law Courts, government offices, and two new wings for Somerset House. The remaining 'estate' could be leased for commercial purposes.

'Supposing at some future period it might be considered advisable for the metropolis that this should be fresh river water instead of tidal water', continued the enthusiastic projector, pointing to the strips of water between the causeways and the foreshores on his plans, 'that could be arranged.' All that would be called for would be locks so as to prevent the water in the centre getting through to the sides.

The Commissioners must have gasped. 'I will read you a paragraph of our instructions', interrupted the Chairman, Sir William Cubitt, sternly, 'from which you will see that this very elaborate and beautiful scheme of yours, full of merit as it is, will hardly come within them.'

'I am not aware, my Lord,' replied Newton, sarcastically ennobling Cubitt, 'that my proposition very far exceeds, if at all, those instructions. . . . But, of course,' he continued huffily, 'after such an expression of opinion from you I cannot seek to occupy your time further.'

'Have you formed an estimate of what it would cost?' enquired one Commissioner innocently.

'Yes', snapped Newton.

'What would be the estimated cost on the Middlesex side?' persisted the same gentleman.

'With submission,' retorted Newton, gathering up his plans, 'I do not think I should be asked to give a reply to this question after the intimation from his Lordship that my examination is discontinued.' Newton withdrew.

The man the Commissioners actually appointed to build the Victoria Embankment was Joseph Bazalgette. As chief engineer of the Metropolitan Board of Works, Bazalgette generally gets all the credit, and at the time this angered some of the people who remembered the visions of the pioneers. Dr Granville (who supported John Martin in 1836) was particularly concerned because he thought praise was going to the wrong people. Without acknowledgement the Board of Works had taken Martin's ideas as well as Granville's statistics to help them. 'Poor Martin was dead and gone and could not protest', Granville wrote bitterly in his memoirs.

Trench was also dead by 1864, and so neither of the great planners of the Thames Quay idea saw the realisation of their dreams. The Victoria Embankment took six years to build and involved the reclamation of thirty-seven acres of mudbanks. With road, railway, sewers and river wall, it was a vast engineering achievement for Bazalgette who, with an Act of Parliament behind him, could overcome all the difficulties that had defeated the early visionaries.

Chapter 9

Many Houses of Parliament

IN October 1834 Parliament suddenly became homeless. A fire started by an over-fuelled stove in the House of Lords swept through the haphazard collection of buildings which had grown up over the centuries in the precincts of the old Palace of Westminster. Taking customary delight in the discomfiture of authority, the London crowd filling nearby streets and windows clapped and cheered as roofs fell in. Three Guards regiments, an attachment of Cavalry and some largely ineffectual fire-engines were able to save the medieval Westminster Hall, the crypt of St Stephen's Chapel, and one or two lesser buildings. The rest were in ashes. Grumbling angrily, members of both the Lords and Commons had to find temporary quarters.

Discomfort spurred the Government into action, and within a few months a competition was announced for the rebuilding of the Houses of Parliament. For architects it was the opportunity of a lifetime, a chance not only to make a reputation but secure immortality. Entries poured in.

The design chosen was by Sir Charles Barry, and the building he created is so familiar a London landmark that, though less than 150 years old, it gives the impression of having been there for ever. Largely forgotten are the ninety-six alternative proposals which might be standing at Westminster today. Little is remembered either of earlier schemes.

Even before the 1834 fire there had been many other plans for new Parliament buildings. For centuries the country had lacked a proper seat of government. Members had always had to make do with improvised meeting places. From the 14th century when the 'Commons' began to be convened with any regularity, they had assembled in the Painted Chamber of the old Palace; then for 200 years in the Chapter House of Westminster Abbey; and from the reign of Edward VI in St Stephen's. This converted chapel, draughty and uncomfortable, became impossibly overcrowded with the arrival of forty-seven Scottish MPs in 1707.

Wren did his best with a conversion that involved installing panelling, balconies and new windows into the Gothic building, but this was never more than a patched-up solution. It was a poor alternative to a much more ambitious plan he had submitted to William III in 1700. This design was for a Parliament House which would have stood on the river about 300 yds north of the present building, roughly on the site of New Scotland Yard. It was to be joined by a long arcaded corridor to the palace which Wren was proposing for the King at the same time (see p. 19). The umbilical symbolism of a corridor attached to the palace, though probably unintentional, was not calculated to appeal to independently minded Parliamentarians.

No more was heard of Wren's scheme, and similarly short-lived was a plan

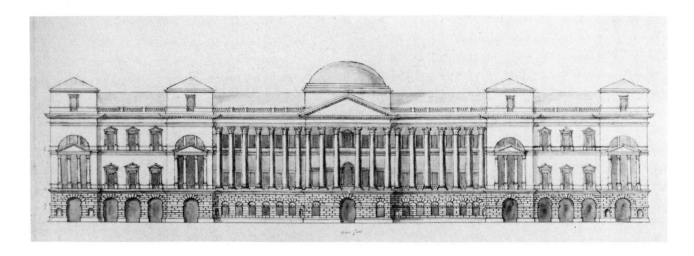

69 William Kent's 1733 design for new Houses of Parliament. War prevented its realisation

by his successor as Surveyor-General, William Benson. Benson overplayed his hand by prophesying that the House of Lords was about to collapse. Both he and his far too opportune plan were dismissed. From a sale catalogue of his drawings prepared after his death it is clear that Hawksmoor made no less than forty-three designs for a Parliament House in 1732 which were submitted to Lord Burlington. Though 'said to be very grand and beautiful', the drawings have disappeared and were apparently shelved in favour of plans drawn up over a period of the next six years by William Kent. It was during this period that Kent, artist and designer of elegant classical interiors, was in great demand by the nobility and carried out internal work on Burlington House, Piccadilly, Chiswick House, Devonshire House and Kensington Palace.

Kent's earliest design (Plate 69) shows a long, low Palladian building with a columned portico which was to stand south of Westminster Hall. With the main façade to the river and with a curved colonnade and the back entrance opposite the Abbey, his first scheme would have required demolition of the existing Lords and the Painted Chamber as well as the occupation of much of Old Palace Yard. In 1739, six years later, Kent revised his design, encouraged by a debate in the House of Commons. The seating arrangement breaks away from the conventional, still surviving, oblong shape in favour of seats tiered like a miniature football stadium with curved ends and straight sides.

Kent's plans were approved by the Speaker, and his Parliament House was on the point of being started when England became involved in foreign wars. London's landscape might be radically different today with a classical instead of a Gothic Palace of Westminster had the country not embarked on the curious conflict with Spain, 'The War of Jenkins's Ear'. When hostilities ended in 1748 the country was too heavily in debt to embark on an expensive building project, and Kent died in the same year with his plans still shelved.

Members of Parliament had to accept more than a century of further discomfort. But although nothing practical was done until after the fire, architects continued to bubble with ideas. Among them was John Soane who, juggling with fanciful schemes in Rome (see Chapter 6), conceived his

'Design for a Senate House' in 1779. With a sublime disregard for existing buildings, he swept away Westminster Hall, demolished other parts of Parliament, and felled Westminster Abbey, all in a single blow. In their place (Plate 70) Soane substituted an elaborate structure which, looking north-east, shows St Paul's and a Triumphal Bridge in the background.

The architect admitted that his Senate House was 'animated by the contemplation of the majestic Ruins of the sublime Works of Imperial Rome'. He never pretended this was anything more than a *capriccio* and did not even bother to explain the functions of the various temple-like buildings, curved colonnades, triumphal arches, sprouting obelisks and scattered statuary. This youthful fantasy was altogether different from the more serious designs he produced at the request of the House of Lords in 1794 when he was Clerk of Works for Westminster.

In these proposals Soane flanks Westminster Hall with long classical buildings and arcades of Corinthian columns. His view from the south-east (Plate 71) with steps leading down to the river shows us, as Kent did, how a classical Westminster Palace would have looked. In a variant of his Royal Academy drawing of 1795 the near building is the House of Lords and there was a similar domed building for the House of Commons at the far end of the colonnade. Although nothing so comprehensive came into being, in 1822 Soane did succeed in adding some extra buildings and an impressive royal entrance and staircase – all to be destroyed in the fire.

70 Sir John Soane's design for a Senate House made while on a travelling scholarship in Rome, 1779. An architectural exercise inspired by the ruins of Imperial Rome, it was made without regard for expense or limitations of space. Westminster Bridge in the background is a Greek Doric variation on Soane's Corinthian Triumphal Bridge (Plate 26), which he has moved a few hundred yards down-river

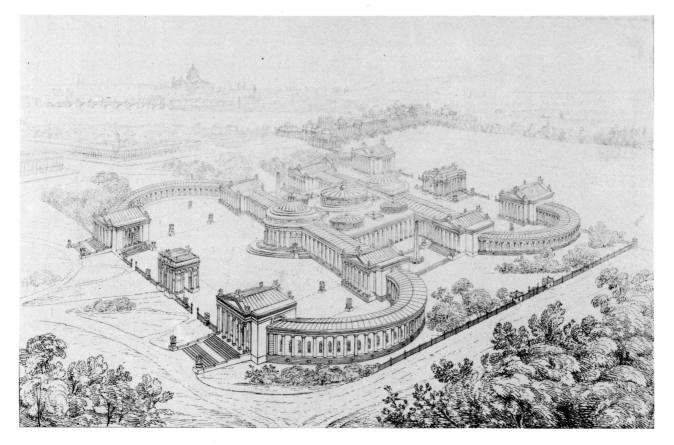

71 *Design for the new House of Lords, visualised as a classical building; south-east view from the river by Sir John Soane in 1794. The end of the Henry VII Chapel of Westminster Abbey is just visible on the far left*

Seven years later we find Colonel Trench as usual in the front of the fray and demanding that the Commons must be 'more commodious and less unwholesome'. For once this architectural meddler was onto a subject near to the hearts of his sweating, tightly packed hearers. The struggle over the Reform Bill when more than 600 members took part in crowded, intensely uncomfortable debates, accentuated the problem, and the cudgels were taken up by Joseph Hume, new Radical Member for Middlesex, who invited thirteen architects to give evidence to a committee of which he was chairman.

Ideas emerged for a number of differently shaped chambers. An octagonal House of Commons was suggested by Rigby Wason, MP, and his architect William Bardwell. This would serve as a reminder of Parliament's medieval, historic home, the Abbey Chapter House. Soane, backed by Francis Goodwin, advocated an oblong shape like the Concert Room in Hanover Square. Colonel Trench's architect, Benjamin Wyatt, made a plea for a semicircular chamber like the Paris Senate. From James Savage, architect of St Luke's, Chelsea, came the suggestion supported by a drawing that the chamber should be round for better acoustics.

All these plans were addled, but discomfort and ever-increasing claustrophobia gave new impetus to various suggestions that Parliament should be moved to a quite different part of London. Trafalgar Square and

Leicester Square were considered, and Green Park was proposed by Sydney Smirke, younger and overshadowed brother of Sir Robert Smirke. William Daniell produced a lithograph (Plate 72) of Smirke's domed New Parliamentary Buildings showing a wide open space approached by lawns, and with 'terraces spreading themselves at its base, and stately walks enriched with sculptures and formal parterres of shrubs'. The nearest neighbouring building would be Buckingham Palace.

Smirke's rural refuge in Green Park was published in April 1834. Six months later came the disastrous fire which put an end to theoretical ideas and demanded practical remedies. With so large an area devastated there was now no necessity to search for an alternative open space.

When Parliament announced its plans, Westminster was automatically readopted as the place to rebuild. This went initially unchallenged, but not so the decision that the style should be 'either Gothic or Elizabethan'. Yet this was a curious reversion to medievalism since nearly all architects had been visualising a classical building up to that time. This choice of style was decided by the proximity to the Abbey and a wish to blend in with the surviving Westminster Hall and ruined St Stephen's. There was also a general, if loosely defined, feeling that there was an 'Englishness' about Gothic.

Until the competition was announced, it looked as though the new Parliament building would be left to Robert Smirke in his capacity of Government Architect to the Office of Works. His solution was a long building, three modest storeys high at the centre and two storeys high at each end. With pointed arches, cusped windows and squat towers rather than pinnacles, this riverfront façade had the bland, unemphatic look of 'Strawberry Hill Gothic'. Rival architects immediately raised an outcry about the 'poverty' of Smirke's taste, and the only way to avert criticism was a competition. The terms were announced in June and July 1835.

The whole business was desperately rushed. The ninety-seven entrants were given only four months to prepare most complicated plans and

72 Green Park was suggested by Sydney Smirke for this Parliamentary building (1834)

drawings. To get through the work Barry allowed himself only four or five hours' sleep a night. John Savage had to submit his drawings unfinished, and Francis Goodwin, Soane's supporter for an oblong Commons, died under the strain. Five Commissioners – the Committee of Taste soon to be reviled as 'gentlemen amateurs' – had only three months to examine 1,400 drawings and reach their decision in Barry's favour. This was in the following February when they declared that his designs bore 'such evident marks of genius and superiority of taste as fully to entitle it to the preference we have given it . . .' This did not satisfy the press or rival architects. Newspapers condemned his designs as 'highly ornamental and meretricious', his drawings as 'dangerously artistic'. He was accused of being the 'tool' of the Commissioners and unfairly favoured by one of them. The qualification of these judges was questioned. It was pointed out that before Chagrin's Paris Senate House was decided upon, sixteen of France's most distinguished architects had travelled all over Europe to study style and design. Here it had been left to a handful of dilettanti connoisseurs.

Not unreasonably, Barry was upset by all this. Though he had never visualised building a new Parliament as his destiny, it so happened that two years earlier he had been travelling to London by coach from Brighton and had seen the red light of the fire in the night sky. He had hurried to Westminster and, as he watched the old Westminster Palace going up in flames, he had envisaged the opportunity this would mean for some architect. Certainly, with eight Gothic churches to his name, he was well qualified for the undertaking. Once the dust had settled on controversy born out of envy, he and his close collaborator, A. W. N. Pugin, were to devote themselves to their masterpiece. It was to involve him until his death twenty-four years later.

Our concern, however, is not with Barry's familiar monument, but with some of those other ninety-six Houses of Parliament that were never built. Of these the nearest contender was the work of John Chessell Buckler, artist, antiquary and architect, who won the second of the four awarded prizes. If he had had his way the building we should have at Westminster (Plate 73) would resemble a Tudor palace or great abbey with a rather more domestic look than Barry's. It would have a modest central tower and a river façade broken up with numerous slightly projecting bays and oriel windows. A low wall and double gateway (where Barry placed the Clock Tower of Big Ben) lead into New Palace Yard. The chambers of the two Houses are parallel to the river but set back and not overlooking it in symmetrical relation to Old Palace Yard. Buckler provided no description of his comfortable looking building, but from the plan it can be seen that corridors are in a grid-pattern and a uniformity further imposed by rooms that, with few exceptions, are strictly rectangular or square.

Right from the start there was a good deal of resentment about the imposition of the Gothic or Elizabethan style. Without necessarily being strict classicists, a number of architects thought the public should be given a chance to decide if other styles were preferable. C. R. Cockerell even forfeited his chance of winning by defying the rules. 'Elizabethan architecture cannot

101

be defined,' he contended, and preferred to submit a very un-Gothic building with a river aspect reminiscent of Greenwich Hospital (Plate 74). Two balancing pavilions, with squat French domes, set back behind flanking buildings on either side, stand sentinel to a wide open approach. This leads up to Cockerell's one concession to Gothic, a tall campanile – 'St Stephen's Bell Tower restored'. From the river there is a vista through the centre of the building to Westminster Abbey.

Most vehement among the disappointed architects was Thomas Hopper, the largely self-taught son of a Rochester surveyor, who as a young man had made a name for himself with a Gothic conservatory designed for the Prince Regent's Carlton House. He disliked competitions, and soon after the results were announced his voice was raised among those of angry dissidents who held a meeting at the Thatched House Tavern, St James's Street. He accused the Commissioners of incompetence, said the site should first have been subjected to an inquiry, and claimed that the Gothic style would not resist London smoke and atmosphere from the river. Nursing so many objections, it seems rather surprising that Hopper took part in the competition at all.

Along with William Wilkins, RA, Lewis Nockalls Cottingham, the defiant Cockerell and many other unsuccessful entrants, Hopper passed a motion that Parliament should be presented with a petition denouncing the competition. This was done a fortnight later, but their demand for a new competition with revised rules under different Commissioners was ignored. Hopper bided his time, and in 1840 published a large portfolio of his designs 'in order that they might be subjected to minute examination'.

These spectacular lithographs show Parliament with a massive square central tower on either side of which are gateways approached from the river by stairs (Plate 75). 'In the original design,' he explained, 'I omitted the principal Centre Tower as it would necessarily be exceedingly expensive; and although an important improvement to the appearance of the Building, it seemed to me more calculated for an Hôtel de Ville than for Houses of Parliament; but as it appears the general opinion is against me, I have annexed it in these Designs in order that they may be judges of with or without a Tower. . . .'

Each competitor was allowed to submit only two elevations – one from the north-east, the other from the south-west. Hopper's south-west view looking across Old Palace Yard is highly original (Plate 76). He has restored St Stephen's which stands at right-angles to the south end of Westminster Hall. This is an act of professional piety for this 14th-century building was architecturally very important. St Stephen's had been the private chapel of the old Palace until 1547 when it was given to the Commons. Only the crypt survived the fire, but Hopper has rebuilt the old chamber (it is the smaller of the ecclesiastical buildings on the left). He went further by duplicating the chapel on the south side so that the two buildings provide a converging approach to the main building. The rest of Hopper's Parliament House was, he asserted, 'Gothic of the pure English of Edward III's time being homogeneous with St Stephen's and the other ancient buildings.'

Antiquarian enthusiasm was also displayed by William Railton (the future

76 *Thomas Hopper's view from Old Palace Yard with two flanking chapels*

77 *William Railton's medieval Gothic design, which won fourth place*

78 *Peter Thompson's south-west view shows Westminster Hall (left) encased in a decorative shell*

102

79 *Parliament as it might have looked from the corner of Whitehall and Bridge Street if Sir Charles Barry's proposal for enclosing New Palace Yard had been adopted. Extensions to the north-west corner were to include a massive gatehouse to be named the Albert Tower, this corresponding with the Victoria Tower at the south-west corner*

designer of Nelson's Column) who won fourth place for a design that attempted the external restoration of the Palace of Westminster as he conceived it to have looked prior to the fire of Henry VIII's time (Plate 77). This he based, presumably, on the ground-plans of the medieval palace measured and drawn a few years earlier by William Capon, designer of the monumental pyramid for Shooters Hill (see p. 76).

Another dedicated antiquary was L. N. Cottingham, one of the Thatched House dissidents. He brought a deep love of Gothic to his design which simulated the style prevailing in the reigns of Edward III and Richard II – 'a period in which', he contended, 'the palatial architecture of England arrived at its highest pitch of splendour.'

If he was not feigning humility, Peter Thompson of Marylebone who described himself as 'a mere carpenter', was one of the few competitors who took the Commissioners' decision with good grace. He published his drawings not, he insisted, 'with the slightest feeling of disappointment or envy'. He had neither speculated nor cared who the successful candidate might be. He didn't want 'appeal from the judgement of the Commissioners'. Over a many-buttressed building hangs an atmosphere of collegiate calm (Plate 78). This south-west view shows Parliament in a rural setting. What we can see of Westminster Hall is encased in an oblong shell which, with its intricate decorative balustrade and crenellated corner towers, might belong to a Byzantine palace.

A limit must be placed on the number of Houses of Parliament that can be resurrected from portfolios of the past, but it is reasonable that Barry should have the last word. Even when he was well started on his huge task variations on his original plans continued to come off the drawing board. The Victoria Tower and the tower for Big Ben were in his submitted plans but the third central tower and spire was an afterthought, or rather was forced on him. Much to his resentment this octagonal lantern over the central hall was insisted on by an engineer, Dr David Boswell Reid, as part of a ventilation system. Barry revised this several times, and a sketch of 1846 makes it a preposterous 253 ft high, 3 ft higher than the Victoria Tower, his greatest pride. In the following year he reduced it to a height of 149 ft which, as he foresaw, made it only half visible from street level outside.

The one great change Barry would have liked to achieve was an extension on the north-east side — that is, the open area of New Palace Yard surrounded by railings on the corner of Bridge Street and Parliament Square. It was an idea which Alfred Barry, his son and biographer, recalls was 'always most in his heart'. To give unity to the 'irregular, disjointed and incongruous character of the present building,' as he put it in 1853, he wanted completely to enclose New Palace Yard with an L-shaped range of matching buildings. They would house government offices and the like. Most importantly, as the drawing shows (Plate 79), at the corner there was to be a really monumental entrance, a grand gate tower which carried a reminder of the one that existed there in Tudor times.

Barry intended this as the dominating ground-level feature of his whole building, and proposed to call it the Albert Tower as a tribute to the Prince Consort's interest in artistic decoration. Barry submitted the idea to Parliament and returned to it again and again. In 1864, after his death, another of his four sons, Edward, once more laid it before Lord Palmerston's Government. But this extremely logical part of the architectural composition remained an unfulfilled dream.

80 Six of the eminent architects, who were rivals in the fiercely contested competitions during the second half of the 19th century. Main contestants for the Royal Exchange (1839) were (A) C. R. Cockerell (1788–1863) and (B) Sir William Tite (1798–1873);

for new Government offices (1857), (C) Sir George Gilbert Scott (1811–78) and (D) Sir Charles Barry (1795–1860);

and for the Law Courts (1866), (E) William Burges (1827–81) and (F) Alfred Waterhouse (1830–1905)

Chapter 10

Battles of the Giants

AFTER 1835 Sir Charles Barry devoted the greater part of his professional life to the New Palace of Westminster, but he somehow managed to find time to design a great many other buildings. With his then resounding reputation it might be supposed that nearly all of them would have been built. But this was not so. Like all architects, he frequently worked on plans that never materialised.

Out of fifty-four commissions prepared by him and his office from then until his death in 1860, twenty-two were never carried out – eleven of them for London. His design for a Law Courts was pigeon-holed; his plan for the redisposition of Government offices was supplanted by the quite impractical scheme of a French architect; when the Crystal Palace was moved to Sydenham his idea that it should be given domes was ignored. None of his suggested improvements for Pall Mall, Piccadilly, Horse Guards or the British Museum ever took place.

Barry was not particularly upset by these rejections. From his early years he had learnt that a great deal of any architect's effort is bound to be fruitless. As well as work for his office, he designed for his own pleasure, and professed that he was incapable of going into a building or town without subconsciously devising improvements. Waiting for Service to start one Sunday in his local church at Clapham he sketched a new design for the chancel in the fly-leaf of his prayer book. At Stoke Newington, Streatham, Kensington and Highgate we should have examples of Barry's ecclesiastical work if his churches had been built. Westminster and Charing Cross Hospitals might have been his, and his Gothic hand seen more plentifully all over London.

With a huge demand for new public buildings, the 19th century offered unprecedented opportunities not only for Barry but for all leading architects. Victorian London had to cope with needs of a population which multiplied four times over to a total of 4,500,000 between 1800 and 1900. There were rich pickings for the designers who sometimes followed their own preferences, or, faced with fierce competition, deliberately shaped their work to suit changes in taste and to catch the public eye. Their offices hummed with work. Pattern-books were raided for styles that varied from Gothic to classical, Italianate to Byzantine. Only Georgian failed to get much of a look in. Not enough profitable elaboration there.

All this activity makes us wonder what might have been built if rich men had not had particular prejudices; if powerful men had nurtured different tastes; what we should have now, for instance, if Lord Palmerston had not insisted on a classical Whitehall. London might be almost unrecognisable today if the assessors of big competitions and private clients had been less uncertain and capricious, and if winning designs had been executed instead of being replaced by the work of other nominees.

In the thirty years after the new Westminster Palace of 1835 there followed a series of major competitions which threw up dozens of completely different buildings to those first chosen. First came the controversial Royal Exchange competition (1839), and next the Trafalgar Square competition (1839). Then, after an eighteen-year gap, there was the Government Offices competition (1857), decisively settled by Palmerston, followed by one for the South Kensington Museum (1864) which resulted in a win by a military man who wasn't really an architect. A National Gallery competition (1866) fizzled out, and in the same year came the most fiercely fought and oddly concluded Law Courts competition. Not one of these epic contests passed without the architectural giants of the day (Plate 80) fighting, sometimes none too honourably, for victory. In nearly every instance the buildings that did not go up were as interesting — sometimes far more so — than those that did.

Architects were bound to enter the battle arena if they were to win the most glittering prizes and the prestige that went with them. But they often detested the conditions, and the way verdicts were left to laymen who, in Gilbert Scott's estimation, 'knew amazingly little about their subject'. Awards by the assessors were sometimes arbitrarily set aside.

For several of these reasons Charles Robert Cockerell adopted a most unorthodox gambit when the competition for the Royal Exchange was announced in 1839. The previous 17th-century building in the City had been burnt down. The City's ancient rivalry with Westminster was perhaps reflected in the decision not to have a Gothic building but instead a Royal Exchange in 'the Grecian, Roman or Italian style'. This attracted 120 entries, but the assessors said they could recommend only one within the specified building cost of £150,000. They put five entrants in order of merit and then named three others, whom they preferred. Unplaced was John Davis Paine's sprawling and domed building (Plate 81) adapted from a previous design for 'a hall of commerce', but obviously so vast that it would have called for the destruction of Cornhill and, quite possibly, the Mansion House and the Bank of England. The assessors worked out that three plans would exceed the stipulated cost. Of these one was by a young unknown, H. B. Richardson. He was placed second.

No sooner were the results announced than it was revealed that Richardson's design was in fact the work of Cockerell. A keen exponent of Greek and Roman styles, he had been irresistibly attracted to the competition from the moment that Richardson, a former pupil of his, came to him for advice about his entry. Cockerell persuaded Richardson to forget his own drawing and to submit instead an elaborate, highly accomplished design which Cockerell prepared and entered under his pupil's name.

It seems very devious, but Cockerell, an implacable critic of competitions, had his reasons. He had recently sacrificed his chances for the new Palace of Westminster by defying the basic rules. He had a number of important buildings to his name, including Harrow Chapel; but when it came to

competitions he was a born loser, as was to be seen later when he failed to win the National Gallery, London University and the Reform Club. Using Richardson as a pseudonym he could cover the possibility of failure.

Now he felt safe to declare himself as responsible for the marvellously ornate building with Graeco-Roman detail that at once attracted great admiration (title-page). With its intricate, elaborate façade, the architect created a Royal Exchange of daring magnificence, which he defined as a 'Triumphal arch expanded and rendered habitable by floors'. Goddess-like, and not unduly over-dressed, female figures seated on six Corinthian columns represented the four quarters of the globe. Loosely draped symbols of South America and Australia completed the set of six. Reminiscent of the temple which he had seen in the Forum of Nerva in Rome, Cockerell's building would have had a space in front – a 'Forum Londinium' – which he considered apt for an Exchange. His interior (Plate 82) is equally grand.

Insisting that it could be built for under £150,000 he begged to be allowed to provide evidence from an estimating surveyor. This was agreed for all three nominees, and Cockerell asked William Tite (with whom he had worked on the London and Westminster Bank, Lothbury) for his help. This was to prove a tactical mistake. Tite had some good friends and many connections in the City. With their help a new arrangement was suggested. First the assessors proposed that Tite and Cockerell should collaborate (which Cockerell declined); next, the two men were invited to compete against each other in a knock-out contest.

The Cockerell faction was darkly suspicious of what it saw as Tite's machinations, and the architect himself was incensed that he was not allowed to submit a large, splendid model. Tite, without a model, said this would be

81 This elaborate design for the Royal Exchange was resurrected in 1838, following the destruction of the building by fire. In fact, the architect, John Davis Paine, had made the drawing as an exercise five years earlier. His Hall of Commerce beneath a great dome surmounted by Atlas is surrounded by coffee-houses, sale-rooms and offices for insurance companies, brokers and underwriters, including Lloyd's

82 *City merchants, resembling Senators in a Roman bath, transact business in C. R. Cockerell's Royal Exchange. But statues in niches are not Roman emperors but British kings and queens. The roof, open to the sky, might have posed construction problems for the architect. (See also title-page illustration)*

unfair. Cockerell's drawing was described as 'a very extraordinary and fine Composition' by one assessor, but something funny took place in the secret conclave of the committee. When the final announcement was made, Tite was declared the winner by thirteen votes to seven. And so today at the hub of the City we have Sir William Tite's grey classical building with its eight-column portico and large pediment, a sombre landmark compared with Cockerell's rash burst of splendour.

The even more famous Victorian architect, George Gilbert Scott, was to experience the effect of personal and powerful influences when he entered for the Whitehall competition of 1857. This was a tripartite contest for a new Foreign Office, a new War Office and the better disposition of Government buildings. It came at the end of nearly thirty years of mounting chaos during which a plan by Decimus Burton was shelved, and also one by James Pennethorne, who had the idea of a single vast building to house the Treasury, Colonial Office, War Office, Board of Trade and Chancellorship of the Exchequer.

The triple competition attracted 218 designs, a few of them from abroad. To prevent a repetition of complaints that the public had no adequate idea of the plans decided for the new Houses of Parliament, the drawings for this latest competition were exhibited in Westminster Hall (Plate 83). Only nineteen of the entries were Gothic because the whisper had gone round that the Government wanted a classical building. Charles Barry was one of the architects who toed the classical line for the good reason that he wanted the new Whitehall buildings facing on to the Thames to give a unified grandeur to the whole stretch of the river from his new Palace of Westminster to a big hotel he planned on the site of the present Whitehall Court (Plate 84).

His ground-plan with its massive and domed Government building (set back to the west of Whitehall with ornamental gardens and a riverside promenade in front of it) seems sensible. He must have been riled to see this rejected in favour of a French plan by Adolphe Crépinet, who wanted to encroach on Parliament Square with buildings, and to provide a monumental approach placed a bridge across the Thames parallel and in absurd proximity to Westminster Bridge.

Barry's son, Edward, had also competed, and took a second prize (they were called premiums then) for a Foreign Office in the plain, heavy Italian style adopted by comfortable Grand Hotels of the period. Among the War Office designs was one by Cuthbert Brodrick which looked suspiciously like his Leeds Town Hall which, slightly elaborated, was exactly what it was. To provide a militant look the architect simply added some sculptured trophies in the heroic Blenheim manner to crown the side pavilions.

Though he was soon to be chastened, Gilbert Scott had reason to expect that his chances were very good. The apostle of High Victorian Gothic, with one of the largest practices in England, he must have felt an almost divine right to win. He had just completed Broad Sanctuary, the turreted gateway to Dean's Yard by Westminster Abbey, and his Gothic Revival church spires

83 The public exhibition of entries for the Government Offices competition in Westminster Hall, May 1857. Great public interest was aroused by the 218 different entries and nearly 2,000 drawings submitted

111

pointed to the sky from Wimbledon to Wembley and West Ham to Ealing.
The Government might think they wanted something classical, but clearly he
had a God-sent mission to persuade them otherwise. To his chagrin his War
Office in French Gothic style was not even placed; and his Foreign Office
won only third prize (Plate 85). Scott did not 'fret at the disappointment' he
tells us in his *Recollections*, but when a few months later he learned that the
Prime Minister had coolly set aside the results and was on the point of
appointing Pennethorne who had not even taken part in the competition, he
felt 'at liberty to stir'.

He stirred to good effect. He badgered the Institute of Architects into
lobbying Parliament, and a select committee was appointed which revealed
that the architectural assessors in the competition, unlike the judges, had
placed Scott second for both buildings. In July 1858 the committee
recommended the Commissioner of Works to choose between Scott's designs
and those of Banks and Barry. In November it was announced that Scott had
been appointed.

Scott's elation did not last for long. Opposition to his plans was voiced in
Parliament by Lord Palmerston and by William Tite (who besides being a
rival architect was MP for Bath). They both complained that Scott's Gothic
windows were too small and would shut out light. Scott was summoned to
see Palmerston. He found him in a jaunty mood, but absolutely firm about
one thing. He would have nothing to do with the Gothic design. He must
insist on the Italian style. Why, exclaimed the Prime Minister, if Scott were
given his head he would 'Gothicize the whole country'!

A battle of attrition was waged for months. Supported by his fellow Goths,
Scott pressed for his style. Palmerston stood firm. Again Scott was
summoned, and the Prime Minister opened with the disarming remark that
after thinking it over he had decided that it was unfair to compel a Gothic
architect to erect a classical building. But before Scott could smile,
Palmerston added that he was thinking of appointing a coadjutor who
would, in fact, make the design. Bottling up his resentment, Scott retired, but
sent Palmerston a letter of protest and wrote to Mr Gladstone for support. To
calm his nerves he took a brief seaside holiday and a course of quinine.

When he returned to London he produced a Venetian-Byzantine
compromise. But Palmerston would have none of it. 'A regular mongrel-

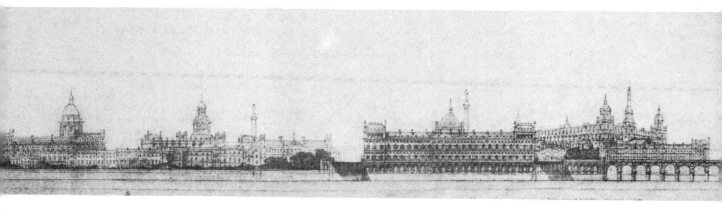

85 *A French chateau Foreign Office. Sir George Gilbert Scott's 1857 competition design included a staircase influenced by the Loire chateau at Blois*

86 *Francis Fowke* (right) *discussing his plans with Henry Cole. As Cole was a museum official his encouragement of Fowke caused suspicion among the unsuccessful competitors*

87 *Designs for museums at South Kensington:* (A) *The proposal (c. 1865) by Capt. Francis Fowke for the Victoria and Albert Museum but completely transformed by Aston Webb in the 1890s;* (B) *Fowke was also responsible for the prize-winning design for the Natural History Museum (1864). This did not materialise either. It was built finally in 1873 by Alfred Waterhouse, though not as in the architect's own drawing* (C) *on the Embankment.*

affair,' he growled. There was nothing for it. Scott had to swallow his pride and produce what Palmerston wanted. After buying some expensive books to brush up his Italian architecture he went to Paris to study the Louvre and other public buildings. The result is the Renaissance-style Foreign Office in Whitehall on the south side of Downing Street and overlooking St James's Park.

One question remains unanswered. If Gilbert Scott had triumphed over Palmerston, should we now have to live with St Pancras Station Hotel towering over Parliament Square? This alarming thought cannot be completely ignored. Legend always insists that Scott transferred his rejected Gothic Foreign Office to Euston Road. This would provide a plausible explanation of how the unlikely combination of a German cathedral and Flemish town hall comes to stand at the gateway to the old Midland Railway. A glance at Scott's competition design for the Foreign Office rules this out, though it is true that elements of it are repeated at St Pancras. The architect himself goes no further than to say '... having been disappointed through Lord Palmerston of my ardent hope for carrying out my style of Government Offices I was glad to be able to erect one building in that style in London.'

As a playground for ideas no part of London offered more scope than the eighty-seven acres of South Kensington, bought by the Commissioners of the Great Exhibition out of the exhibition's profits. For a decade they pondered ideas for colleges, institutes, a concert hall, and a museum which would match the imaginative success of the Crystal Palace. Their actual achievements were impressive, but before the present Natural History Museum, Victoria and Albert Museum and other buildings for learned organisations came into existence a great many plans were mooted. The V. and A. would have looked very different had an 1865 scheme, proposed by Captain Francis Fowke (Plate 86), been adopted (Plate 87A).

One large, all-embracing museum was the subject of an open competition in 1864. There were thirty-six entries, few by well-known architects, and only two of them were Gothic. The museum was to become the one on the present Natural History site and posed a number of problems because it was planned not for one collection but several. The zoological and natural history exhibits were to be transferred from the British Museum in Bloomsbury and housed there; then other collections were to fill galleries which would be added piecemeal. Soon seen to be impracticable, this was changed to the present arrangement of separate museums.

The prize for what was to become the Natural History Museum was won by the same Francis Fowke, Captain in the Royal Engineers, who within a few months was also to submit his design for the V. and A. The award at once caused an outcry from other competitors. In their opinion he wasn't a professional architect, and because of his earlier association with Prince Albert and the Commissioners they viewed his success with suspicion. That he was the inventor of the bellows camera and an Army fire-engine added nothing to his credibility.

Building News found his proposed museum (Plate 87B) 'unchaste but effective' and the *Athenaeum* called it 'a splendid design', but objections

A

B

C

88 A new National Gallery proposed for Trafalgar Square in 1867; E. M. Barry's design was denounced as 'a strong plagiarism upon St Paul's Cathedral'

were lodged that he had not observed the competition rules. Fowke agreed to conform, but before he could adjust his plan he died. A distressed Queen Victoria expressed the hope that a plan by a friend of her late husband would not be tampered with. But few of Fowke's ideas appeared in the redesigned version, a Byzantine building in terracotta and brick, produced by Alfred Waterhouse, a bright young architect from Manchester.

Building of the Natural History Museum, as it came to be called, did not start until 1873, and one cause of the delay was the idea of moving the entire museum from Kensington to the Victoria Embankment, a scheme for which Waterhouse prepared a drawing (Plate 87c). The plan was discarded but the Embankment, just then being completed, was also at different times suggested as a home for the Law Courts and the National Gallery.

Almost from the time it opened in 1838 the National Gallery had been troubled by lack of space. Originally a very shallow building, it did not stretch back to Orange Street as it does now. More space would be available in Kensington, and in 1853 the Prince Consort had asked Sir Charles Barry if he thought the gallery should be moved there. Barry considered Kensington too far west for general convenience and suggested instead a remodelling of the 'useless portico and other columns and projections' to triple the wall space. This, like the later Embankment idea, never happened.

Improvement for the National Gallery was exactly the kind of thing to excite Colonel Trench. Always on the lookout for a chance to improve something which no one particularly objected to, he wanted to put fifteen fluted columns round the base of the dome and an onion-shaped feature on top of it. More constructively in 1866 six architects were invited to submit plans that went beyond conversion to actual rebuilding.

116

By this time Sir Charles Barry was dead, but carrying on the family tradition his son Edward proposed a huge classical building with a central dome (which seems to incorporate Trench's columns) and four smaller domes at each corner (Plate 88). Although embellished with a pallisade of Corinthian columns and enlivened with statuary and decorative friezes, the whole effect is decidedly ponderous and was criticised as a plagiarism of St Paul's. Even more intimidating was the design of Cuthbert Brodrick (placed fifth in the War Office competition) who faced his building with so massive a phalanx of columns that it would have taken a very intrepid art lover indeed to gain entrance (Plate 89). As if the whole effect were not sufficiently Grecian, the architect heaps Pelion on Ossa with a large pedimented temple on top of the main structure. The *Ecclesiologist* saw the design as 'the Bank of England exaggerated with a Noah's Ark stuck up a-top'.

The assessors rejected these and all other designs, and so, along with the columns he had incorporated from Carlton House, the work of William Wilkins, the original architect, was allowed to rest in peace. The only really attractive alternative to the National Gallery was the Palace of Fine Arts in Kensington Gardens suggested by Joseph Mitchell (Plate 90).

Mitchell's gallery, approached by a broad avenue of trees should, he suggested, be part of a royal palace, 'the new repository for the national collection of works of art similar to the Louvre in Paris'. It would have been like the present Queen's Gallery in relation to Buckingham Palace on a much larger scale. Mitchell gives no details (the building was in fact dreamed up as a culmination of his railway through Hyde Park), but his vista gives his Palace of Fine Arts a grandeur comparable to the garden approach to Versailles.

89 Cuthbert Brodrick's Leeds Town Hall, adapted for the War Office in Whitehall (but rejected), rears its head again – this time in Trafalgar Square with a temple superstructure as the National Gallery. The Ecclesiologist, *which favoured Gothic, commented: 'A more inartistic display of pillars, arranged as thick as strawberries, we have never seen'*

90 *View of a grand drive through Hyde Park to Joseph Mitchell's Palace of Fine Arts. Well screened by trees is a railway station on the right*

In 1867, the year new plans for the National Gallery went into limbo, public interest switched to a far more spectacular project. The Law Courts in the Strand were, after the new Palace of Westminster, London's most important building of the century. They were long overdue because the previous law courts surrounding the old Houses of Parliament ('a mere

excrescence upon Westminster Hall', Charles Barry called them) had been destroyed with other buildings in the fire of 1834. Barry had not been able to find space for courts in his new Palace plan, and in 1842 had proposed building a court-house in Lincoln's Inn Fields. To show that he wasn't totally under the spell of Gothic, he chose the Greek style he had so long discarded,

91 G. E. Street (1824–81), who won the Law Courts competition in 1866

and the result gave the impression that the British Museum had settled among the leafy foliage of the square. Foliage was possibly its undoing. Public objection was raised to confiscation of one of the 'lungs of London', and Lincoln's Inn Fields was saved for recreation and lunchtime basketball for present-day office girls.

During the following fifteen years the lack of adequate courts had become critical, and in 1857 the Government, under pressure from the law, acquired land between Carey Street and the Strand, a site within a lazy lawyer's range of the Inns of Court. Invitations to take part in the competition went to eleven leading architects, five of them veterans of the Government Offices battle.

With contestants like George Gilbert Scott, William Burges, Edward Barry and Alfred Waterhouse, the scene was set for a titanic struggle. The senior men, Scott and H. F. Lockwood, were in their mid-fifties. The up-and-coming challengers, Barry and Waterhouse, were thirty-seven. A former assistant of Scott, George Edmund Street, who had only just put up his plate in London, aged thirty-three, was an outsider (Plate 91). He had come seventh in the Foreign Office competition.

Though the elder Barry had favoured a classical Law Courts, Gothic was, by common consent, the choice for the building in the Strand; a nod, perhaps, towards Westminster as historic seat of law. The basic requirement was twenty-four courts, and over 1,300 rooms. An imposing entrance hall was not specifically called for, but was incorporated in designs to strike a note of awesome dignity. The great external problem was the extremely long Strand frontage – it is only twenty-four yards less than the Parliament riverfront – which had to avoid monotony yet not overwhelm the passing public with excessive Gothic decoration.

As we know, G. E. Street got the commission. But he was never actually named the winner. In Victorian competitions victory was never conceded easily. Street had to endure months of uncertainty, and was to see the prize almost slip through his fingers. Even after the award was indisputably his, he was required to redraw the Law Courts for the Embankment, and that done (and discarded), to replan the building on a reduced scale for a smaller area in the Strand.

From the start there was the usual humming and hawing by the assessors. Among them were Mr Gladstone, then Chancellor of the Exchequer, and Sir Alexander Cockburn, Lord Chief Justice. The laymen, advised by two shrewd architects, were divided among themselves. Fortunately the drawings originally displayed to the public in a specially built gallery in Lincoln's Inn have survived, so we are able to make an assessment of what might have been.

Though Street was eventually selected, the judges preferred the plan submitted by Edward Barry (Plate 92), and the main award might have gone to him had they cared more for his detail. Like his father's river front, Barry's Strand frontage was in late Gothic style which by a vagary of taste was going through a phase of unpopularity. It could have been a further mistake – and certainly was hardly original – to include a similar clock tower to Big Ben,

already established as a London landmark. A dome, looking like a Prussian officer's helmet with a spike on top, caused people to wonder why this classical feature, reminiscent of St Paul's, was included in his design.

Favourite with the lay assessors was Scott, followed by Waterhouse. Scott's entry has been described as a combination of Brussels Town Hall and the Doges' Palace, with the strangely incongruous addition of a Bridge of Sighs (Plate 93). A striking interior feature is a dome in the central hall with a strong Byzantine influence and a scene of the Last Judgement, certainly an apt warning in a Law Court. Obviously more flexible since his brush with Palmerston, Scott humbly wrote in his report: 'I should be quite ready, if it were thought too ornate, to adopt a severer tone.'

Waterhouse won the regard of the professional judges with a seductively attractive watercolour which he made of his building as it would be seen from the river (Plate 94). This obscures the lower Strand front, but shows a prodigiously tall tower to the west as well as a dozen other towers, spires and turrets which break the skyline and anticipate the skyscraper silhouette of London today. Inside, Waterhouse's inventiveness is seen in his central hall with a glass and iron-ribbed semicircular roof which owes something to Paxton and may well have been influenced by the *galleria* which was then being built in Milan (Plate 95).

Among the others who took the £800 premium paid to all entrants was William Burges, whose huge chateau reflects his lifetime love affair with medievalism. With the band-box appearance of a French fortress over-restored by Viollet-le-Duc, his bird's eye view (Plate 96) smacks of Disney to the modern eye, and one half expects to see Snow White on the battlements.

92 E. M. Barry's Law Courts for the Strand borrowed Gothic inspiration from his father's Houses of Parliament, including a Big Ben clock tower

93 Sir George Gilbert Scott's Law Courts featured a Bridge of Sighs across an interior street to add to the effect of a Venetian palace

94 Alfred Waterhouse's 'skyscraper' design for Law Courts on the Embankment (1866–7). Temple Bar, transferred from the Strand, stands on the waterfront

96 Bird's-eye view of William Burges's Law Courts (1866) in 12th-century French Gothic style. 'Eccentric and wild' was the opinion of Sir George Gilbert Scott, a rival competitor

If the choice had gone to the building with the greatest unity, all-round use of height and an overall compactness, the winner would have been J. P. Seddon, architect of the Campo Santo, the most spectacular funeral monument for Westminster (see Chapter 12). The triple main entrance is under a tower, and this gives access to a Great Hall which stretches the entire depth of the building. By using the whole depth of the site Seddon achieves an appearance of squareness (where the others are oblong). The long hall provides entrances to all the courts. At the back overlooking Carey Street the highest tower with windows that suggest a modern hotel block is for offices and a depository for records.

When the judges were at last agreed, they made a compromise suggestion. They wanted the Law Courts to be the work of two architects and suggested to the Treasury that both Barry and Street should be commissioned to work in association. The Treasury did not like this, nor seemingly did Barry. As the majority favourite, Gilbert Scott was also incensed by what he considered an injustice. In the end the commission went to Street alone. He was bedevilled by the brainwave, which came to nothing, of re-siting the Law Courts on the Embankment (in the area running back to the Strand from the present Temple Station) and further aggravated by then being given a smaller budget, and having radically to alter his original conception to suit a smaller Strand site. When Street died after two strokes in 1881, still in his fifties and with his Law Courts unfinished, he was the victim of accumulated responsibility.

In an attempt to put an end to injustices which so embittered their members the Royal Institute of British Architects (founded in 1835) belatedly set about the reform of competitions. New conditions were in force for the next major public building, County Hall. Replacing the effective but corrupt Metropolitan Board of Works in 1888, the London County Council was initially housed in cramped premises in Spring Gardens tucked away beside Trafalgar Square. The press immediately demanded that this new reforming body should have a town hall worthy of London.

Architects scarcely needed prompting. By April of the next year Ernest Rüntz, designer of the Gaiety Theatre, after 'labour long and arduous', had already prepared large, detailed drawings in the style of the 'French Renaissance of the François Premier period', equally popular, he maintained, with classic and Gothic enthusiasts. The major question was where to put it, and Rüntz opted for the extreme easterly end of the Victoria Embankment. This was a fundamental error. To trespass on the boundaries of the still independent City of London was a presumption calculated to make the entire Court of Aldermen choke in their turtle soup.

Sites in the Adelphi and Parliament Street were considered, the latter opposed as an imprudent encroachment on Westminster. The new LCC seemed to have no friends, a dilemma solved by Alfred Rosling Bennett, an electrical engineer who placed his County Hall on a new bridge over the

95 Central Hall of Alfred Waterhouse's Law Courts. With its cast-iron and glass roof it would have resembled Paddington Station. Three storeys of consulting rooms with windows looking into the hall were to be situated on either side

97 Alfred Bennett's proposed
County Hall on a new Temple
Bridge would have straddled
tramways as well as the Thames

Thames. Bennett's 'Temple Bridge' was a long Gothic structure stretching from north to south banks with a steeple resembling St Dunstan-in-the-East's in the centre. An uneasy blending of ancient and modern was achieved by roads with tramways which passed slap through the medieval building (Plate 97).

Another bridge for central London was sorely needed, but not surprisingly Bennett's was not considered and a County Hall competition was announced in 1907. Ninety-nine rather sober and generally unadventurous designs were submitted. Sir Edwin Lutyens, famous for his vernacular country houses was later invited. When his symmetrical plan with a river front recessed between flanking blocks was rejected, he was bitterly disappointed. Only the building by E. A. Rickards (Plate 98) caused much of a stir. This was because the architect of the Methodist Central Hall, Tothill Street, made a great baroque tower the main feature, a disagreeable challenge, thought Parliament, to Big Ben.

In the end the competition was won by an unknown young man, Ralph Knott, who had prepared the plans in his own time while working in the office of Sir Aston Webb. Although Webb acted as an assessor of the competition, and was known to be Knott's principal, his impartiality was never questioned. Competitions were now respectable. If not exactly bold, Knott's County Hall in Lambeth has a light delicacy, but it is hard not to sigh romantically for Bennett's turreted fantasy which would have straddled the Thames after the manner of Old London Bridge.

98 A baroque County Hall designed by E. A. Rickards in 1907. A more modest but not entirely dissimilar recessed centre features in Ralph Knott's County Hall as actually built

Chapter 11

Railway Mania

O N 14 December 1836, London's first railway, the London and Greenwich, was opened in an atmosphere of carnival excitement. The large crowd which had assembled at London Bridge Station cheered the Lord Mayor as he boarded a carriage. A bugler blew his horn; a band dressed as Yeomen of the Guard seated on top of another carriage began to play; and the train pulled by the locomotive *Royal William* proudly moved off for Deptford.

Raised on arches like a Roman aqueduct, the four miles of track crossed bridges supported on Doric columns. With the staircase of Deptford Station modelled on a monument of the Acropolis, there was a touch of fantasy about the London and Greenwich Railway that set the tone for dozens of bizarre ideas during the next twenty-five years.

Even while the line was being completed, moves were afoot for a second railway which would snake its way from Deptford through south-east London – Peckham, Camberwell and Kennington – to a terminus on the Lambeth side of Westminster Bridge. The station was to be just across the water from Barry's new Houses of Parliament, then under construction. The Westminster Bridge and Deptford Railway was to have separate tracks as far as Deptford where it would converge with the 1836 line from London Bridge, and together they would use the tracks that would by then have extended to Greenwich.

Greenwich was not to be the end. Proposals were being made to carry it on still further under the name of the Greenwich and Gravesend Railway. Local palpitations and quarterdeck fury from retired naval officers were aroused because this extension would advance across Greenwich Park.

How the Westminster Bridge and Deptford scheme – announced in 1835 – might have appeared we know from two attractive prints. A bird's-eye view (Plate 99) shows the railway raised on arches passing in a wide curve through Southwark and Lambeth to an impressive, domed station on the site of the present St Thomas's Hospital. A lithograph depicts the scene beneath the arches (Plate 100). Under a vaulted roof, as splendid as that of a baroque cathedral, there were flanking rows of shops as elegant as those in Burlington Arcade. At the Deptford end of the line the arches were to have a more domestic use: fitting snugly under them would be a continuous line of bijou villas – one to an arch – flanked by a tree-lined boulevard which, the prospectus declared, would rival Paris (Plate 102).

The designer of the Westminster Bridge and Deptford Railway scheme was John Davis Paine, architect later of the terminus of the St Petersburg and Tsarskoe Selo Railway in Russia. His work included designs for one of the

99 The Westminster Bridge, Deptford & Greenwich Railway, viewed from the Duke of York's Column looking across Horse Guards Parade to John Davis Paine's terminus. The scheme was denounced as a gambling and speculative undertaking. The same company promised 'a direct London and continental railway communication' – with a Channel Tunnel, it is presumed

grandest of all proposed Royal Exchanges (Chapter 10) and for the Goodwin Sands lighthouse. In March 1837, two years after the original announcement and eight months before the Greenwich line opened, Paine's proposals received a mortal blow. The company was accused in the House of Commons of procuring fictitious signatures to the Parliamentary application and paying certain people for signing the deed. The company secretary protested innocence, but the application was turned down, as were efforts to revive the project a couple of years later.

At the other end of the line, the Greenwich and Gravesend Railway scheme also failed, the result not of any hanky-panky by over-zealous speculators, but of opposition from the local lobby. Despite the obvious benefits, not everyone in Greenwich favoured the original line, as a writer to a local paper, the *Mosquito*, buzzed loudly. His cry of pain referred to '. . . this infernal Greenwich railway with all its thundering steam engines and omnibusters, just ready to open and destroy our rural town of Greenwich with red hot cinders and hot water. . . Too late . . . what have we let come amongst us?' How far more awful was this new proposal – invasion of the park and peace shattered – to connect with Gravesend of all places.

100 Interior view of the arcade beneath the Westminster Bridge, Deptford & Greenwich Railway viaduct. Vacant ground on either side was to be leased for shops

101 *The Greenwich & Gravesend Railroad as it would have appeared in Greenwich Park from near the foot of the Observatory Hill. The railway's opponents claimed it would desecrate the Sabbath and that its colonnade would afford shelter and opportunity for offences against propriety and good morals*

Sensing what they were up against, the new company's directors embarked on a campaign to win local approval. Early in 1835 they produced a large print of their intended ornamental viaduct across the park. It was an impressive affair (Plate 101). Tuscan columns carry the railway on a line that runs parallel to the colonnade of the Queen's House, but well to the south of it. In the centre is a dignified if extraneous pavilion. The artist is careful to show no dreaded 'omnibuster' on its progress to undesirable Gravesend.

This quasi-classical bid for respectability did not impress the Royal Naval Hospital whose peace would be most affected. An Admiralty representative is said to have obtained an injunction for all copies of the print to be destroyed on the grounds that they were illegal propaganda. This was quickly followed by the publication of a whole catalogue of objections. Among them was the awful possibility that '. . . the colonnade underneath the viaduct will afford opportunities to the holiday-folk and the frequenters of the Park to practise indecencies'. King William IV, his sister Princess Sophia (as Honorary Ranger of Greenwich Park), and several members of Parliament were petitioned, and in the face of so much hostility the Bill authorising the Gravesend extension was withdrawn.

But the battle was not over. In the autumn of the same year, 1835, a new company was formed which commissioned a professor to carry out vibration tests to forestall objections that the railway would disturb Greenwich Observatory. He reported that there would be no inconvenience to the Observatory instruments provided that the Astronomer Royal was allowed to signal all trains to a halt for one minute twice every evening for readings to be taken. To win over the naval authorities the company suggested that it might place '. . . niches at stated intervals between the massive piers . . . wherein are to be placed busts of our most celebrated bygone Admirals, leaving ones for the reception of future naval heroes'. The viaduct was to be

surmounted by '. . . a colossal statue of his present Majesty in full Naval uniform'.

None of this palpable window-dressing deflected the Admiralty or the local press. A new Bill was given a First Reading in 1836, but a mountain of petitions successfully prevented any extension, and once the South Eastern Railway line to Dover was authorised the company's campaign ceased. Not until 1878 was the Greenwich line extended by the expedient of tunnelling under the park to Maze Hill.

To the north of London, while all this was going on, the first link with a provincial town – the London and Birmingham Railway – was under construction. The terminus was to be at Euston on the New Road (now Euston Road), then the outward limit of built-up London. The decision not to bring the station right into the centre of the city was regretted by many people and prompted an ambitious scheme – the first of a great many proposals to centralise London's termini.

Among the first to come up with practical proposals was George Remington, whose firm in July 1835 issued a prospectus for an extension of the still uncompleted main line. The London Grand Junction Railway, as he called it, was to run from Camden Town (the junction of the London and Birmingham and Great Western Railways) to the Thames. The route: Camden Town – Battle Bridge (St Pancras) – Clerkenwell – Snow Hill (Holborn) – the Thames (at Blackfriars) – 'a magnificent uninterrupted entrance to the City of London from the Northern and Western parts of the Empire . . .' Between St Pancras and Holborn there was to be a viaduct for carriages and pedestrians, below which would be a 'sub-railway' for trains.

This plan had to be radically modified. On the advice of George Rennie, the 'sub-railway' was abandoned ('altogether too novel'). The railway, instead of a carriageway, was to be constructed along the top of the viaduct. The terminus was to be Skinner Street, Holborn, not the river at Puddle Dock, Blackfriars. As the published print shows (Plate 103), the extension would have ended just by St Sepulchre's Church, Newgate, at the point where today Snow Hill joins Holborn Viaduct. Out of view to the north is Camden Town, and then, in a gentle curve, the railway crosses Euston Road and, following Farringdon Road, ends at Holborn. Rennie was particularly fond of arches which he had admired on the London and Greenwich line – 'The eye dwells with pleasure on the undulating line of the arches – and when the series is of some length the effect is still better. The admiration excited by the Aqueducts at Rome and Lisbon is a proof of this.'

All appeared set. On 22 February 1837, *The Times* announced that the first stone of the London Grand Junction Railway would be laid that day in Ampton Street, off Gray's Inn Road. No viaduct or railway in fact materialised and the route was not adopted until later with the building of the little-known goods line under Holborn Viaduct, the only surface line from north to south through the centre of London.

103 To bring northern railway lines right into the City, George Remington Jnr. proposed the London Grand Junction Railway. This would have run from Skinner Street, near Newgate, to Camden Town, linking up with the Great Western Railway and the London & Birmingham. The construction of the intended station (not shown in this view) would have entailed the demolition of the railway stairs and the Saracen's Head tavern adjoining St Sepulchre's on the right

But it is no good being impatient at the sudden and often unaccountable way so many 19th-century schemes disappeared into thin air. Railway projects had a particularly high fatality rate. The truth seems to be that, fascinated by the arrival of trains, railway mania seized the imagination of engineers, architects, planners, cranks and speculators. They saw gold in the iron rails, and for three decades the rail rush was on. Rivalry was intense; no scheme was too preposterous. Parliament was inundated with proposals, some supported by drawings and estimates, others with hardly more than a quickly printed prospectus, the names of companies' directors, and vague guarantees that capital was available. In 1863 no less than fifty-five proposed London railway schemes were deposited in the Private Bill office of the Commons. The rejection of most of them was inevitably summary, and verged at times on the testy.

Once the main lines from and into London had been built – the eight principal ones were established between 1835 and 1840 – and as soon as the termini were opened (between 1836 and 1854) planners were left with only two outlets for their enterprises. One was to find a system for linking all the termini together; the other for making the various lines converge into one central station. There was no lack of ingenuity, but promoters obviously had trouble in finding adequate terminology to distinguish the different projects. It is difficult not to be confused in sorting out the London Grand Junction from the Grand Central Railway Station, or the Grand Central Terminus (Smithfield) from the Great Central Terminus (Elephant and Castle). The Crystal Way has to be disentangled from the Great Victorian Way (both encased in glass), and each differentiated from the Metropolitan Super-Way. And this is only the start of the problems of understanding the various overlapping schemes.

The most persistent campaigner for linking up the various lines and bringing them into one central station, was a City solicitor, Charles Pearson. Articled in 1816 when he was twenty-three, Pearson quickly built up a large, lucrative practice, became a member of the Court of Common Council, City Solicitor and MP for Lambeth. Whatever cause he identified himself with, he fought with great passion and tenacity. Early in his career he campaigned for the rights of Jews and Catholics, and later for London railways.

Pearson's idea was not dissimilar to George Remington's. Indeed, at one stage the two men seem to have worked together. Pearson's railway would start at Battle Bridge, just to the north of modern St Pancras Station, and have its terminus on either side of Farringdon Street just north of Holborn. Carriages would be brought down on the last stage of their journey on an endless rope powered by a stationary engine. But in 1845 Pearson decided that it would be better worked by atmospheric pressure and enclosed in an arcade, the roof of which could conveniently be used as a street. Farringdon Market, he suggested, should be bought by the City Corporation as a site for what he called Grand Central Terminus.

Two things made Pearson's plan unusual. One was using the Fleet River (by then transformed into a subterranean canal) to carry goods even beyond his terminus to the river at Blackfriars. The other was his Suburban

104 On an upper level on either side of the street James Clephan's London Railway would have linked all the existing London termini. The architect's view shows its two pneumatic tubes in cross-section. Another version with three railway lines – the London Union Railway – would have entirely covered over the lower roadway

Residences for London Mechanics. In a village five to eight miles outside the city 10,000 houses and gardens were to be built for the poorer artisans made homeless when his large terminus swept away such notorious rookeries as Chick Lane. The village, with a private station as its centre, was designed with straight roads radiating out like the rays of the sun, a model suburb equipped with churches, schools, shops and public gardens – the shape of things to come conceived nearly a century before H. G. Wells.

Pearson's plan was one of so many rival schemes put forward in the 1840s that the Government in self-defence set up a Royal Commission to report on them. Among the most interesting was a proposal by James Clephan, an architect whose odd qualifications were that he had rebuilt Wrest Park, the great Bedfordshire house and ornamental grounds designed in 18th-century style. Clephan, who called his idea simply the London Railway, wanted to link all the existing termini in a great ten-mile circle.

A delightful print (Plate 104) shows the elevated railway carried on the roof of a shopping arcade, running sedately down both sides of a street; from

133

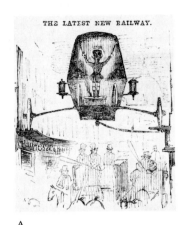

A

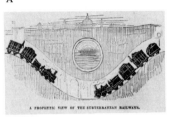

B

105 (A-C) Punch *in 1846 offered some railway suggestions*

C

the upper and balconied windows people look out apparently untroubled by the trains which are noiselessly powered by a pneumatic system. This would be connected to St Katherine and London Docks and link up to the south with rails (wooden, to keep noise to a minimum) over Southwark and Waterloo Bridges. His scheme required no central terminus. Verdict of the Committee: *As its proprietors contemplate occupying two of the bridges over the Thames and passing through the centre of the Metropolis in the most objectionable way, we consider this scheme altogether inadmissible.*

An alternative, comparatively modest scheme was suggested by John Martin, the visionary landscape artist who in the previous decade had advocated elaborate plans for a quay along the Thames (see Chapter 8). Martin was still preoccupied with utilising the river. His idea was to join up the railways with an encircling line which, coming in from east and west on the north side of the Thames, would meet on a stretch alongside the water. Loading and unloading from goods trains and ships would be made possible by permanent, floating piers. These piers, explained Martin, were tantamount to a terminal station about three miles long.

A similar encircling line would be built to the south of the river (presumably joined to the northern circuit by bridges) with a Great Central Terminus at the Elephant and Castle. There would be intermediate stations at every great road crossed by the railway. The London Connecting Railway and Railway Transit Line had been registered as a company and could, Martin believed, 'be the most profitable in all England'. Verdict of the Committee: *It appears that Mr. Martin has neither prepared detailed estimates nor surveys of any part of the scheme he has submitted to us, and therefore it is not possible to enter minutely into its merits. But it is quite evident that to carry it into execution could require an enormous outlay of capital, and we can conceive no commensurate advantages...*

Another riverside scheme also involved a line alongside the water, but the Central Terminus Company whose main spokesman was Thomas Page, engineer to the Great Western, proposed the construction of three grandiose stations. Only slightly less elaborate than the future St Pancras, they had domed turrets, rows of Gothic windows, terraces and a vast central entrance, and were to be placed between Hungerford Bridge and Waterloo Bridge (to serve the GWR), between Blackfriars and Southwark Bridges (Birmingham Line), and between Southwark and London Bridges (Northern and Eastern Lines). The idea of even one such station balefully dominating a section of the waterfront was bad enough. Imagination quails at the thought of the embankment between Charing Cross and London Bridge accommodating *three* St Pancras Stations. Verdict of the Committee: *A great public evil.*

Many other schemes examined in 1846 were equally bizarre, and *Punch* threw a few bright suggestions into the debate. An elevated railway could be slung on suspension bridges between City churches, tower to tower, and ending with St Paul's, a convenient way to accelerate the mails (Plate 105c). If a subterranean passage were preferred, trains could burrow down through domestic coal cellars deeply enough to pass under impeding sewers (Plate 105b). Perhaps best of all, the magazine considered, would be the Shop Ledge Line down streets in which coaches with wheels on widely expanding axles that stretched across the whole width of the thoroughfare would pass high above horse-drawn coaches (Plate 105a). This anticipated by well over a century the futuristic Regent Street Monorail of 1967 (see p. 191).

Ridicule and an unexpected drying-up of finance in the late 1840s after the first surge of railway mania put an end to a great many ideas. But by 1854 confidence in railway investment had to some extent been restored. In that year the Select Committee on Metropolitan Communications called in and examined a number of promoters. Among them was John Pym, an amateur mercantile enthusiast who eight years before had proposed a City Junction Railway to run through Regent's Park from the north to a Central Station by the Bank of England in the City. The scheme he now outlined to the Committee was quite different, but audaciously revolutionary. This was for a Metropolitan Super-Way (Plate 106), a tubular iron construction on columns which would connect all the most important parts of London.

Looking a little like the future New York elevated railway, Pym's Super-Way was to be run by a cable on a stationary engine or by magnetic power. Stations would be established at all principal streets, and passengers would be lifted and lowered to the ground in 'chambers by the aid of machinery' – an early form of lift. The line would be open from 6 a.m. to 10 p.m. with trains running at five-minute intervals. Second-class fares for all distances: 1d.

In 1851 Remington, thwarted earlier in his plan for a terminus at Holborn,

106 John Pym's Metropolitan Super-Way, reminiscent of New York's elevated railway. Connecting all the most important parts of London, the line was to consist of a tubular way similar to the Britannia Bridge on the Chester & Holyhead Railway. Its carriages would by propelled by cable or magnetism. The stations would also be sub-post-offices

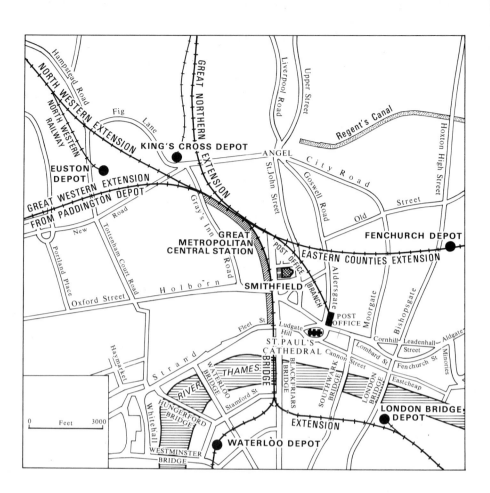

107 How the railways would
have reached the Great
Metropolitan Central Station at
Smithfield

returned to the idea of a central station into which railways would run from
all over the country. He issued a prospectus for his Metropolitan Railway
Union and Central Station, an improved and elaborated version of his
original scheme. This time the so-called Great Metropolitan Central Station
was to be near Smithfield Market. The old termini would become 'depots'
with a series of extensions bringing the trains to the single station – from
Paddington, Euston, King's Cross and Bishopsgate. A new bridge at
Blackfriars would carry extensions from London Bridge and Waterloo. His
plan (Plate 107) also envisaged a short branch line on which all mail coaches
would run into the Aldersgate Main Post Office. A generalised idea, rather
than a specific view (Plate 109), shows Remington's railway bringing trains
into the central station by a 'cut and cover' track which runs down the
middle of a wide thoroughfare. This second scheme enjoyed no more success
than the first, and clearly, while it might have been ideal for the time,
tremendous problems would have arisen as railway traffic increased.

In Remington's scheme we see the slowly developing idea of the
Underground, which was at the back of Charles Pearson's mind as early as
the 1830s. This was to take actual shape in London's first underground, the
Metropolitan from Paddington, via King's Cross, to Farringdon Street,

136

started in 1860. Two other more fanciful schemes for easing London's communications came up for consideration three years later – 1854 – and both showed the influence of the Great Exhibition and the Crystal Palace. Indeed, one of them was called the Crystal Way (Plate 108) and had the backing of several members of the Crystal Palace Company; the other, the Great Victorian Way, was designed by the Crystal Palace's architect, Sir Joseph Paxton.

The Crystal Way was the brainchild of William Moseley, the designer of several unsatisfactory Sussex churches, the Middlesex House of Detention, and a number of lunatic asylums. His line with its fairytale name sounds a happier conception, but trying to understand it threatens to qualify one for a Moseley asylum. The Crystal Way would stretch from Cheapside in the City to Oxford Circus in the West End with a branch line from near Seven Dials to Piccadilly. With a shopping arcade above the railway, it turned upside down

109 In George Remington's scheme all lines north of the river were to converge in the Fleet valley near Smithfield. This view with St Paul's in the background is hard to place topographically; presumably it is looking south roughly down the line of Farringdon Street. A branch running further south was to be carried across Fleet Street and over the Thames at Blackfriars to connect with all the railways south of the river

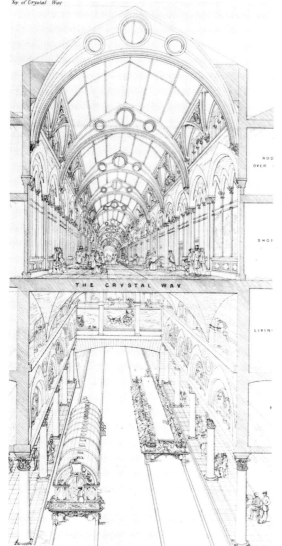

THE CRYSTAL WAY

108 The Crystal Way, designed by William Moseley, would have stretched from Cheapside to Oxford Circus and Piccadilly. This cross-section shows how it was crossed by roads and incorporated a shopping arcade above, and an atmospheric railway below

137

110 *The Thames Viaduct Railway, running down the middle of the river on cylindrical cast-iron piers, has its terminus on London Bridge (left), then passes over Southwark and Blackfriars bridges before curving away to Westminster, the other terminus. This view looking south from the City shows (l – r) the spires of St James Garlickhithe, St Mary Somerset and St Benet, Paul's Wharf, in the foreground, and factories belching smoke at Puddle Dock and on the Surrey side. In the early 1850s, long before its proposal, Robert Stephenson gave the scheme his sanction and approval*

the older schemes of Paine (Westminster Bridge Railway) and Clephan (the London Railway).

Moseley's glass-enclosed, shop-lined arcade was not only above the railway; it was 25 ft above street level. Pedestrians would climb up to reach the arcade, and there was to be a penny charge. If they went down, they reached the platforms 12 ft below street level to board trains propelled by atmospheric pressure. Four hundred buildings would have had to be demolished to build this system.

The most novel (and to us impenetrable) feature of the Crystal Way is how it operated and the way carriages did not have to stop at stations. Moseley himself went before the Select Committee on Metropolitan Communications to explain his claim.

'Do you calculate on going the whole distance [Cheapside to Oxford Circus] in five minutes including stoppages?' he was asked.

'The whole distance without stopping,' replied Moseley. 'To take up passengers at the stations it is proposed that the carriages which have been left by the train as it passed in the opposite direction [for the trains would be formed like the links of a chain] working on a sort of supplemented tube, should be liberated by the weight of the co-running train passing over a weigh-bridge, or by some other contrivance, in sufficient time so as to get its velocity before the other train comes up.

'I have no doubt whatever,' he added a bit lamely, 'but some arrangement of that kind could be made.'

It is to be hoped that the Committee were able to follow the argument better than we can today, because even after concentrated study of the drawings and Moseley's verbatim evidence, the present writers are quite unable to follow how the trains and 'non-stop' carriages would work in practice. An expert consulted at the Science Museum, South Kensington, confesses himself similarly baffled.

Paxton's Great Victorian Way would have made use of glass in a similar fashion. Over ten miles long, this girdle round the whole of central London was to be 72 ft wide – the same as the transept of the Crystal Palace.

It would house eight lines, a roadway for public and private carriages, as

well as shops and houses. Inside this covered Way the atmosphere would be as pure as in the country. The temperature would be regulated to 'give to the whole of London a new source of comfort and enjoyment ...' and would 'prevent many infirm persons being obliged to go into foreign countries in the winter'.

In the section of the Way crossing Kensington Gardens there were to be no buildings, because Paxton was anxious to create the appearance of an elongated Crystal Palace. In bad weather this part of the glass house was to be available to pedestrians of the right social position and used by equestrians as an alternative to Rotten Row. Except for a crossing of the Thames and a loop through Southwark, the Great Victorian Way prophetically took much the same course round London as the Inner Circle Line in the 1880s.

Almost equally extravagant, and also encroaching on the Park, was the scheme suggested in 1857 by a Scottish engineer. Living in Inverness, and thus safely distanced from the London he proposed to cut neatly in half, Joseph Mitchell decided that a railway line, four miles long, was needed, running in a straight line from Bishopsgate to Kensington.

Alongside a road, the line would 'convey passengers from one end of London to the other, at railway speed, with great economy, comfort and convenience'. There were to be six stations on the route, and two branch lines, so that all London's termini, except London Bridge, would be linked.

Mitchell claimed his route would only require demolition of property of 'comparatively inferior value', a rather arbitrary assessment since it cut slap through Grosvenor Square. Any objections to a railway in Hyde Park were countered by sinking the track below ground level and behind a screen of shrubbery.

The one redeeming feature of the disruptive conception was seen in a lithograph which accompanied the published proposal (see pp. 118–19). The terminus is just short of the Serpentine, and there is a pleasant bridge across the water. A broad avenue leads up to the Round Pond and a magnificent Palace of Fine Arts – a view which has a touch of grandeur and magic.

In the next ten years there was little abatement in the ideas proposed for new railway schemes. In the 1860s they became even more numerous when the once-incredible idea of running a railway under the streets had become a reality with the building of the Metropolitan. A map published by Edward Stanford shows that no less than fifty-five railways were proposed during the 1864 session of Parliament. These included an Oxford Street and City Railway (foreshadowing the Central Line) and the Paddington to Charing Cross Line, which would have cut a disfiguring gash right across Hyde Park.

The most sensational railway proposal of the session, however, was that of James Samuel and John M. Heppel. Samuel, a Glaswegian engineer, was later to plan railways in Asia Minor and become consultant to Mexican railways. He combined with Heppel to remove one great obstacle to all new railways — compensation for demolition. Their solution was to build where no building existed. The Thames Viaduct Railway (Plate 110) marched like a stilted giant down the centre of the Thames.

This system linking the Houses of Parliament, the Law Courts and all the chief centres of commerce would be built, it was claimed, in two years without obstructing a single existing road. 'The overcrowded mis-called thoroughfares could be relieved, a crying nuisance abated and an urgent need satisfied.'

Samuel and Heppel admitted that their Thames Viaduct looked somewhat novel, but maintained that there would be 'intelligent support' once the many advantages were appreciated. An obstruction to navigation? No. By keeping down the centre of the river, it was less of a menace to shipping than bridges. Ugly? Not at all. Of lighter and more ornamental design than Hungerford Bridge, the viaduct's appearance would be enhanced by elevation and length.

Trains running by day and night between London Bridge and Westminster would make the whole journey in five minutes (express) and ten minutes (stopping at each bridge and intermediary stations). Fares: First Class, 2d; Second Class, 1d.

With the building of the various Underground lines towards the end of the century and their extensions which have continued ever since, practical development replaced theoretical ideas. But the constantly recurring idea of a surface line which would link the various railways was revived in 1911. A plan for a semicircular line, 57 miles long, connecting all railways north of the Thames was put before a Select Committee in that year. It was openly declared to be a method of moving troops from Aldershot and Salisbury to the docks without going through London. The loop began at Feltham, and passed through Northolt, Hendon and Barking to reach Tilbury. As if visualising the possibilities of the Great War three years off, the War Office was said to be 'not only watching its progress but actively supporting it'.

Chapter 12

Pyramids, Mausoleums, and Anti-Vampire Devices

THE Victorians seem to have been half in love with death, which was just as well since they had a great deal of it to contend with. By the middle of the 19th century 52,000 funerals were taking place every year in London, and the population was multiplying out of all proportion to the accommodation available for its dead. In the City's tiny churchyards grave-diggers resorted to heaping fresh corpses into old graves. The ever-growing mounds of bodies caused graveyards to rise high above street level. Shallow interments greatly convenienced body-snatchers, and relatives of the dead, returning to churchyards, were frequently appalled to find earth thrown back and coffins empty.

Especially in times of cholera epidemics it was feared that rotting and exposed corpses would spread pestilential disease. The genuine concern of a sanitary reformer such as Edwin Chadwick about the threat to public health was magnified in the popular imagination by sensational stories. Workmen engaged in removing bodies from a vault at St Dunstan's, according to a typical story, were seized with 'instant trembling', the foetid atmosphere causing their tongues to fur over, a condition associated with the plague. 'The aperture was instantly closed and the men have slowly recovered,' it was reported with relief, but Londoners were left shuddering. Apprehension became the spur for action.

Two centuries earlier John Evelyn had foreseen the problem of overcrowded churchyards and had proposed a gated enclosure, one mile long, to the north of the City, its walls adorned with monuments and inscriptions apt for contemplation. Wren, too, had proposed cemeteries set away from town centres with finely designed monuments and mausoleums. The scale of the scandal in the early 19th century prompted action by Londoners already humiliated by the example set by the Parisians with their celebrated Père Lachaise cemetery. Napoleon had ordered the cemetery as one of four to be built outside the walls of Paris, and, magnificently landscaped out of the gardens of a former mansion, this graveyard showed what could be accomplished. London followed suit with three startlingly innovative schemes put forward in the 1820s.

In 1824 an Inner Temple barrister named George Frederick Carden, who had undertaken a gruesome personal investigation of London churchyards, proposed a plan for an extensive burial ground – a British Père Lachaise – and petitioned Parliament in the following year to enquire officially into the

111 *The Grand National Cemetery, a Graeco-Roman vision, was to cover 150 acres (42 acres within the central double cloisters) by Primrose Hill or possibly at Kidbrooke. The cemetery's practical intention was advertised as 'the prevention of the Danger and Inconvenience of burying the Dead within the Metropolis'. Investors were offered 16,000 shares at £25 each*

gross evils of the present system. His tastefully laid-out cemetery would be surrounded by a high ornamental wall 'watched and guarded as to prevent the possibility of the sepulchres within being violated'. Vaults and catacombs would be provided for general use through parishes and public bodies while individuals would be free to erect mausoleums and monuments after their own fancy. The cemetery, Carden hoped, would be sited near Primrose Hill.

A rival, far more extravagant, scheme for a 'Grand National Cemetery' was advanced with equal passion by the architect Francis Goodwin. The public was invited to see the drawings at the National Cemetery Office in Parliament

142

Street. His wildly classical burial ground would also be outside central London and would cover an area of 150 acres (Plate 111). The site was unspecified – probably purposely – but he may have had Primrose Hill in mind, though the curve of the river suggests the Kidbrooke area south of Shooters Hill. The most striking features in his design were to be confined to 42 acres. Here, surrounded by a double cloister affording 'a promenade in the case of unfavourable weather', would be a church modelled on the Parthenon, together with facsimiles of the Temple of the Vestal Virgins in the Roman Forum, and the Erechtheum on the Athenian Acropolis. Four copies of the Tower of the Winds in Athens were to stand, one at each corner of the

143

cloister. The whole of this stunning arrangement would be concluded with a long, magnificent crescent encompassing a replica of Trajan's Column. The space beneath the cloister would be for catacombs. The three entrances were to be modelled on the Athens Propylaea and the Roman arches of Constantine and Septimus Severus. This inner area would be reserved for the very wealthy and 'great and distinguished persons whose wisdom, bravery, genius and talent have conspicuously contributed to the glory of the country'. Beyond the inner 42 acres, for people of moderate means, would be a second region of tombs laid out in luxurious Père Lachaise style. And beyond that division, a third would be reserved for the 'humbler class'.

Goodwin's Graeco-Roman vision had to compete with the third grand proposal of the period – Thomas Willson's. For Willson the answer was nothing other than one enormous pyramid (Plate 112). With a base roughly the same size as Russell Square, Bloomsbury, this structure – higher than St Paul's and larger in volume than the Great Pyramid itself – would ingeniously provide a last resting place for a total of 5,167,104 Londoners. Like Carden's General Cemetery as originally planned it would be sited near Primrose Hill and thus dominate the north London skyline.

Willson was not new to the game. Winner of a Gold Medal at the Royal Academy Schools, he had already designed an unexecuted mausoleum for Lord Nelson, an unrealised National Mausoleum for Naval and Military Heroes, and an earlier and even vaster pyramid than the one described in his c.1829 prospectus. The edifice which he envisaged for Primrose Hill would be constructed of brick with granite facing. Entering through its lofty portals, mourners would first come across a small plain chapel, a register office, and four 'neat dwellings' for the Keeper, the Clerk, the Sexton and the Superintendent. The entrances to the pyramid would be four in number, one in the centre of each side. Inside the pyramid the main avenues would lead to 'a central shaft of general ventilation'. Surrounding this shaft, gently inclined planes in lieu of stairs would enable the undertakers to move coffins around from one level to another. In all, the pyramid would contain 215,296 catacombs. Each catacomb accommodated twenty-four large coffins, and after all the interments the two dozen would be sealed up for eternity.

Consisting of row upon row of small groined alcoves, in cross-section Willson's pyramid would resemble a beehive. 'To trace the length of its shadow at sun-rise and at eve,' Willson lyrically predicted, 'and to toil up its singular passages to the summit, will beguile the hours of the curious and impress feelings of solemn awe and admiration upon every beholder.' The whole would form 'a *coup d'oeil* of sepulchral magnificence unequalled in the world'. A contrast, indeed, this hygienic pyramid, to the pestiferous city graveyards where even consecrated bells could no longer be relied upon to protect the souls of the departed from 'foul fiends of the air', or their remains 'against the horrid ravages of obscene vampires underground'.

Willson continually stressed the aesthetic qualities of his pyramid ('the graceful proportions are particularly adapted to sepulchral solemnity'), its historical importance ('an impressive *memento mori* to every passing age') and its civic appeal ('the grand Mausoleum will go far towards the glory of

112 Sections through Thomas Willson's pyramid cemetery, showing the alcoves for the storage of bodies. The scale of the pyramid may be judged from the size of the diminutive figures on the side of the front pyramid

Section

London!'). As for hygiene ('every deposit hermetically sealed for ever'), there would be purity of atmosphere surrounding the pyramid for which 'the author of the Project is willing to answer with his life'.

But the appeal of the pyramid was not just aesthetic. Each stage constituted a freehold estate obtainable from the Pyramid General Cemetery Office, and investment in it would make men rich. Willson flourished the figures. The catacombs were to be rented to parishes or individual families at £50 per vault or at an outright sale of at least £10. More than 40,000 corpses could confidently be expected to turn up each year. The saving compared with ordinary burial costs would benefit London to the tune of £12,500 a year. As for investors, they could expect a final profit of £10,764,800. The wise would do well to apply for 'The Five Per Cent Pyramid Stock' at once.

In May 1829 Willson announced in the press that he would be making an application to Parliament for a charter to carry his pyramid into effect. In the following year, however, Carden presented a second petition to Parliament calling once again for a 'British Père Lachaise', where people were at liberty to erect what individual monuments they liked. At a meeting of the shareholders of the company Willson defended his pyramid with vigour but conceded defeat and withdrew his campaign so as not to prejudice Carden's chances. As a result Royal assent was given in 1832 to a 'Bill for Establishing a General Cemetery for the Interment of the Dead in the Neighbourhood of the Metropolis'. Fifty-four acres of land were purchased, not at Primrose Hill, but to the north of Paddington at Kensal Green.

A place of rest one might suppose would inspire tranquil development. In fact Kensal Green soon developed into a battleground on which architects bludgeoned their opponents in a new round of the Battle of the Styles. H. E.

Kendall, a medievalist, won the competition for landscaping the ground and designing the buildings. His chapel, on gently rising ground, would have been a fairy-tale building of points and pinnacles (Plate 113). The Harrow Road entrance was to consist of a lofty gateway with a Gothic arch flanked by towers and crenellated walls. From the Grand Union Canal black-draped barges would approach the ornate water-gate (Plate 114) like gondolas arriving at the Venetian island cemetery of San Michele; Paddington Basin would be a second Rio della Misericordia. At a meeting of the Cemetery Company in March 1832, however, the Chairman swung the vote in favour of his own Greek Revival preferences. Doric and Ionic won the day.

Between 1832 and 1847 seven further commercial cemetery companies were authorised by Parliament in the London area, and Cities of the Dead, not too dissimilar to All Souls, Kensal Green, were laid out at Norwood, Highgate, Brompton, Nunhead, Abney Park and Tower Hamlets. But so rapid was the growth of London's population, and so devastating the ravages of the great cholera epidemic of the 1840s, that Parliament was soon compelled to search for yet another extensive burial ground. In December 1849 the great social reformer, Edwin Chadwick, placed before the Government a scheme whereby funerals would be made a public service, interments in churchyards and private burial grounds would cease, and joint-stock company cemeteries would be closed down. In future interments would take place only in National Cemeteries. Kensal Green would become the Great Western National Cemetery. And to provide a burial ground on the other side of London a Great Eastern Cemetery would be laid out at Abbey Wood.

Abbey Wood was a natural choice. A beauty spot, well treed, and with monastic remains providing what was then judged the appropriate atmosphere, it lay close to the Thames. For Chadwick the river would serve

114 A water-gate allowing access into Kensal Green Cemetery from the Grand Junction Canal for waterborne funerals

147

as a 'Silent Highway' and from eight London 'reception houses', an average of ninety-six corpses a day would be floated in specially adapted steamboats. He bombarded bishops and MPs with proposals ranging from the arrangement of corpses to the style of the funeral chapel. He outlined his plans to the Earl of Carlisle, then promoting the Public Health Bill in Parliament. Confronted with a profusion of premature detail, the Earl confessed himself quite staggered by talk of a chapel with a dome of stained glass, floors paved with encaustic tiles, and stalls for mourners hung with rich cloth and emblazoned with the arms of the Metropolitan parishes. Chadwick wanted an effigy of an apostle in terracotta, a glass-covered approach for wet weather, and arrival avenues lined with colossal statues. A remarkable effort of constructive thought, the Earl conceded, but at the same time a great imprudence.

Chadwick's critics judged it more than imprudent. They found serious faults on hygienic grounds. Upon medical authority it could be stated that twelve-thirteenths of every decomposed human body passed into the air. As a result 62,000 decomposing corpses buried annually at Abbey Wood would produce 3,038,000 cubic feet of dangerous gases all to be blown towards Greenwich and then London by the prevailing winds. Poisons would be swept up river on every flood tide. A minimum of twenty-four miles from London, not fifteen, was crucial for so vast a cemetery.

So Abbey Wood with its monastic ruins was abandoned and left to the future mixed blessing of Thamesmead. Kent's loss became Surrey's gain. Chadwick's Metropolitan Interment Act was found to be impracticable and in 1852 was repealed. But in the same year the London Necropolis and National Mausoleum Company acquired 2,000 acres of land at Brookwood near Woking. As its name implied the Company intended to lay out a cemetery – large enough for 400 years – but there was also to be a National Mausoleum, a gigantic building set up with a maze of chapels, vaults, private mausoleums and catacombs. A railway would transport funeral parties swiftly on oiled axles from the Necropolis Station at Waterloo to Woking. This railway was constructed, and, looking out of trains taking them past London's relief cemetery, today's passengers can reflect on the enterprise of the Victorians in uniting the Locomotive with the service of God.

The desire to see loved ones buried with the utmost decorum in hygienic, landscaped cemeteries rather than thrown into pestilential churchyards now led people to ponder how the bodies of the nation's great men might more honourably be disposed of. 'Where are the tombs of our heroes and statesmen? Where are the monuments to those eminent men whose exertions or whose genius have bequeathed to their country the inheritance of a noble name . . . ?' asked Sydney Smirke. 'Alas for patriotism and gratitude of our country! In reply to these questions we point to Westminster Abbey, where, by slinking down a bye lane and creeping through a wicket of a back door, the enquiring stranger will (on payment of twopence) be admitted to survey, in a corner of the south transept, a more motley, ill-assorted, and graceless collection of bad sculpture than ever dishonoured the workshop of a marble mason.'

Francis Goodwin had hoped to resolve the problem by earmarking the spectacular heart of his Grecian Grand National Cemetery for those who had most conspicuously contributed to their country's glory. Smirke's triumphal solution in the 1830s was a miniature Salisbury Cathedral to be built 'in a treed spot sloping towards the water and backed by venerable trees' on the north bank of the Serpentine (Plate 115). Here, in 'long aisles and cloistered arcades', would be deposited mortal remains and monumental effigies of all deemed worthy. In a melancholy print of this 'lofty pile of antique architecture' the funereal purpose of the building is suggested by the ferryman in the foreground. A modern Charon, he seems to be ready to row two visitors across London's Styx to Smirke's Hades on the other side.

Briefly an idea was entertained of devoting a small portion of the new Palace of Westminster to the reception of public monuments of great men. It was also noted that at Regensburg on the banks of the Danube King Ludwig of Bavaria had recently erected a 'Walhalla' with a 'Hall of Expectation' beneath to serve as a repository for busts of eminent living nationals whose remains on decease would be deposited upstairs. This notion rather appealed to an *Athenaeum* contributor who, supported by *Art Union*, suggested a 'British Walhalla', as part of the British Museum. Two wings, one classical, the other Gothic, 'grouping with, though detached from, the main building', would house the busts of those who had distinguished themselves in Literature, Art, and Science.

In the 1850s Sir George Gilbert Scott joined the campaign with his own idea for a national monument, and chose Westminster as the logical place.

Generally it was felt that a national shrine should retain a close association with the Abbey, which had housed the tombs of famous men since Tudor times, but was now uncomfortably full. The only available site was immediately south of the Henry VII Chapel, facing the Houses of Parliament across Old Palace Yard. Today this is an open grass area where a statue of George V stands, but at the time was cluttered with domestic buildings including a terrace of pleasant Georgian houses in Abingdon Street. Scott chose this as the place for 'a wide and lofty cloister of great length' which at first he saw simply as a good place in which to house the 'more offensive' monuments in the Abbey. In years to come he was to elaborate this plan with drawings for a long neo-Gothic building stretching as far south as Great College Street.

It was in this area, running south and east of the Chapter House, that architects were to exercise their ingenuity for half a century to create a shrine variously called a Campo Santo, New Valhalla, Monumental Chapel, National Mortuary, and Imperial Mausoleum. A modest suggestion for an extra aisle in the Abbey itself, which the architect and restorer J. L. Pearson wanted to graft onto the north side of the nave, was rejected, as was Edward J. Tarver's idea for a 'wreath' of chapels set between the flying buttresses surrounding the Chapter House and joined to it by bridges.

Much public discussion and newspaper criticism greeted all these ideas. At one time it was hoped that the great national monument would be built to mark Queen Victoria's Golden Jubilee, but in 1888 ideas were still in the melting pot. Yearly the situation grew worse as the last remaining burial places in the Abbey were filled, and busts, statues and tablets continued to proliferate. The alternative of memorial windows and floor brasses took the strain, but left the problem unsolved. Bureaucracy fell back on its last refuge – a Royal Commission.

In 1891, after more than a year, the Commissioners published their report. Their dissension was clear from the way they presented evidence instead of reaching a conclusion. They were torn between two main possibilities – both of enormous cost and with inevitable drawbacks. One of these schemes was for a chapel to be built on the site of the monastic refectory owned by Westminster School. The school demurred. A £30,000 Valhalla was all very well, but they had just built a boys' latrine there.

Parliament declined to arbitrate, and even when Yates Thompson, wealthy book-collector and philanthropist, offered to subscribe £38,000 in 1894, they wouldn't agree. A year later the demolition of a number of buildings on the west side of Old Palace Yard made the area ripe for development. But Parliament was saved by the Boer War. Difficult decisions always tend to be shelved during wars and forgotten after them.

It was an amateur, a doctor named David Walsh, who reopened the debate in 1903 with a new scheme for a pyramid, this time to be raised 'say in Hyde Park', where it would be visible to the greater part of London. Illustrations in the *Strand Magazine* reveal a structure of singular ugliness. The building would not run down sheer to the ground but stand on a square pediment reaching to a third of its total height. On the south side would be the main

entrance, a monumental doorway led up to by steps and supported by massive square pillars. Large sloping windows punctured its sides to allow light into the main chamber. Within, at the very heart of the building, would stand a Stonehenge Druidical arch. In a subterranean chamber posterity would discover the tombs of the Kings and Queens of England. To finance the erection of the pyramid Dr Walsh suggested that the population of the United Kingdom and the Empire should be invited to pay for bricks, each costing one penny. The humblest could contribute one brick for the great monument. Wealthier members of the community could subscribe to a hundred, a thousand, a hundred thousand, or even a million bricks.

Perhaps it was the sheer hideousness of Walsh's National Monument that in 1904 caused the Westminster Campo Santo to rear its head again in a defiant burst of unparalleled grandeur. In 1890 John Pollard Seddon, Diocesan Architect for London, and Laurence Harvey, Instructor of Scientific Masonry at the City and Guilds, had submitted an elaborate and expensive scheme to the Royal Commissioners incorporating a system of ambulatories, a cluster of chapels round the Chapter House, and a massive *campo santo*, or sacred shrine, in Abingdon Street. Eleven years later Edward

116 Bird's-eye view of J. P. Seddon and E. B. Lamb's Imperial Monumental Halls and Tower (1904), viewed from a point above New Scotland Yard. The Halls (with side-chapels) can be seen extending south of the soaring 550-ft Tower down Abingdon Street. Parliament's Victoria Tower is dwarfed. Westminster Abbey is provided with an extra, central tower to lessen the shattering impact

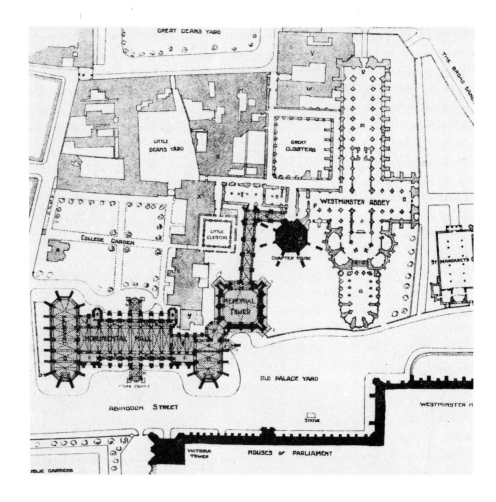

117 Plan of the Imperial Monumental Halls and Tower and the approach from Westminster Abbey

B. Lamb had exhibited 'a design for a National Monument to British Heroes' at the Royal Academy which to some extent fell in with Seddon's ideas. The two men now worked together on an elaborate version of the earlier Seddon-Harvey scheme. The new designs were exhibited in a studio near Sloane Square. One of Lamb's drawings (Plate 116) showed the scene as it would appear from below Westminster Bridge. It is a view of such photographic realism and the proposed buildings fit in so splendidly with the surrounding Westminster architecture, that we have to look twice to realise that the gigantic building does not really exist.

The dominating feature of Seddon and Lamb's Imperial Monumental Halls is the great tower, 550 ft tall, that dwarfs Big Ben and rises more than 100 ft higher than the Victoria Tower. Westminster Abbey nestles at its feet. The main approach is by a right-angle cloister which leads from the Great Cloister of the Abbey to a reception hall, 64 ft across, in the base of the tower (Plate 117). A series of galleries for monuments occupy the inside of the tower and there are rooms above for records. At the top of the tower is an ambulatory, 70 ft square, and above that a lantern constructed to hold bells.

From the Memorial Tower a funeral cortège would move into the Great Monumental Hall that extends 192 ft to Great College Street and culminates in a double transept, 157 ft long. Leading off the Monumental Hall are minor halls for 'monuments of high art to eminent men and women of all parts of the British Empire ... a worthy centre in the metropolis of the Empire "upon which the sun never sets"'.

Seddon and Harvey had been told in 1890 that they had priced themselves out with a similar scheme that would have cost £780,000. Now the *Builder* commented severely that the tower had 'a little too much of the megalomania about it'. Seddon and Lamb can hardly have cared. They had enjoyed one wild fling. All architectural inhibitions had been discarded. Though they must have known it was doomed to be a nine-days' wonder they could delight in having proposed just about the most preposterous folly in London's history.

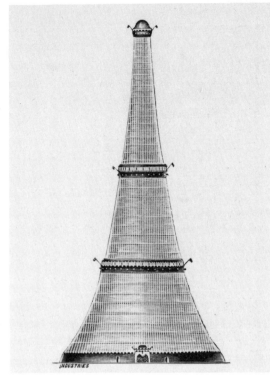

118 (l.) Albert Brunel's 'upright Tower of Pisa' design

119 (r.) Steel and glass tower, 1,234 ft high, with twelve pneumatic lifts

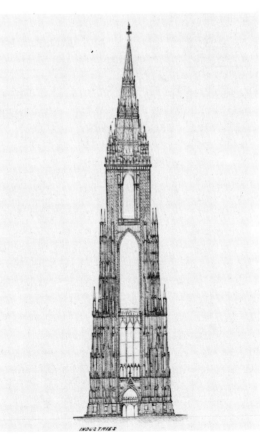

120 (l.) 'Tower of Babel' with outside spiral gradient for a train

121 (r.) Gothic cathedral tower with spire, 1,550 ft high, of iron and steel

Chapter 13

The Eiffel Tower at Wembley

ANCIENT rivalry between England and France has been kept simmering by our subconscious resentment that the French, defeated in war, have shown an impertinent refusal to accept our superiority when it comes to the arts of peace. But towards the end of the last century it seemed as if this sorry state of affairs was to be ended by a small, but decisive British triumph. Victories at Agincourt and Waterloo were to be pressed home on the Field of Wembley.

Revenge was long overdue. Blatantly, as it seemed to true British hearts, the French had laid out Paris to make London look inferior. It had been particularly galling that within a few decades of Bonaparte's overthrow fresh plans were afoot to render the French capital even more sumptuous than London. There were those elegant quays and plentiful bridges to shame the Thames. Versailles and the Tuileries were an irksome reminder of the inadequacy of Buckingham Palace. Not content with existing Grands Boulevards, Napoleon III began to create broad new avenues while London's traffic remained snarled up in tortuously narrow streets. Why was Baron Haussmann able to design a Paris of such unparalleled magnificence during the Second Empire when Wren and Nash had been so largely frustrated?

This intolerable position seemed as if it might be slightly rectified by the building of Nelson's Column in 1843. At least that was higher than any monument in Paris. But the pride in which London might have indulged was shortlived. Within half a century of our raising of the 170-ft Corinthian column in Trafalgar Square (a neatly named reminder of the French defeat), the old enemy hit back. They dwarfed it with the 984-ft Eiffel Tower.

Fortunately this moment of architectural crisis found the man. A reprisal came in the same year, 1889, with an announcement that London, too, intended to build a great tower. The promoter of the scheme, Sir Edward Watkin, MP, became the hero of the hour, and his Metropolitan Tower Construction Company was greeted as enthusiastically as a victorious fleet.

To rub salt into the French wound, Watkin published his intention of building a London 'Eiffel Tower' that was going to be 150 ft taller than its Paris rival. 'Anything Paris can do, London can do bigger!' was the triumphant boast as the foundations for the four massive steel legs of the tower were laid at Wembley Park in 1891. But, as we shall see, the cry was premature. Patriotic euphoria was not to last for long.

Sir Edward (Plate 122) was an engineer of wide vision. Although most of

122 Sir Edward Watkin

155

123 *Second Prize design modelled on the Eiffel Tower but with six Gothic towers and gatehouses round the base*

124 *The winning design with similar silhouette to the Paris prototype; the original six legs were modified to four*

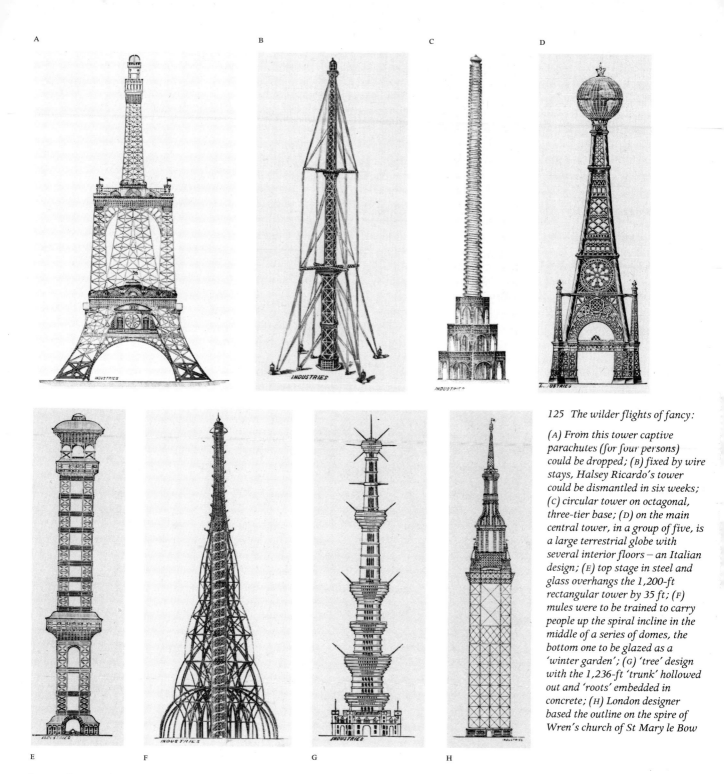

A   B   C   D

125 *The wilder flights of fancy:*

(A) From this tower captive parachutes (for four persons) could be dropped; (B) fixed by wire stays, Halsey Ricardo's tower could be dismantled in six weeks; (C) circular tower on octagonal, three-tier base; (D) on the main central tower, in a group of five, is a large terrestrial globe with several interior floors – an Italian design; (E) top stage in steel and glass overhangs the 1,200-ft rectangular tower by 35 ft; (F) mules were to be trained to carry people up the spiral incline in the middle of a series of domes, the bottom one to be glazed as a 'winter garden'; (G) 'tree' design with the 1,236-ft 'trunk' hollowed out and 'roots' embedded in concrete; (H) London designer based the outline on the spire of Wren's church of St Mary le Bow

E   F   G   H

his early and middle life was devoted to railways, he was a man whose ideas spread in various directions. He was an early advocate of Saturday half-holidays and the building of public parks. In 1869 he pioneered the idea of a Channel Tunnel, and ran into trouble by excavating a trial shaft on the Kent foreshore without Crown permission. The Paris Exhibition of 1889 and the tower designed by Gustav Eiffel in the Champ-de-Mars had a great impact on him. If it could be done in Paris, why not London? This was the tallest building in the world, but why shouldn't one go higher? There was a question of the vast expense, but once he heard that two-thirds of the Eiffel Tower's cost had been recovered in the first year, Watkin's mind was made up.

A decision had to be reached about the kind of tower, and where exactly it should be built. Among other railway appointments, Watkin was Chairman of the Metropolitan Railway which a few years before had extended its north-eastern line from Baker Street past Willesden to Harrow. This ran through unspoilt woodland country, enhanced by a tributary of the River Brent, and was already popular with day visitors keen to get out of central London. Watkin decided that if he could acquire the 280 acres of land and convert it into a pleasure park, Wembley would be the perfect place for his tower.

All that would be needed would be to open an intermediate station — Wembley Park was the obvious name — so that the crowds could get there. The huge structure, visible from miles around, would be its own constant advertisement. The commercial advantages to the railway were obvious, and the Chairman of the newly formed Metropolitan Tower Construction Company (Watkin) had no difficulty in persuading the Chairman of the Metropolitan Railway Company (Watkin) that money would be well invested in the new venture. The land was purchased.

What kind of tower? Making a surprising gesture of Anglo-French amity, Watkin first invited Gustav Eiffel to design the tower for Wembley. But Eiffel declined on the patriotic grounds that 'if I, after erecting my Tower on French soil, were to erect one in England, they would not think me so good a Frenchman as I hope I am'. It was the mildest of snubs, and Watkin neatly deflected it 'as a bit of pleasantry' — a flattering tribute to the capabilities of British engineers. Very well, they would launch a competition.

The Tower Construction Company advertised for designs in November 1889 offering prizes of 500 guineas and 250 guineas. Drawings came in from Germany, Sweden, Italy, Austria and Turkey as well as from Britain and from as far away as the United States and Australia. France was not to be left out and an architect from Rouen, Albert Brunel, submitted a design for a circular building 574 ft in diameter and more than double the height of the Eiffel Tower that was likened to the leaning Tower of Pisa — 'only that it stands upright'. This entry (Plate 118) was to be built in solid granite weighing 200,000 tons at a cost of £1,000,000.

Fancy took many wild and imaginative flights among the sixty-eight proposals. In what became known as the 'Tower of Babel' (Plate 120) category because of outside spiral staircases, the most elaborate was submitted by S. Fisher of London, and covered an area so vast that it permitted a spiral road and railway of $2\frac{1}{2}$ miles (gradient 1 in 20) to the top. One feature of the elaborate tower by J. M. Harrison-Vasey (Plate 125A) was a captive parachute (to hold four persons) attached to a corner tower, but it is not clear if the designer regarded this as a sideshow or emergency escape.

GENERAL VIEW
OF
WEMBLEY PARK,
AS SEEN FROM RAILWAY STATION,
SHEWING TOWER AS IT WILL
APPEAR WHEN COMPLETE.
TOTAL HEIGHT 1150 FEET.

SKETCH PLAN
SHEWING PROXIMITY
OF PARK TO STATION.
FROM BAKER S.T

WEMBLEY PARK STATION

126 Prospectus for the Wembley Park Tower showing the ornamental ground and boating lake with the tower on the horizon as it was going to look on completion

A Poland Street architect sacrificed frivolity to functional purpose with model lodgings, offices, and pubs served by twelve automatic lifts (Plate 119). The downward motion of these lifts would supply pure air ('laid on by pipe as gas is') to what was virtually a city in the sky. There must be a library, patent office, courts of administration, county council offices, scientific institutions and (wrote the entrant warming to his theme) 'all other measures tending to civilise and educate the civilised world'. In case of war it would be used for signalling, he added as an afterthought.

Barely suppressed fanaticism was observable in a design submitted from an ironworks on the Thames at Blackwall by the President of the London Vegetarian Society. This provided for a colony of aerial vegetarians. They would derive nutrition from fruit and vegetables grown in gardens hanging, presumably in the style of Babylon, on the first level. 'Ye Vegetarian Tower' was shaped like an Egyptian monolith, and at its summit was the Great Pyramid of Giza, one-twelfth full size. On the fourth level there was a temple (sect unspecified); on the fifth an international store; and above that a hotel, club, flats and chambers, 'the smokeless, fogless atmosphere of which should command a rent proportional to their Alpine altitude'.

The principal judge, Sir Benjamin Baker, a distinguished civil engineer, and Fellow of the Royal Society, had to sort his way among towers prodigally endowed with theatres, concert halls, glass-covered winter gardens and even complete villages. Uninhibited by any worry about cost, one competitor suggested a tower covering $8\frac{1}{4}$ acres at its base. Quirky names abounded.

127 *Photograph of the Wembley
Eiffel Tower as it appeared
shortly before being demolished by
explosives in 1907. The Tower
should have reached a height of
1,150 ft – 165 ft higher than its
Paris rival. In fact, it never rose
beyond the first stage of 155 ft*

There was the Rose, Thistle and Shamrock Tower, the Circumferentially,
Radially and Diagonally Bound Tower, and one for which it was necessary to
take a deep breath – the Muniment of Hieroglyphics Emblematical of British
History During Queen Victoria's Reign Tower. Sir Benjamin and his fellow
judges must have been relieved to escape from this lunatic fringe and
consider the handful of serious designs. They quickly came round to the idea
that for grace and beauty it was hard to excel the basic shape of the Eiffel
Tower with its four splayed legs merging into a vertical shaft. As a result, the
winner looked uncommonly like the Paris prototype.

One runner-up by a Dutch architect, Max em Ende, broke away with a
building that resembled nothing so much as a French cathedral spire, but was
far too ecclesiastical to appeal to holiday-makers (Plate 121). The winners of
the second prize, Webster and Haigh, mounted an Eiffel Tower, not on legs
but on an elaborate Gothic gatehouse with buttresses to strengthen the six
vertical towers round the base (Plate 123).

The winning design with its open-work metal lattice-work looked in
silhouette almost identical to the Paris tower, except that for extra height it
rose to four stages instead of three. Originally it was planned by Messrs A. D.
Stewart, J. M. Maclaren and W. Dunn, a firm of London architects, as an
octagonal tower standing on six splayed legs (Plate 124). But before building
started, they had modified this to four, further confirmation that Eiffel's
concept was virtually unbeatable.

The added height was to provide more facilities 'for the healthy recreation
of the million', and pleasure-seekers could expect restaurants, a theatre,
shops, Turkish baths, promenades and winter gardens at various stages. An
observatory was planned for the summit because freedom from mists at that
altitude would mean the stars could be clearly photographed. A
meteorological office would record wind velocities and scientists carry out
micrographic studies of the air for the existence of bacilli. Exactly what

germs would be doing flying about more than 1,000 ft in the air was not made plain, and seemed at odds with the suggestion that a kind of informal sanatorium would also be established. In Paris, doctors had recommended visits to the top of the Eiffel Tower as a 'pure air cure' for pneumonia patients, and the London promoters advocated that their tower should similarly 'be utilised in the interests of suffering humanity'.

With this combination of old-style showmanship, piously professed altruism and a hope of big dividends, the Metropolitan Tower Construction Company started work, and by July 1891 was reported to be making 'visible progress'. Foundation holes, 35 ft deep, were dug at the four corners of the 250-ft square base and filled with concrete for the legs of the tower which it was estimated would weigh 3,000 tons. Short stretches of temporary track were laid to each base branching off the Metropolitan Line to carry steel girders forged at the Newton Heath Ironworks in Manchester right to the site. Landscaping started on the park which, with its boating lake, waterfall and leafy walks, was to be the setting for Watkin's Tower (Plate 126).

A year later the park was said to be complete, but little progress had been made to the tower. A shareholders' meeting heard the rather ominous statement that work could soon go ahead now that the kind of tower had been 'practically settled'. Wasn't it a bit late in the day for there to be any uncertainty on that score? The Chairman, Sir Edward Watkin, dismissed this question along with fears expressed about finance. Shareholders were assured that there was plenty of capital for the next stage of the operations. The meeting would be pleased to hear that the tower would be able to take three times as many visitors as the one in Paris. A vital means of approach, the new Wembley Park Station, would be opened in a few weeks. Revenue would start coming in with the opening of the park in the following spring. As to when the tower itself would be finished – well, in about eighteen months, the Chairman thought.

This prediction was wildly optimistic. Thirteen months later – September 1893 – the tower had reached a height of 62 ft, and the company reported that the design had been 'considerably modified'. Some 150 men were at work, and the contractors said they hoped to be finished within a year, but when the park was actually opened in May 1894 the public found that the tower had only reached the first stage of about 155 ft. Disappointment was reflected in the numbers who paid to go up to that level. Out of 100,000 visitors during the first six months only 18,500 made the ascent. Their initial curiosity to see the building partially satisfied, few people bothered to go back to Wembley.

Behind the scenes things were far from well. The tower was beginning to be called 'The Shareholders' Dismay', and with reason. It could no longer be concealed that the Metropolitan Tower Construction Company had never had enough capital. Their subscriptions amounted to only £27,000. To this the Metropolitan Railway had added £60,000. If the price of the still unpaid-for land (£33,000) were added to the cost, a total of £72,000 had already been spent. This left the company a balance of £15,000 to complete a job which had virtually only just begun.

To make things worse, public opinion began to turn against the 'London

Stump' which, along with 'Sir Edward's Pride and Folly', was a new nickname. At the start it had been widely assumed that Queen Victoria would be asked to give her name to the tower. There was no question of that now. The *Building News*, previously quite friendly, began to carp. 'In less than another hundred years,' asserted a writer, 'the perpetrators of an unfinished ugliness like the Wembley Tower will, I trust, have to pay a handsome rent to the public for spoiling views in such a lovely locality.' The magazine reckoned that about £100,000 had been spent to reach only one stage, and that few people would care if it went no higher. At least another £200,000 would be needed to complete the tower. Even then, people began to ask, who would pay money for a view at the top of a far too distant London?

At the end of 1894 all work suddenly stopped. The tower which was to have risen proudly to 1,150 ft never went above 155 ft. It remained a dispiriting silhouette on the skyline for a further thirteen years (Plate 127). Rusting and derelict, London's defiant gesture to Paris remained there simply because it was too costly to demolish. As scrap, the metal would hardly fetch more than £9,000. Then, in 1906, the Tower Construction Company, renamed the Wembley Park Estate Company, started a programme of house building and decided to get rid of the spectre at the feast. About forty men went to work with sledgehammers to knock out the bolts and rivets holding the structure together. It was a perilous undertaking as the loosened girders crashed onto the concrete below.

In July 1907, the demolition was finished by dynamite. Explosives were put under each of the four legs. The Manchester firm of Heenan & Froude which had tended the birth of the tower administered the last rites. The noise was heard for miles and there was a good deal of flying debris. Fewer than a dozen people were on the site, and no one was hurt. Sir Edward Watkin, MP, was not among those who witnessed the end. He had died six years earlier. Some people were to say that he was to be vindicated, and his whole enterprise justified, by the success of the British Empire Exhibition held there in 1924. But if it were standing today, Watkin's Folly would be something of an inconvenience. The tower would be right in the middle of Wembley Stadium.

Chapter 14

Strange Roads and
a Westminster Scandal

LET us confess at once that the immensely important (and to most people immensely boring) subject of London's roads is going to get short shrift. Traffic solutions, like large-scale building schemes, contribute little to urban gaiety. Even so we should not be thanked if we failed to record the attempt to create a London Champs-Elysées, a Regent Street across Smithfield Market and a Burlington Arcade for the City. The most magnificent entrance conceived for a city since the days of the Caesars can hardly be ignored. Time must be found to consider the dubious behaviour of the MP who tried to push a great new crescent-shaped street through the heart of Westminster. The momentous Bressey/Lutyens Report just before the Second World War simply has to be reviewed.

After John Gwynn's prophetic vision for London and Westminster in 1766 (p. 56) the only important street schemes for nearly a century were those of John Nash, which, since they materialised, are outside our survey. Colonel Trench's preposterous 1823 plan for a two-mile boulevard from St Paul's to Hyde Park (p. 58) has a nice touch of higher lunacy about it but was naturally dismissed as wildly impracticable. So, ultimately, was John Soane's Grand National Entry into the Metropolis (Plate 128) even though it was attuned to late Hanoverian illusions of grandeur.

George III first asked Soane to design a gateway into London to replace the simple wooden gates and pair of toll-keepers' cottages that stood at Hyde Park Corner at the beginning of the 19th century. A whole series of monumental entrances were designed by various architects for the point where the Great West Road at Knightsbridge meets Piccadilly and the royal route to St James's and Buckingham Palace. Robert Wetten's we have already seen (Plate 53).

Soane returned to the project with a more elaborate design prepared under the eye of the Duke of Wellington. Finally he came up with his Grand National Entry, a vast gateway which was, as he put it, 'intended to combine the classical simplicity of Grecian architecture, the magnificence of Roman architecture and the fanciful intricacy and playful effects of Gothic architecture'. We look in vain for simplicity or any sign of Gothic in the marzipan splendour of an edifice suitable for an Indian durbar. Calculated though it was to knock out the eye of every awe-struck traveller arriving from the west, the Grand National Entry was manifestly the kind of thing destined never to be built.

128 *Sir John Soane's Grand National Entry into the Metropolis. A crowd watches a regiment of guards marching through the central archway from the direction of Knightsbridge. In the romantic Piranesi tradition, fragments of proposed sculpture and ironwork lie scattered in the foreground*

Soane makes most other Regency enterprises seem small beer. There was, however, a minor attempt by the City to create its own curved quadrant in 1824, clearly aping Nash's Regent Street completed four years earlier. The idea put up by Samuel Acton, Surveyor of the City's Sewers, was, in fact, just outside the City boundary to the north-west. His 'Design for Improving the Public Ways' was a new road from Fleet Market (today's Farringdon Street) constructed 'in a curvilinear direction' to St John Street. This 'immediate commodious access to Islington' was a straight crib of Nash's Quadrant even to a colonnade of Ionic columns.

In his published proposals, Acton admitted the colonnade would be 'rather expensive' and that it would be cheaper to carry an umbrella, but he thought this part of London deserved something impressive. The City had buildings of unquestionable beauty, he argued, but when it came to shops there was 'not one street at which, with any degree of satisfaction, we could ask a Foreigner to look'.

Acton's New Street was to start where Farringdon Street is now crossed by Holborn Viaduct. Leaving Snow Hill on the right, it cuts through the west end of present-day Smithfield Meat Market, and comes out at the southern end of St John's Street.

'Surely it will not be thought too extravagant a stretch of architectural feeling', said Acton, 'to ask that one of the chief Cities of the World should possess this little portion of modest decoration. . .' But his scheme never got off the paper even though the Surveyor was shrewd enough to suggest that it would be a great commercial advantage as people coming to shop from north London would head into the City instead of the West End.

The idea of providing a better approach to the City from the north was also behind a proposal three years later, in 1827, for an arcade between London Wall (at the intersection with Moorgate Street) and Bartholomew Lane immediately to the east of the Bank of England. In Paris arcades were already fashionable, and the City's direct inspiration was Burlington Arcade, the shopping precinct in Piccadilly completed in 1819 to which it was compared in the prospectus.

The arcade was described as particularly attractive to 'Families residing in the Suburbs of London' who would be set down in carriages at the entrance and, who then, their shopping done, 'might be re-conveyed to their homes without suffering the dangers and molestations of which Ladies, in particular, are continually and fairly complaining'.

Where Burlington Arcade had seventy shops, the London Arcade would contain 112 'of good dimensions with Two Stories above them'. They were designed by Stephen Geary, an architect whose office was in this immediate area of proposed demolition. As well as shops there would be chambers and counting houses and other premises likely to be popular in an area 'frequented by men of the greatest wealth in the kingdom'. In 1833, two years after the proposal to form the 'City of London Arcade Company', a petition to build it was presented to Parliament by proprietors and inhabitants of the lanes, alleys, yards and courts in the area. It was ordered to 'lie upon the table' – the formal graveyard of so many lost causes.

By the early part of the 19th century the pattern of London was in so inflexible a straitjacket that virtually only one area remained available for large-scale development. This was the land between Buckingham Palace and the Thames, consisting of low-lying marshy fields near the river, and insanitary streets immediately south of the palace, which George IV had once ingeniously proposed should be razed to the ground. The whole district would then be laid out with spacious streets crossing each other at right angles in a formal gridiron pattern. But the King was too old and tired to press on with the idea, and it was not until 1832, two years after his death, that an ambitious plan was promoted which would have transformed the whole area of Westminster between the Houses of Parliament and Buckingham Palace.

The scheme was put forward by Peter Rigby Wason, MP, who was Chairman of a Select Committee appointed to 'inquire into the most economical and eligible mode of improving the approaches to the Houses of Parliament'. Rather as Colonel Trench retained Benjamin and Philip Wyatt as his architects to implement his theories, so Rigby Wason kept William Bardwell in tow. Wason, MP for Ipswich, was a barrister with a number of reforming bees in his bonnet, among them universal suffrage, triennial Parliaments and the removal of bishops from the House of Lords. Bardwell from Suffolk was an exhibitor of architectural schemes at the Royal Academy. Together, in later years, they were to work on an ambitious project for erecting a scientific and artistic institution as a memorial to Prince Albert on the site of Burlington House. They submitted a scheme for the new Houses of Parliament. When Wason was appointed Chairman of the Select Committee for Improvements in Westminster, he 'directed' Bardwell to prepare a plan. Obviously they worked it out together, and later eyebrows were to be raised over certain suspicious features devised by this two-man team.

It was a very elaborate piece of town planning which Rigby Wason unfolded to a suitably impressed committee in June 1832. The whole area of small streets, stagnant ditches and cesspools was transformed by building a road, nearly a mile long, from Westminster Abbey to Lower Grosvenor Place in Belgravia. This continued in a wide arc at the back of the Palace grounds to Hyde Park Corner. Three huge squares wiped out the ill-favoured and confused network of streets between Birdcage Walk and what is now Victoria Street.

The long curved street, 90 ft wide, was to follow much the same course as Victoria Street. A bird's-eye view, as if from the top of the Abbey (Plate 129), shows the street curving from Broad Sanctuary in the direction of Buckingham Palace. In the foreground, on either side of a wide entrance to the thoroughfare, are two imposing classical buildings intended to stand where Great Smith Street and Central Hall are today. The square building set diagonally on the left in the middle distance is Tothill Fields Prison, and the large enclosed building beyond it, a new barracks that was a feature of the plan. To flatter the recently crowned William IV, the new thoroughfare was to be named Great William Street.

The street is impressive in itself, but the dominating features of the Wason/Bardwell scheme are the three great squares of terraced houses branching off to the right and stretching up to St James's Park. In between the public building facing us on the right and the first terrace is an indeterminate group of buildings, which looks foreshortened and ill at ease in the grand plan. Wason and Bardwell have allowed them to survive, probably because Park Street and Queen Street (now merged into Queen Anne's Gate) on the extreme right contain such fine houses that only a maniac would be foolish enough to threaten them. Also, Bardwell happened to live there.

The square nearest us was to be called Parliament Square, and is on the site of present-day Caxton Hall, St James's Underground Station and Queen Anne's Mansions. Within reasonable distance of the House, this was intended primarily for MPs. There were to be gardens in the middle and a church at the end. King's Square, next along, would have taken in the middle section of Buckingham Gate and Petty France. The third – Queen's Square – is where Palace Street and the Westminster Theatre are today.

Each square, 860 ft long, was to be about two-thirds of the length of Eaton Square which was then being built. William Cubitt, the Eaton Square contractor, was invited by the Select Committee to give them his expert views. His enthusiasm was only to be expected of someone who might well have envisaged handsome pickings for his firm from an extension of the Cubitts' Belgravia and Pimlico interests. The scheme, he assured the Committee, would render the neighbourhood better for the Palace, improve the air, and provide ideal lodgings for MPs.

Select Committees take their time, and during the next six years of

deliberations, the architect and MP energetically improved their plan so as to remain in the public eye. They considered (but rejected as too expensive) a proposal that the street should be built in Gothic style in keeping with Westminster Abbey. Then in 1838, just when they hoped that the matured, constantly revised ideas would be adopted, the blow fell. There were accusations of corruption.

The first hint of trouble came when the Committee heard that an attempt had been made to buy a piece of land – an orchard – at the back of the Tothill Fields Prison. This was where an important part of the street development was to occur. The would-be purchaser, it was revealed, was Rigby Wason. Wason was further accused of conspiring to make the street curve so as to take in land he had bought. An enormous sum, it was asserted, had been invested by the MP 'speculatively here and there'.

It sounded damning, but Wason came back with prompt refutations. He stated that at the time of drawing up the plans, he had no property in Westminster. Worried for the future of his scheme, he had purchased the

129 Victoria transformed: the Rigby Wason/William Bardwell view shows a new thoroughfare running from Broad Sanctuary near the Abbey to Pimlico. In the foreground to the left of the street would be the Judges' Chambers and Record Office, and on the right the Stationery, Alien and other offices. The main features were to be the three long 'squares'. Bardwell laboured for six years maturing and perfecting this Westminster improvement plan, publishing maps, views, advertisements and pamphlets to keep the project in the public mind

land years later 'without the slightest intention of personal advantage' and had offered it to the Government for the price he had paid. As for the suggestion that he had bent the street to serve his own ends, well, he argued, wasn't a curved street architecturally admirable?

Wason's purchase might be suspicious, but it was not legally actionable. However, his probity was in doubt. He could no longer serve on the Select Committee, and when a report was published in 1838 his plan was not included. It had been removed 'surreptitiously,' he declared angrily. The barracks, which he planned for the area where he had bought land, were built – as Wellington Barracks – on their present site fronting Birdcage Walk. Nothing at all came of the magnificent squares which would have given dignity to a part of Westminster that has remained in a state of undistinguished confusion ever since.

The idea of a new thoroughfare survived, however, in the slightly changed form of Victoria Street. Work started a few years later, in 1845, with the name altered from Great William Street in acknowledgment of the new sovereign. As if in silent criticism of Rigby Wason, the sweeping curve was straightened out but even so the street follows pretty much the same line from Broad Sanctuary as far as Francis Street after which, instead of curving north to Lower Grosvenor Street, it goes on to Victoria Station.

By now Wason had ceased to be an MP, and the credit for Victoria Street went to Sir Edwin Pearson, a zealous Commissioner of Westminster Improvements. It was completed in 1851, but nothing came of the proposal that bronze statues of Queen Victoria and the Westminster printer, William Caxton, should be erected at the Parliament end, and that the street should be extended to Westminster Bridge with an avenue lined by great statesmen such as Pitt, Fox, Canning and Peel.

After Victoria Street there was little room for planning in central districts. They had to look further afield, and in the middle of the century the romantic neo-classicist, C. R. Cockerell, proposed a rural walkway north of Regent's Park. He wanted to see a curved, tree-lined avenue, 300 ft wide, circling eastwards through the then only partially laid-out fields of Belsize Park. Cockerell's 1853 road would have come out half-way up Haverstock Hill by 'the existing beautiful Belsize Avenue' and part of its purpose was to enhance the attractions and value of the surrounding land where houses were soon to be built. Crossing Haverstock Hill the walkway would link up with the Heath by way of Hampstead Green.

This scheme to provide a magnificent park-ride or boulevard up to Hampstead was more elaborately developed, on a different axis, about a year later by W. H. Twentyman. With great pomp and circumstance his 'Royal Champs-Elysées' was begun on the north side of Regent's Park with an Arc de Triomphe just to the west of the Zoo (Plate 130). An avenue lined on each side by a double row of trees wound a gentle snake-like course north-eastwards. Swiss Cottage lay to the left, and it followed a line roughly parallel and just to the right of Finchley Road. Hampstead village on the right was by-passed, and the 'Royal Champs-Elysées' emerged on the west side of the Heath on the line of Redington Road. In his evocative view the artist places a

Proposed

ROYAL CHAMPS ELYSEES

Orphan School

Tudera

130 Royal Champs-Elysées,
designed by W. H. Twentyman,
connecting Regent's Park to
Hampstead (c. 1854). A stairway
led to a pagoda on Primrose Hill
which could be visited by
pedestrians to admire the view

pagoda on the top of Primrose Hill, yet another alternative to the pyramid, casino, botanical conservatory and statues of Shakespeare proposed at different times. Lithographed plans survive, but of W. H. Twentyman who inspired it little appears known. The originator of London's Champs-Elysées seems to have been swallowed up as completely as his *divertissement*.

While these proposals were being made for outer thoroughfares that never materialised, Londoners in the centre of the city were faced with mounting traffic congestion. With slow-moving horse vehicles, delays were as frustrating as they are today. When a horse fell, as frequently happened on slippery roads, the pile-up of traffic was serious. This prompted schemes for underground roads (Plate 131) which looked effective, but would have created a ventilation problem. Bridges were suggested for 'the benefit of nervous humanity' whom the *City Press* in 1862 described as quaking when faced with 'van-demons, spinning hansoms, ponderous omnibuses, jingling

169

131 Gaslit subterranean streets
for London to accommodate gas-
and water-pipes and telegraph-
wires and to relieve respectable
streets above of heavy and
obnoxious traffic

METROPOLITAN TRAFFIC RELIEF.

cabs and mud'. Even 'a well braced Londoner' often quaked; what was needed were aerial bridges 'charging a toll of one halfpenny each person (with yearly tickets at a low rate)'. The problem was passed to the City Commissioners of Sewers whose findings were published a year later.

Seven main points of congestion in the City were enumerated and the pros and cons debated. Subways produced problems because of existing underground pipes and sewers, and were not favoured by the police who thought people would crowd into them to shelter from the rain and they would be 'a lurking place for thieves, or the means of their escape'. Solid bridges with a headroom of 18 ft requiring thirty-eight steps would be cumbersome and unsightly. The best bridge solution, 'designed for the safety of ladies and children crossing crowded streets', was in cast iron with spiral stairways which were suggested and patented by Thomas Dunn. Attractive coloured views of Dunn's bridges at the Mansion House, Fenchurch Street and Ludgate Circus (Plate 132) demonstrate how they would function. The decisive argument against these crossings was that there was infinitely less danger to life and limb in braving the traffic than would occur in falling down the steps.

In the West End, traffic congestion was serious at Piccadilly Circus where four streets converged, and was made even worse in 1886 by the creation of

Shaftesbury Avenue. 'Piccadilly Circus is a beautiful mess,' a member of the old London County Council once said, and this opinion has been expressed with increasing alarm for over 160 years. Ever since Nash's little Regency circus was converted into a sprawling triangle it has been a controversial storm-centre and a battleground for planners.

The most spectacular proposals did not emerge until the 1950s, but from the beginning of the century suggestions were put forward to ease traffic difficulties as motorcars began to weave among hansoms and horse buses. In 1904 Norman Shaw came out of virtual retirement, invited by Sir Aston Webb, President of the RIBA, to prepare a scheme. Then over seventy, the architect of New Scotland Yard made a number of revolutionary suggestions. Among them was a proposal to rebuild the County Fire Office on the north side, 65 ft back from its present position. As a building quite detached from Regent Street this was to have a monumental loggia approached by a flight of steps, and a forecourt in front of the steps was to be the new setting for Eros removed from the middle of the Circus.

This plan, preserved by the RIBA, also reveals a less happy idea. Where

132 Design for a cast-iron aerial footbridge for Ludgate Circus (1863), patented by Thomas Dunn

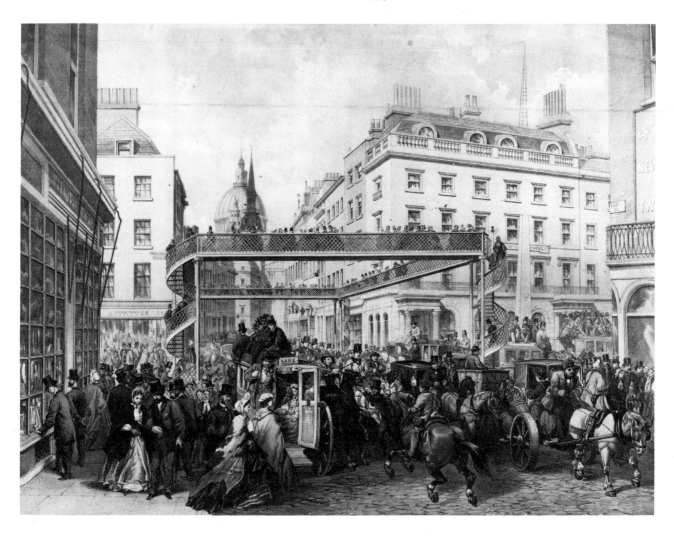

*133 Reginald Blomfield's
Piccadilly Circus, a revised 1920s
version of his earlier proposal*

Eros had previously stood Shaw placed a large island block to face and harmonise with Swan & Edgar. But far from widening out the Circus, this would obviously have created a bottleneck. Reginald Blomfield, called in for suggestions after Shaw's death in 1912, described this middle-of-the-Circus building as 'deplorable', and said it was 'enough to kill the scheme'.

Later, Shaw produced a more practical scheme with the Fire Office set back, but this time only enough to make a straight continuation of the north side possible. The Circus would have become a large piazza, 300 ft from east to west and 266 ft from north to south, but this excellent idea was foiled by the Treasury which refused to finance any architectural improvements, as such, and demanded that changes must also be a good investment.

Blomfield, Norman Shaw's pupil, followed his old master's idea in extending the Circus into a rectangle, and his scheme, of which Plate 133 shows a 1920s variation, had a similar building to Swan & Edgar in place of the London Pavilion. But when the architect learnt that the theatre's lease did not expire until 1962, he rather lost heart, and the idea was not pushed further.

In October 1910, another plan for Piccadilly Circus (Plate 134) appeared in an unconventional manner. It was not commissioned or even solicited. The drawing simply arrived on the desk of the Lord Mayor in his capacity as Chairman of the Edward VII Memorial Committee, accompanied by a letter with a funeral-black border. 'My Lord Mayor,' the writer began, 'May I be allowed to suggest a monumental work which might be a suitable Memorial to his late Majesty King Edward VII?' The letter was signed John Murray, FRIBA.

Murray worked for the Crown Commissioners, and like Blomfield he wanted to demolish the London Pavilion and create an oblong traffic area — a Piccadilly Square. The buildings on the north were to be replaced by a

Shakespeare Memorial Theatre and a National Opera House. As a central feature, Murray suggested an equestrian statue of Edward VII. Eros was to be 'removed and re-erected in one of the Parks where the water could be fully turned on and fulfil its original intention'.

Nothing came of Murray's plan, and it appears to have been completely forgotten until 1959, when the Crown Commissioners were asked if by any chance drawings still existed. They said they doubted it, but made a search, and after a few days produced the perspective from which may be judged how the Circus would have looked. Transformed from a hotch-potch of varying architectural styles and freed from chewing-gum advertisements, Murray's scheme would not please those who say that they want to preserve the 'honest vulgarity' of Piccadilly Circus. By modern standards it may seem ponderous. But we can see the unified appearance that would have been achieved.

Not all the Circus schemes suggested in the first half of the century were strictly traditional. Two very advanced proposals appeared as early as 1910 and 1912. In the first, the whole of the Circus was to be roofed over to form a rotunda which would contain a shopping arcade at first-floor level. The second featured archways that were to be built across the streets into the Circus. These would be reached by moving staircases and there were to be colonnades of shops at a high level. Years ahead of their time, these essentially modern concepts do not seem to belong to the pre-1914 era; their place is in the ranks of all the plans for the Circus which so startled London in 1959 and the years that followed.

Before postwar Piccadilly madness set in there was one other idea for turning the Circus into a dignified rectangular piazza. In 1942 a planning committee set up by the Royal Academy produced a Utopian report (Chapter

134 John Murray's proposal for Piccadilly Circus (1910), laid out as King Edward VII Square with an equestrian statue of the monarch to replace Eros! On the north side a Shakespeare Theatre and a National Opera House

15), in which appeared a bird's-eye view of the Circus, symmetrical, and with a building on the north side large enough to be a palace which is set back behind a screened forecourt (Plate 135). It is flanked by the Fire Office and a matching arcaded building on the other side. Shaftesbury Avenue has had to be diverted through a square (not in the drawing) into Coventry Street which cuts through a demolished London Pavilion.

The drawing is credited to A. C. Webb, and it seems likely that the artist based it on a proposal made four years earlier by Sir Charles Bressey. Bressey was Vice-Chairman of the Royal Academy Committee, and it would have been only natural for him to want to see fresh life given to an idea incorporated in the highway scheme he had produced in 1938.

It is generally thought that the important plans advocated by Bressey and Lutyens in their 1938 *Highway Development Survey for Greater London* were killed by the war. Hostilities undoubtedly prevented any hope of their fulfilment, but they had been formally rejected by the LCC six months earlier. The Bressey Report has been most unfairly forgotten, yet it was a highly acclaimed plan at the time, and, as we can now see, foreshadowed in outline and sometimes in detail the later, better-remembered, plans of Sir Patrick Abercrombie and others.

Bressey was a civil engineer who had joined the Ministry of Transport on its formation in 1919, and on his retirement in 1935 he started on his scheme to solve London's increasing traffic problems. This was no theoretical exercise. Leslie Hore-Belisha, the dynamic and controversial Minister of Transport, was asking for practical solutions. When the 40,000-word report was published it was hailed as a panacea for London's ills, and the Government was expected to finance a large part of the £120,000,000 outlay. The author was talked of as a saviour on whom would be bestowed 'almost certain immortality'.

Over a period of thirty years London was to be transformed with broad traffic arteries radiating from the centre to all the great trunk roads. There were to be new bridges, overhead roads and tunnels. The Embankment was to be extended and tree-fringed boulevards were to encircle the city. An area of 2000 square miles of London and Greater London was affected; 150 local authorities and regional planning committees were to be involved; a population of 9,000,000 people of whom 250,000 were vehicle owners, were swept along in a tide of enthusiasm.

For the first time the term 'ring roads' came into common usage, and, ahead of Abercrombie, three of these orbital roads were suggested as essential to deflect traffic from the centre of London. Cutting right across London from Western Avenue at Hammersmith to Eastern Avenue in Essex was to be a 12-mile arterial road passing north of the City and parallel to Oxford Street. The Embankment was to be extended so that it ran the whole way from the Tower to Putney Bridge. Congestion in Westminster was to be reduced by a new Mayfair-Soho route, which ran partly in a tunnel, under Regent Street.

Most ambitious of all Bressey's proposed innovations was an overhead, high-level road with four traffic lanes joining the Barnet bypass with Croydon. This would have provided a fast through route from St Albans to

Redhill. The viaduct, crossing the Thames at Blackfriars, was to have led to London's airport, a journey which would have taken only twenty minutes.

In the heady excitement with which the Bressey Report was received ('It should be undertaken at once,' declared the Automobile Association) a note of caution was struck by Herbert Morrison, leader of the LCC. He was worried about cost, and months later was compelled to announce that the LCC had had to reject the plan because the Ministry of Transport were offering only a 60 per cent grant. A mild, softly spoken man with a sardonic sense of humour which he needed, Bressey accepted the rejection with apparent equanimity. The outbreak of war so soon afterwards prevented much chance of his voice being heard. He did, however, remind the public of his plan. When the report was published the main objection was the extensive demolition needed to build his roads. 'Today, this objection will, alas! carry less weight,' he wrote in a letter to *The Times*, in November 1940, pointing out that bomb damage had already done much of the clearing. Now, he said, was the time to see future highway planning in the light of changes brought about by war. But nothing was done. The opportunity was lost.

In the last paragraph of his report, Bressey offered a general warning that serves as an epitaph for many frustrated plans: 'So imperative, however, is the need for prompt action that Londoners would be better advised to embark immediately upon useful schemes, admittedly imperfect, rather than wait for the emergence of some faultless ideal which will have ceased to be attainable long before it has received approval.'

135 Royal Academy scheme (1942) for rebuilding Piccadilly Circus after the Second World War

175

LONDON REPLANNED

LONDON : COUNTRY LIFE LIMITED

Price Two Shillings and Sixpence

136 Cover of London Replanned, *published 1942, shows St Paul's
at the end of a vista from a riverside stairway*

Chapter 15

Frustrated Post-War Plans

PLANS for the post-Second World War development of London started long before the end of the war itself. They grew out of the smoking rubble left by the German Luftwaffe. Around St Paul's 164 acres were in ruins, and with hardly a district undamaged there was a practical as well as a psychological reason for planning the future.

Behind the large windows of Burlington House, taped against blast, one group of architects saw history repeating itself and a chance for reconstruction similar to that offered but lost after the Great Fire. They made a point of reproducing Wren's 1666 scheme when in October 1942 they published *London Replanned*, a thirty-page outline of their ideas. As might be expected of the Royal Academy Planning Committee their suggestions, though imaginative, were coloured by the traditions of the past.

They were the heads of their profession, and mostly elderly. The Chairman, Sir Edwin Lutyens, at seventy-three the Grand Old Man of British architecture, wrote in his foreword: 'It is certain that reconstruction and replanning must take place, not only owing to war damage, but in order to relieve the intolerable confusion which has arisen from the use by 20th-century mechanical traffic of a plan devised, so far as it was devised, for the relatively primitive requirements of a far smaller community.' While stressing the need for greater public control, the sixty-seven-year-old Vice-Chairman, Sir Charles Bressey, warned: 'It is not sufficient to slash a new street across a town-map (however indispensable it may be to traffic) leaving jagged fragments of severed building-plots to become the sites of "flat-iron" skyscrapers and other monstrosities.'

Lending their advice were such formidable figures as A. E. Richardson, Giles Gilbert Scott, Vincent Harris, Edward Maufe, Louis de Soissons and Patrick Abercrombie, who was already at work on his famous *Greater London Plan* (1944). The picture on the cover of the report (Plate 136), showing a vista of St Paul's from a monumental river stairway between classical pavilions, typifies their idealism. Every one of the dozen major proposals they advocated is a splendid conception. Not one has been realised. Expansive prospects and gracious buildings, embracing symmetry and employing Portland stone, were for what they called 'A Nobler City', a city for which there would never be enough money and which were destined, anyway, to be out of tune with the new styles and thought in architecture.

Though the drawings were very much what one might expect from a committee chosen by the Royal Academy many of the ideas were far from fuddy-duddy. There was a fundamentally sound scheme for connecting all the main railway terminals by a new Underground railway and a ring road,

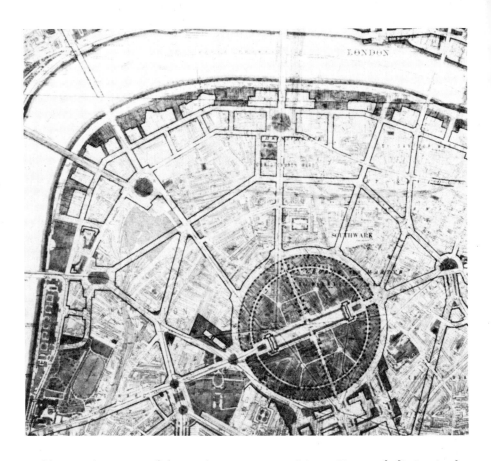

and by moving some of the stations to new positions. To people living in the long-neglected area south of the Thames a new park at St George's Circus, Southwark, would have been a wonderful boon. Circular, a quarter of a mile in diameter, this park (Plate 137) would have given people in an overcrowded, architecturally nondescript area a place for recreation the same shape and slightly larger than Queen Mary's Garden, Regent's Park. Pugin's St George's Cathedral and the Imperial War Museum would have been just outside its south-western perimeter. Like the spokes of a wheel roads from Waterloo, Blackfriars, the Borough and Westminster Bridge would have been joined by a road encircling the park which became in a sense a great roundabout.

Another park or open space on Tower Hill was designed to provide a garden from All Hallows Barking Church to the Mint; there was to be a large roundabout at the Strand junction of Waterloo Bridge and another ('Southwark Circus') just south of London Bridge, which involved moving the station a little to the east. This new, enlarged London Bridge Station would have acted as a vast terminus for all South Eastern lines including Waterloo, Charing Cross and Blackfriars.

With a prophetic eye the Academy Committee had seen that Covent Garden was outdated as a market, and envisaged the area as a Music and Drama Centre (Plate 138A). The site of the market became a garden with the old colonnades preserved. A new Opera House with a classical portico stands

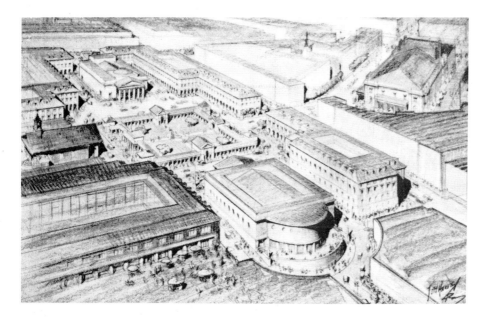

on the north side of the square, a Concert Hall to the south. This scheme anticipated the endlessly debated plans for the £160 million 'comprehensive redevelopment' of Covent Garden in the early 1970s when the market moved to Nine Elms. Another drawing, 'An Approach to the British Museum', shows all the shops in the Museum Street area swept away, a prophetic vision of the furiously opposed scheme during the 1960s to make room for a Museum extension (Plate 138B).

Most ambitious of all the Committee's proposals, and very much in the academic tradition, was a new approach to St Paul's from the west. 'Had Sir Christopher Wren been allowed this situation, he would have had much more room for the Ornament of the West End ... and he would have added a

139 St Paul's given increased isolation and dignity with a semicircular piazza reminiscent of St Peter's, Rome. Ludgate Circus in the foreground is opened out into a tree-lined square. The elevated railway, Holborn to Blackfriars, has disappeared. From London Replanned *(1942)*

circular piazza to it,' wrote Defoe in 1725, and this is the inspiration of P. D. Hepworth's prospect (Plate 139). Ludgate Hill has become a wide straight avenue lined with trees, and in the open space round the Cathedral the Deanery and Chapter House are retained. The through roads from Ludgate Hill to Cheapside and Cannon Street are diverted to follow the lines of Paternoster Row and Carter Lane. In the foreground Ludgate Circus is opened out into a fine tree-lined square to cope with modern traffic. Blackfriars railway bridge has vanished. Along with the station it is re-sited at London Bridge.

The 'Western Approach' which gives St Paul's the dignity of St Peter's in Rome would have required an unthinkable amount of demolition. To the north German fire bombs had destroyed much of the old Paternoster Row area and there was also considerable damage to buildings to the east. But the destruction paved the way for only a slightly improved ambiance for the Cathedral. Leaping ahead from this wartime view of a 'worthy setting', practical reality was achieved in 1955 by William Holford when he was approached by the City to redesign the precincts.

Holford, then Professor of Town Planning at University College, London, and later created a life peer, combined a classical training with a modern outlook. He was advanced but 'respectable', the perfect architect to give public bodies the impression that they were being daring and realistic both at the same time. His idea was to create a pedestrian area in front of St Paul's. Ludgate Hill/Cannon Street traffic was to be diverted south along a widened Carter Lane. On the north side, Temple Bar in its endless search for a suitable home would find a place as an entrance screen to St Paul's Churchyard. Behind the east end the new Cathedral Choir School, incorporating the tower of the bombed Church of St Augustine Watling Street, would serve as what Holford called a 'buffer' between the Cathedral and the new curved Bank of England building.

Only part of Holford's precinct has come into being: the Choir School and the building to the north-west in front of his modern Paternoster Place. Temple Bar, of course, has not yet been brought to St Paul's Churchyard, though this site was approved by the Corporation of London in 1979. But this is unimportant compared to the great loss – the failure to create a large pedestrian concourse in front of the Cathedral which would have been possible by taking traffic down Carter Lane.

Returning to the war years, one of the strangest possibilities was that Nelson's Column might have been removed from Trafalgar Square. This was planned in August 1940, but no one in Britain knew about it. The idea was simply in the minds of the would-be conquerors. Both Hitler and Mussolini had great schemes for the post-war aggrandisement of their capitals and, although Hitler's favourite architect, Albert Speer, did not go so far as to draw up plans for a subjugated London, the removal of the column to Berlin was proposed as a matter of policy. This is revealed in the captured plans of Department III of the S.S. 'Since the Battle of Trafalgar the Nelson Column has represented for England a symbol of British naval might and world domination,' reads the document. 'It would be an impressive way of underlining the German victory if the Nelson Column were to be transferred to Berlin.'

140 Sir Patrick Abercrombie (1879–1957), whose foresighted road schemes for post-war London did not materialise

In London, as opposed to Berlin, planners were looking more positively to the future in the mid-1940s. Building not concerned with the war effort was prohibited, so there would be a backlog of essential work when peace came. It was also a time for imaginative thinking. In 1943 the LCC published the *County of London Plan* by J. H. Forshaw and Patrick Abercrombie and a year later Abercrombie (Plate 140), Holford's predecessor as Professor of Town Planning at London University, produced his *Greater London Plan* (1944). The City and Westminster followed with their proposals in 1944 and 1948 respectively. Heavy with statistics, graphs and diagrams, most of these impressive volumes are now only likely to interest somebody curious to study how far achievement fell short of intention. The way well-argued propositions came to nothing makes melancholy reading.

Of all the problems that bedevil planners, roads and traffic are the worst. They can also be exceedingly tedious unless you personally find that a new arterial road is about to come slap through your sittingroom. Roads make politicians shudder. Governments hate them; they eat up vast sums of money and never win a vote at the polls. The trouble is that traffic difficulties won't go away, as can be discovered by anyone who takes the time to lift the Abercrombie Report from the shelf where it has been gathering dust for nearly forty years. It is a chronicle of lost opportunities.

Some of Professor Abercrombie's ideas have become outdated with changing conditions, but the more London snarls up, and long articulated trucks make their inappropriate journeys through overcrowded streets, the more we can see their lost potential and the relief that would have been provided by the five concentric ring roads round London he proposed. These were not, he pointed out, for 'continuous gyratory purpose'; they were 'a series of cross roads connecting the radial roads'. The ring roads would divert traffic to express arterial motorways radiating out to

Edinburgh, Birmingham, Portsmouth and other main cities. It would be unnecessary for heavy transport to travel through the centre of London.

The importance of at least four of these five proposed ring roads can be clearly appreciated by stating their intention and briefly describing the outcome. The outer ring was to make a huge circle with a radius of about 20 miles from Charing Cross with St Albans and Sevenoaks on its north and south perimeter. All that has come of this is a still far from complete M25, roughly on the same line, broken at intervals, and every mile due for adoption hotly contested locally.

Five miles closer in was to be an express arterial ring road of major importance. It would cut its way through the Home Counties following an almost entirely new route. The perimeter line was to pass close by Dartford – Farnborough – Chessington – Hampton Court (Thames crossing) – Heston – Ruislip – Stanmore – Barnet – Enfield – Romford – Purfleet (Dartford Tunnel). Dartford Tunnel was built, but the road peters out seven miles south of Dartford and four miles north of it. The road it should serve simply doesn't exist.

Abercrombie's principal ring road was much closer in, and was to be used by circulating dock traffic to filter off radial roads. This objective is now outdated but, had the road been built, it would now be an invaluable route for motorists wishing to avoid central London. Passing by tunnel under the river from the Isle of Dogs, the road would have followed the approximate route: New Cross Gate – Denmark Hill – Coldharbour Lane – Clapham Common north side – a new Battersea Bridge – Chelsea – Kensington – Fulham (following existing railway line) – Camden Town – Victoria Park – Poplar – Isle of Dogs. Such a road would have been expensive immediately after the war. Now the cost and public outrage at the destruction of homes make it unthinkable.

To increase the speed and flow of traffic in central London, Abercrombie devised an inner ring, the western perimeter of which went through a tunnel under the centre of Hyde Park linking Knightsbridge and Bayswater. The river was crossed at Vauxhall and by a new tunnel just east of Tower Bridge. To make the use of this innermost ring road even more flexible, especially from east to west, it was bisected by other tunnels. One was destined to pass almost under Buckingham Palace – a serious tactical mistake Abercrombie ruefully admitted later. Not a yard of this route materialised.

So evaporated the road dreams of 1943. They never generated the necessary post-war impetus. They never overcame public apathy and the disinclination of successive governments to handle a very hot potato indeed. Though their immense advantage is obvious to every haulage company, to hundreds of thousands of people these ring roads, or 'motor-boxes', would have meant only one thing: destruction of their homes. The problem remains.

While the war in Europe was in its final year, two private architects, Kenneth Lindy and Winton Lewis, added what they called a 'sketch proposal' for the post-war City. They wanted to make space and create vistas for important buildings so that they were not swallowed up among

141 A pointed 500-ft skyscraper (1944), resembling the New York Woolworth building, was to be a new office block for the City Corporation behind Guildhall

increasingly tall surrounding buildings. They concentrated on three main points of focus: St Paul's, Guildhall and 'Bank Place', as they termed the Bank – Royal Exchange – Mansion House area. They placed these focal points at the end of streets laid out in a cruciform pattern. Saint Paul's was at the base of the cross, 'Bank Place' at the top. Guildhall was at the end of one transverse arm, balanced at the other end by a double pylon on the river which they named 'Guildhall Steps'.

From these river steps there was a wide processional way to Guildhall 'to eliminate the impression of the Guildhall being hidden away in a side street'. The approach was enhanced by a square forecourt in which the 15th-century Great Hall crouches as if between the knees of a kneeling giant. The architects' most revolutionary idea was to rehouse the miscellaneous

departments of the Corporation in a skyscraper. This monumental building, with a pointed tower reminiscent of the New York Woolworth Building, was to be up to 500 ft tall (Plate 141).

Saint Paul's would stand free in a vast elipse which, seen from the air, would make the Cathedral appear to be sitting in a Roman amphitheatre. 'Bank Place' at the top of a straight avenue and ornamental canal from the Cathedral was to be laid out in a regular fan shape round which were grouped the Royal Exchange, Bank and Mansion House. This required demolition of the Globe Assurance Building.

'Aviation must not be forgotten,' wrote Lindy and Lewis, and because the City was too small for runways long enough to take planes, they did not suggest anything so extensive as Charles Glover's King's Cross Air Terminus (p. 212). Their idea was a more modest helicopter landing platform set on the cross-shaped roof which projected from a central tower of Liverpool Street Station to four freestanding towers (Plate 142).

A heliport was also a feature of a huge kidney-shaped fun palace designed in 1946 by Mischa Black, the sprightly industrial architect, for the part of South Bank to be occupied by the Festival of Britain five years later. From Hilton Wright's fantastic drawing the details of what appears to be a curvilinear Crystal Palace are not clear; but this is a way-out example of how for a decade or more an increasing amount of interest was focusing on the south side of the river. Except for County Hall there was not at this time a single building of consequence on the Lambeth shore below Westminster Bridge. A recurring question was why London must continue to look south onto a frontage of untidy wharves and gaunt warehouses.

In the 1942 *London Replanned* Professor A. E. Richardson had drawn a bird's-eye view from Westminster showing the great Surrey loop redeveloped with a southern Embankment. Fine buildings and tree-lined avenues made a strenuous bid to turn the run-down area into 'the geographical hub of the Metropolis'. This was a visual elaboration of the hopes expressed by Herbert Morrison when he was Leader of the LCC in 1935. He wanted to rebuild unused industrial property and then lease sites for hotels, flats and offices 'architecturally suitable to a new and more dignified south London'. Between then and 1950 no fewer than seven uncommissioned schemes for South Bank were published. With remarkable prescience, thirty years ahead of the event, William Goodesmith proposed a National Theatre only a few hundred yards from its present site, on the spot where the Festival Hall now stands.

Ideas for rejuvenating South Bank were not universally welcomed. The Royal Academy Committee's 1942 plan and Richardson's drawing provoked the *Architectural Journal* to complain that London was being treated as though it were Buenos Aires, and, going to the opposite geographical extreme in the *Observer*, Osbert Lancaster likened the buildings to 'several reproductions of Stockholm Town Hall'. However, Forshaw and Abercrombie devoted a whole section of their 1943 report to the South Bank and produced a plan which included varied recreational facilities. With gardens, a youth centre, swimming pool, bandstand and two theatres, they set out to 'recapture some of its former lively spirit' when it was London's playground in Shakespeare's day. Though not now particularly exciting – simply because of what has been achieved since – this scheme was extremely imaginative at the time.

More extravagantly entertaining was the fantastic plan for the whole area by Clive Entwhistle that was published in the *Architectural Review* in 1949. 'Unashamedly in the Le Corbusier manner', the architect turned South Bank into a setting for Orwell's *1984*. The view looking east from Westminster has a vista down a wide promenade with St Paul's in the far distance. Here was to be a People's University of the Arts and Sciences, and a pyramid-shaped building (on today's Queen Elizabeth Hall site) that was to be a museum. Behind a National Theatre stood a science museum. Between the pyramid museum and County Hall was a concert hall seating 7,000. Bandstands and restaurants along the river front struck a note of undergraduate gaiety.

Professor Abercrombie was frustrated in his attempt to create an Embankment along the City frontage of the river – it was part of an east-west road he wanted to join up with his inner ring road – but he was generous enough to give his approval one year before his death to another Embankment scheme. In a plan projected by the London *Evening News* in 1956 he discerned elements as valuable, and in some ways simpler and better than in the version he had worked out during the war with J. H. Forshaw.

This scheme was the brainchild of Brian Harpur, then General Manager of the newspaper. From his office overlooking the Embankment just west of Blackfriars, Harpur saw constantly snarled-up rush-hour traffic. This gave him the idea for a second highway to be built outside, and running parallel with, the existing Embankment to allow fast-moving traffic on each of the roads. From his brother, an engineer, he knew that a cantilever construction would permit the building out of the road over the water without obstructing the flow of the Thames – still a point of contention with the river authorities as it had been in Trench's time.

The Riverside Highway was schemed as an artery to move motorists in and out of central London at the rate of 2,800 vehicles an hour. Among many problems was what to do at Westminster because of the obstruction of the Houses of Parliament. The same difficulty had faced John Gwynn in 1766 (p. 82). Gwynn had simply taken his quay further out into the river, and so circumvented Parliament. The newspaper's solution was to have a lowered section of 300 yds covered with a garden so that the amenities of MPs on the terrace would not be spoilt (Plate 143).

Although it was worked out in great detail, and a major engineering firm declared it practicable for £8,000,000, the planners never quite solved the problem of what would happen at the Chelsea end without a further continuation to the west. After exciting considerable interest, much praise and a little criticism, the Riverside Highway slowly faded away to join the notable company of unrealised dreams. But the *Evening News* had the satisfaction of seeing the idea for an underpass at Blackfriars copied almost exactly a few years later.

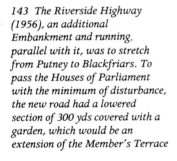

143 The Riverside Highway (1956), an additional Embankment and running. parallel with it, was to stretch from Putney to Blackfriars. To pass the Houses of Parliament with the minimum of disturbance, the new road had a lowered section of 300 yds covered with a garden, which would be an extension of the Member's Terrace

Chapter 16

The Great Piccadilly Circus Rumpus

OF all the schemes for post-war London, none can hope to equal the long-running farce of Piccadilly Circus. It has been described as 'a story of greed, ghastly errors, tragic delays, planning bureaucracy and wasted chances'. This only touched the fringes of the accumulating enormities.

The pre-war saga of the Circus and attempts to alter it by Shaw, Murray, Blomfield and Bressey (Chapter 14) were only prologues to the swelling act. Although much had been happening backstage for some years, as far as the public is concerned the curtain rises on 27 October 1959. It goes up with a flourish to discover, centre stage, a colourful character with a carnation in his buttonhole. That day a Birmingham property speculator, Jack Cotton, called a press conference at the Criterion Restaurant to announce that he was about to start building a huge office tower block on the north side of Piccadilly Circus. It was to be 172 ft tall. Proudly Cotton unveiled the model. There was a moment's astonished pause before he was besieged by questions from the assembled journalists. There was consternation when it became clear that this was not just some flight of fancy, but an actual building for which the developer had official permission. Demolition gangs had already moved in. Work was to begin almost immediately. The contractors had set themselves 120 weeks to turn the site into a massive block of shops, offices, exhibition galleries, restaurants and car parks.

At a spot which for reasons unknown is hallowed by all Londoners and provides a magnet for overseas visitors, there was to rise a vast square tower. From the model it could be seen to be squat despite its prodigious height (Plate 144). The whole of the front was a windowless blank. An area, 100 ft tall, was to be covered with illuminated advertisements. More coloured lights and crude advertising were to fill great slabs on the side walls.

'The Monster of Piccadilly Circus', as it was dubbed by the *Spectator*, rested on a podium designed with no architectural relevance except to follow the line of the pavement. On the roof was the propeller of a vast helicopter, or so it appeared. In fact it was a revolving crane, 93 ft long, to be used for putting up neon signs.

The smiling Mr Cotton must have been dumbfounded at the reaction to the building with which he had hoped to bless London, but which in the next few days created such an almighty rumpus. The press showered it with abuse. Letters poured into *The Times*. Questions were asked in the House

144 *'The Monster of Piccadilly Circus': a drawing of the model that caused the 1959 uproar. The 172-ft block of offices, shops and amenities was to be built on the north side of the Circus. The propeller-shaped feature on the roof was a revolving crane for putting up neon signs on the 100-ft-tall area reserved for them*

about this 'vulgar and unimaginative' building. In the Lords a peer stood up to demand: 'What has London in all its glorious history done to deserve this fate?'

Cotton could hardly believe what had hit him. After years of waiting, a vast investment of money and the purchase of 150 properties he had received the sanction of the LCC. In the previous March the Town Planning Committee had ended its report: 'We consider the building can take its place as a satisfactory element in the redevelopment of the Circus.' And now all this! Had Cotton kept quiet for only a few more days, and had he not called that press conference, it is virtually certain that his building would be standing in Piccadilly Circus today. Formal planning permission would have been in his hand, and no power could have stopped him. But with London baying for his blood, the Minister of Housing looked round desperately for a loophole. He found it in a quibble about car parking. The application was 'called in'.

Sighs of relief were drowned by gasps of dismay as people realised the implications. Only at the eleventh hour had they learnt what was going on behind their backs. That plans were afoot for the Circus had been known for about seven years. But rumour, vague interim reports and the news that the authorities were constantly changing their minds had lulled curiosity.

Jack Cotton had fought a long battle. He had come to London in 1952 and had bought the $\frac{1}{4}$-acre Monico site (named after the famous restaurant) for the then very large sum of £500,000. He had done so in anticipation of high profits in the boom that was certain to follow the eventual removal of building restrictions. The next year he submitted plans to the LCC, which was dismayed to be faced with so tall a building – then 160 ft – but was also worried because the Circus was a listed priority among traffic bottlenecks to be dealt with. The architects' department, headed by Leslie Martin, was concerned that the building on the Monico site should be an integral part of a master plan. Twenty acres round the Circus were needed to create a 'Comprehensive Development Area' and, lacking the money for this, the Council encouraged Cotton to buy up the necessary property. He encountered pockets of resistance, and his hopes were further blighted when traffic engineers reported to the LCC that the existing roundabout was out of date and that congestion would get worse. More road space was needed; not Mr Cotton's building.

If you take Lower Regent Street as the main axis to the Circus with Piccadilly and Coventry Street going off it at right angles, it is evident that the Monico site and the London Pavilion are impediments to any logical development. A rectangular coherence can only be achieved by extending the north side on a line with the arcaded Fire Office. This means cutting off the nose on the Glasshouse Street/Shaftesbury Avenue corner, demolishing the London Pavilion and extending the line to the Trocadero.

The necessity for this has been obvious to all planners from Norman Shaw onwards, but only in 1958, six years after Cotton had bought the site and was demanding his pound of flesh, did the LCC stop looking at the Circus buildings in isolation and get out a comprehensive plan. Overhead walkways

145 Sir William Holford prepared a number of schemes for Piccadilly Circus. Here he is with the model of his 1962 proposal in which the Circus was turned into a rectangular space enclosed by high buildings, and Eros was placed on a slightly raised piazza. This piazza had a shallow chequerboard pool that could be frozen for skating. 1: The Monico block; 2: 180-ft tower; 3: Trocadero block; 4: London Pavilion, turned into a restaurant on stilts; 5: Criterion block, with the subterranean theatre preserved; 6: pedestrian piazza with Eros and chequerboard pool. This pedestrian area in front of the Criterion and with the statue on it is a feature of the latest GLC plan published in December 1980

were devised to link the three surrounding island blocks, but this scheme did not suit Cotton and was little favoured by the traffic experts.

Cotton kept submitting new plans, and in 1958 his sixth was turned down by the LCC because of its excessive height, bulk and generally inelegant shape. At this point the LCC's head architect, Hubert Bennett, took a hand in the design, and a combined plan with Cotton's own architects closely following advice from County Hall was eventually passed. Ironically, it was an even taller building than the one Cotton had originally asked for. This was 'The Monster of Piccadilly Circus' which so horrified London in November 1959.

Faced with a barrage of criticism, Cotton hastily prepared a revised elevation of his much-ridiculed building. It was simply a cosmetic job, with the crane removed and the advertisements toned down. The misty wash-and-line drawing made the London Pavilion site look garish by contrast. The podium was lowered and – a major concession – the building lined up with the Fire Office. It remained an eyesore. The Royal Fine Arts Commissioners (to whom the plans were now belatedly shown) were seemingly so stunned that they made only minor criticisms and asked to see further plans. Probably the Commissioners knew they had no need to wield a bludgeon. The Monster was all but slain. After a public enquiry Cotton's building was rejected out of hand as falling 'below the high standard needed'.

Advertisements 'would be too dominating' and traffic and pedestrian difficulties remain unsolved.

A 'comprehensive' plan was the next demand, and the LCC called in the ever-reliable William Holford to prepare a co-ordinated scheme. He switched with dexterity from God and St Paul's to Mammon and the Circus. Within a few months of his appointment in June 1960, Holford had produced his first sketches and model showing a tall office block to the south (Criterion side), a pedestrian bridge over Jermyn Street, a raised piazza and Eros built over a flower shop. Attuning to commercial values, he declared: 'I believe it would pay.'

Still in the game, but losing heart, Cotton announced that he had commissioned Walter Gropius to prepare a design. This was early in 1961 but nothing by the great German architect was ever published. The next scheme, fourteen months later from Holford, proved to be a radical rethinking of the whole problem. Piccadilly Circus was transformed (Plate 145). The lopsided triangle had been changed into a rectangle enclosed by tall buildings. Most of the ground-level area was filled by a slightly raised piazza which was, in effect, joined to the new Criterion block on the south. Eros stood on this raised piazza and there was a shallow chequer-board pool which could be frozen for exhibition figure-skating – seemingly an impracticable idea until one remembers the small rink at the Rockefeller Center in New York.

Stairs and escalators carried people from the piazza up to high platform levels to the east where they would find a new London Pavilion. No longer a theatre, this had become 'a very open, almost transparent building with an open ground floor' raised on stilts with a coffee bar and three floors of restaurants. The platform, 23 ft wide, provided a pedestrian link with the new horizontal Monico building to the north which had shops and offices above them. A platform bridge to the south linked up with the Criterion block, also horizontal, with shop, restaurant, office and flat space. The old subterranean Criterion Theatre was retained.

On the west side of the square, Piccadilly, Swan & Edgar, Regent Street and the Fire Office remained untouched. There were to be three tall 'light and airy' blocks on the Trocadero site and, on the corner of Haymarket and Jermyn Street, a tower with office, luxury flats and showrooms. Apart from the skating rink, Holford's one frivolity was a slim 180-ft tower, 'a vertical feature' inspired, he said, by St Mark's campanile in Venice. Standing on a traffic island at the foot of Shaftesbury Avenue, this floodlit steeple was to be surmounted by the sign of Piccadilly – a starched and pleated ruff or 'pickadilla' that traditionally gives the area its name.

It was a bold, very lively conception in the Festival of Britain idiom. More practically, a one-way traffic flow on two sides allowed for a 20 per cent increase of vehicles. Holford had good reason to expect a favourable reception. The LCC conceded that it was 'gay and lively' and represented 'the spirit of the age'. But though this piazza plan pleased all but the diehards, it foundered. After more than a year's deliberation, the plan was rejected because it did not make enough provision for the expected increase of traffic.

The architect was incensed. It was impossible, he said, to reconcile traffic with 'a place of attraction and resort'. Something had to be done to divert traffic outside the Circus. If the principles of his plan were rejected he threatened to resign. But the traffic was not diverted and Holford did not resign. He bided his time and, in association with various working parties, he and other architects developed an even more revolutionary plan. If the problem could not be resolved *outwards* it must be settled by going *upwards*. From this evolved the two-level Piccadilly Circus: traffic on the existing ground-level, people on a concourse above. This plan was offered to the public in the summer of 1968.

One lesson learnt from the 1959 Cotton fiasco was that Londoners must have some say about what happens in places about which they have a sentimental concern. If nothing else, the Piccadilly Circus row ended the secrecy with which speculators and official bodies cloaked their activities before presenting the public with a *fait accompli*.

For ten days in July 1968 the GLC and Westminster City Council (which had now taken over the responsibility for the future of the Circus) gave the public a chance to see the plans and consider if they would enjoy walking on an upper deck, 26 ft above street level, with traffic circulating below them. The statue of Eros was to be on the higher level. Though completely different, the surrounding buildings were really only alternative exercises in architectural design, variations of Holford's earlier suggestions. The most controversial was a bronze and glass tower, thirty storeys high, on the

Criterion site which was criticised by the Royal Fine Arts Commissioners. They mildly pointed out that this skyscraper, twice the height of Nelson's Column, 'would conflict with the existing scale and character of the area immediately to the south and west'. But the gargantuan tower and practically everything else about the plan masterminded by Dennis Lennon can now be seen as an irrelevancy. The vital question was the two-level concept. London was amused and intrigued, but was not, it seems, ready for so bold and irreversible an innovation.

A sober footnote is provided by a decision reached for the Circus in 1978. Twenty years of high-powered planning for a brave new Piccadilly Circus simply went up in smoke; they evaporated following a decision that the old shape, familiar elevations, and single level were to be retained. Over the next five years changes are to be made. There will be tinkering with various buildings. But fundamentally the Circus is to remain the same even to the garish Coca-Cola advertisement. Popular prejudice will see that it continues to be the vulgar, disorganised, tatty and unaccountably much-loved place it has been for a century.

After the Piccadilly battle everything is bound to be an anti-climax. But just a few other interesting plans have made their bid for attention, only to be put down, in the last few years. First we move into the realm of what might seem like fantasy, but should be considered with a tolerably straight face. The Overhead Monorail in Regent Street (Plate 146) is not a Wellsian concept, a clip from *The Shape of Things to Come*. It comes from a 'feasibility study' produced by the GLC Department of Highways and Transportation in 1967.

The word 'Confidential' is stamped on the cover of the report which suggests that perhaps the author feared that Londoners, faced with such an alarming possibility, might take to the hills. A serious document researched from the Seattle World Fair to Disneyland, the report explores the possibility of overhead routes not only in Regent Street but all over London. Look out, Edgware Road, Piccadilly and Fleet Street! At peak hours up to 30,000 comfortably seated customers must be carried in each direction at 50 mph in 'aesthetically pleasing conditions'. It is a tall order. Things went awry in Tokyo where a similar monorail was built. Will there (the report ponders) be 'a pattern of demand'? An oversight in research will require an addendum in the next edition of the study. This is 'The New Aerial Omnibus' (Plate 105A) which *Punch* discovered was 'the only method of surmounting the difficulties of transit' in London – in 1846.

Transport of a more extensive, but slightly less outlandish sort was part of a mammoth project which has come to nothing at Hammersmith Broadway. The scheme burst on the architectural world with the splendour of a comet in 1978, and then was not so much killed as allowed to fade away twelve months later.

For several years London Transport had considered the idea of demolishing Hammersmith bus station (feeding fourteen routes) and the Underground (Piccadilly and District lines), both of which are more than somewhat out of date. Anything to improve the suicidal traffic roundabout would also be a bonus. In 1977 Norman Foster, who happily combines avant-garde ideas with a conventional architectural practice, was commissioned to produce plans for an ambitious, multi-purpose Hammersmith Centre (Plate 147).

Round the edge of the site, 3.7 acres in size and embracing the whole of Hammersmith Broadway, was to be an unbroken circle of office blocks. They would surround and be above the flat roof of the bus station. This huge open space, the size of Trafalgar Square, was to be enclosed in a translucent bubble stretched between the roof of the offices. Made of a lightweight glass-fibre membrane with heat-regulating properties, the bubble, supported by tension cables, would shelter the entire podium area from the weather.

The resulting indoor public plaza would accommodate exhibition and concert areas, pubs, restaurants, lecture halls, a gymnasium, squash courts, shops and an ice rink. There would be a decorative sprinkling of trees. Access to the offices was supplied by four steel lifts at the corners of the site. The section drawing gives the impression that the background is transparent like the roof, but this blank area consists of offices such as those shown at the sides.

Because of the facilities provided by Foster (needed to make the scheme financially self-supporting) the basic function of providing a transport station is somewhat obscured. Lines of buses can be observed below the main floor and there is a glimpse of trains in subterranean rabbit holes. A helicopter, inevitable symbol of a brave new world, comes in to land on a platform supported on what appears to be a very fragile roof.

Hammersmith and Fulham Borough Council gave planning permission, but when the architect was asked to cut down the amenities by a Dutch-based firm of developers he declined saying he didn't want his original concept diluted out of existence. After an outlay of about £1,000,000 to architect and technical consultants, Norman Foster was sacked. He was left with one minor satisfaction: his Hammersmith Centre is one of the few modern buildings for which prominent local residents have held protest meetings not against but in favour.

Another non-starter – even though it was not due to be completed until 1988 – is the Olympic City which might have been built on the site of the Royal Victoria Docks. So vast a project needed ten years of preparation, and in 1978 the GLC began to study the scheme for a 1988 London Olympics.

The proposed dockland site on the river at Canning Town was 214 acres, i.e. about a third of the size of the City of London. A vast outlay of £750,000,000 for staging the games was needed for a transformation that included filling in the Royal Victoria Dock basin. Among the facilities were to have been a stadium for as many as 100,000 spectators, an indoor arena seating 15,000 and a velodome (banked arena for cycle racing) to seat 6,000.

To bring people to the games the Jubilee Line was to have been extended to the Olympic Village (accommodation for 12,000 competitors and team officials). Car parking facilities had to be found for 5,000 cars and 1,000 coaches.

Olympic City might have turned the depressed area of dockland round Canning Town into a boom town. Ripples of prosperity from money

147 *Hammersmith Broadway transformed. The plans for the scheme, prepared by Foster Associates in 1977, were rejected after costing about £1,000,000 in fees to the architect and consultants*

provided by foreign visitors would have spread out over the whole of East London north of the Thames. Rough plans were made for the position of stadiums, an International Centre and other features of the Olympic Park, but the whole scheme was killed by a combined Conservative and Labour vote of the GLC. Both parties came out against holding the 1988 Olympics in

London. 'I say we should go for the Olympics, and damn the expense,' asserted a Conservative member; but the Soviet takeover of Afghanistan caused too many uncertainties about the future of the Olympic Games. The idea was abandoned early in 1980, doubtless to the relief of members of the GLC Architects' Department. Their hair would have turned white to a man.

*148 A perspective view of Wren's
original design for Greenwich
Hospital*

Chapter 17

The Awkward Squad

ANY attempt to give unity to the varied schemes which follow or impose on them anything more than a chronological discipline would be difficult. A Mansion House heavy with Masonic symbolism; a peculiar place and elevation for Temple Bar, that Wandering Jew among London buildings; a gentlemen's club that looks like a fairy-tale vision of Camelot; the twisting course of the Thames transformed into a straight canal; the Mausoleum at Halicarnassus (or something very like it) poised on the roof of a London store; a Georgian crescent magically transported from its spiritual home in Bath to suburban Upper Norwood; all these, and more, are unruly recruits to an Awkward Squad.

A WREN *FAUX PAS* AND LES INVALIDES FOR GREENWICH

When the Tudor palace of Placentia at Greenwich fell into ruin during the Commonwealth and was finally demolished there was considerable uncertainty about what would happen on the site. The decision in the reign of William and Mary to build a home for sailors led Wren to put forward a disastrous idea and apparently inspired a grandiose alternative by Johann Bodt.

Wren's *faux pas* was to suggest a large building with a dome and quadrant colonnades linking it to flanking wings that would completely block the river view of the Queen's House (Plate 148). This was sometime before 1694, and Queen Mary's angry reaction to this insult to the home of her ancestors and to the architect, Inigo Jones, caused Wren to change his design to the one finally adopted. This leaves a gap, 115 ft wide, between the buildings so that the Queen's House is not obscured.

Bodt's suggestion was even more ruthless. Bodt, the Huguenot military engineer involved in Whitehall buildings for William III, produced an aerial panorama of a palatial building marked 'Plan d'une maison des Invalides pour le Roy Guillaume'. Greenwich is not specified, and the river not shown, but in the 1690s when Bodt was in England the King and Queen Mary had Greenwich in mind for a seamen's hospital. Conceived on a heroic scale, Bodt's 'Invalides' would have stretched back over the present Woolwich Road and would have involved the demolition of the Queen's House. As happened over Wren's first plan, any interference with the Inigo Jones building would have ensured its rejection.

Little more about Bodt's scheme can be discovered because the original drawing was in a Dresden museum and was probably destroyed in the 1945 bombing. Fortunately it was photographed in 1932, and Sir Nikolaus Pevsner reproduced it in the *Architectural Review* in 1961.

AN ECCENTRIC MANSION HOUSE

149 Design by Batty Langley for the Lord Mayor's Mansion House (1735), to be erected in Leadenhall

Early in the 18th century the City decided that the Lord Mayor should have an official home. The idea had been in the air since shortly after the Great Fire, and in 1735 a site was chosen – the Stocks Market – at the junction of Poultry, Cornhill and Threadneedle Street.

The Mansion House Committee, consisting of the Lord Mayor, five aldermen and twelve commoners, invited a number of architects to submit designs. Among them were Giacomo Leoni; John James, a colleague of Hawksmoor; James Gibbs, the designer of St Martin-in-the-Fields; and the City Surveyor, George Dance the Elder.

News that the City was thinking of erecting a palace for its titular head immediately created ironical comment from Westminster where stories were concocted about its progress. A design by the dead Palladio, it was asserted, had been submitted by Lord Burlington. The Corporation were supposed to have solemnly queried whether Palladio was a Freeman of the City. This academic point was said to have been cut short by a worthy deputy alderman who had pointed out that as a Papist Palladio would be ineligible anyway.

In fact, the strangest of the designs was that of Batty Langley who had not been asked to compete at all. Langley, a designer of 'grottos, cascades, caves, temples, pavilions, and other rural buildings of pleasure' was, he told the committee with disarming self-confidence, 'able to compose a Design for a Mansion House with greater Magnificence, Grandeur, and Beauty than has been yet express'd in any, nay even in all the Public Buildings of the City taken together'.

A distinctly theatrical affair, Langley's Mansion House sported twin domes and a series of vast open windows and doorways – totally impractical for London conditions. As a Freemason he introduced a superabundance of Corinthian columns (equated with beauty in Masonic symbolism) as well as statues of the four cardinal virtues, Temperance, Justice, Prudence, and Fortitude (Plate 149).

If some members of the committee were fellow Masons, it did him little good. It was Dance's plans for the Stocks Market site that were recommended to the Court of Common Council. Dance's Mansion House, which still stands, was completed and first occupied in 1751. Gibbs was awarded 100 guineas, James 75 guineas; Leoni 50 guineas, and Langley a mere 20 guineas.

ADAM AND LINCOLN'S INN

150 Robert Adam's palatial building for Lincoln's Inn

If Robert Adam had not submitted so spectacular and costly a design, and if at the time the Adam brothers had not been preoccupied with the problems of the Adelphi, London today might possess a building comparable to Somerset House. Vast and palatial, it would fill the whole of the east frontage of Lincoln's Inn Fields and back onto Chancery Lane.

In April 1771 the Benchers of Lincoln's Inn asked Adam and three other architects to 'draw up proper plans' for the rebuilding of the old part of the Inn. They were James Paine, Matthew Brettingham and Robert Taylor, all deeply involved in the English Palladian tradition. The Society of Lincoln's Inn needed more legal chambers for its members, and probably had in mind a new library and a great hall like those of other inns of court.

The Society's records show that nine months later Taylor alone was in the running, yet until July the following year, 1772, the restricted competition was apparently still open. Around this time Adam and, no doubt, his brother

James prepared the great building which, with a frontage of 700 ft, resembles a palace (Plate 150) with ornamental gardens facing Lincoln's Inn Fields.

In today's context, Adam's building, 100 ft longer than Somerset House, but not so deep, must be visualised as occupying virtually the whole of the eastern side of Lincoln's Inn. The building would stretch from Holborn, through Old Square and encompass a large part of New Square. Adam's detailed plans have disappeared, but it is a fair assumption that the main entrance under the six-columned portico led into a domed ante-room beyond which was the hall and common room. It was essential to preserve the early 17th-century chapel by Inigo Jones, and this is masked by the recess and portico, right foreground, and was to be encased (as the Chancery Lane view shows) in a classical shell. The further matching recess fronts a balancing building of equal size that would have been ideal as the library.

The building is not as solid as it appears. Behind the impressive façade are four large open courtyards occupying almost as much space as the building itself. It could well be that the discrepancy between elaborate superficial design and actual accommodation was a factor in deciding the Benchers against Adam. They chose instead Robert Taylor's compact, unadorned and rather dull block, now called Stone Buildings. Completed in 1774, this only extends to half its intended length.

So prodigious and expensive a scheme may have frightened the Benchers. They may also have preferred to retain the medieval flavour of the Inn which meant that Lincoln's Inn ended up with blocks of Victorian Gothic chambers and the awkwardly placed hall and library of 1843. Instead of two monumental classical buildings which it might have had, London has only one. Four years later in 1776 William Chambers was able to take the architectural lead from Adam, his great rival, with his creation of Somerset House.

STRAIGHTENING THE THAMES

A plan to straighten the Thames was one outcome of attempts to enlarge and improve anchorage, quays and warehouses for merchant ships bringing their cargoes up the Thames to London.

A House of Commons Committee, which sat for twenty-five days in 1796, heard many proposals including suggestions for huge docks for Rotherhithe and the Isle of Dogs, subsequently to be built. But the most ambitious and ingenious of all ideas was that of Willey Reveley, architect and engineer, who wanted to straighten out the curving river. To provide three huge docks and, even more importantly, to reduce the sailing time up the river, Reveley suggested channelling from Woolwich Reach right across the Isle of Dogs and what subsequently became Surrey Docks to bring the new canal out in the Pool of London at Wapping. The $\frac{3}{4}$-mile channel joining up Blackwall and Limehouse Reaches would alone have been invaluable in taking off hours of sailing time involved in going round the great loop of Greenwich Reach against adverse winds. As Reveley's plan indicates (Plate 151) this channel would have become the main course of the river and would have left the

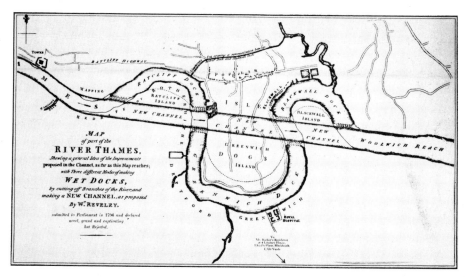

151 The 'New Channel', designed
by Willey Reveley (1796) to
straighten out the Thames

great horseshoe and two smaller horseshoes for conversion into docks.

It seems such an admirable idea that it is hard to accept that this 'novel, grand and captivating' scheme was rejected simply because it was too difficult an engineering feat. But this was the only explanation offered.

TREVITHICK'S REFORM COLUMN

In 1831 London had a chance to forestall Paris by putting up a structure which would have been four times higher than the future Eiffel Tower. In that year a Cornish engineer and inventor, Richard Trevithick, had the idea for a colossal tower to celebrate the Reform Bill shortly due to be passed. It was to symbolise 'the beauty, strength and unaffected grandeur of the British Constitution'.

There was little unaffected grandeur about the monument itself. This was clear from the drawings and explanations issued by Trevithick from an address in Highgate. His Reform Column made of cast iron was to be 1,000 ft tall and covered in gold. To illustrate its splendour the engineer prepared an engraving (Plate 152) in which the column soared high above the Monument (210 ft), St Paul's (420 ft) and the Great Pyramid (500 ft). It was to be the tallest pillar ever erected anywhere in the world.

At this flourishing period of new ideas, no scheme however eccentric seems to have lacked noble patrons, and three dukes and an earl were among those who promised Trevithick their support. Support was certainly needed for the column was to be built of 1,500 huge cast-iron squares each weighing about 3 tons which had to be hauled up and screwed in place.

A great feature was to be the air lift for carrying people to the top. Up sightseers would go riding on 'an air cushion' controlled by a Trevithick steam engine at the base. Then 'having from the loftiest pedestal of human art surveyed imperial London' they would be lowered 'to the every-day level at a safe speed regulated by valves closed by such simple acts as rising from the seat'. The rate of descent would be about 3 ft a second with (the nervous were assured) 'the same shock at the bottom as jumping off a 9-inch door-stop'.

The Reform Bill went through as expected, in June 1832, and in the

152 Trevithick's Reform Column
seen in relation to the Great
Pyramid, St Paul's and the
Monument

following March plans for the column were submitted to William IV. Two months later Trevithick, who never received the proper rewards for his inventions, died penniless, and was buried without a single relative present in an unmarked pauper's grave at Dartford in Kent. His Reform Column died with him, and was only to be remembered thirty-nine years later when it was suggested – and rejected – as a suitable memorial for Prince Albert.

MAUSOLEUM FOR NEWTON'S HOUSE

153 Mausoleum for Newton's House (top and lower r.), inspired by the primitive Franciscan chapel at Assisi (lower l.).

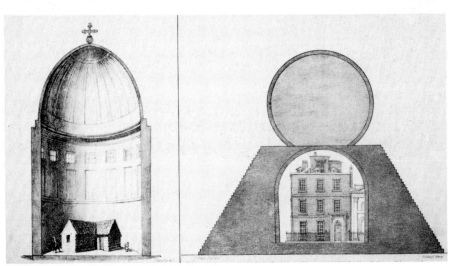

In June 1834, the artist and lithographer, George Scharf, received a visitor from Ireland at his studio off Tottenham Court Road. He was a Mr T. Steele, MA, of Magdalene College, Cambridge, and he had a curious request.

Would Mr Scharf prepare a detailed drawing of a proposed plan for a national monument to Sir Isaac Newton? Since Newton had died more than a hundred years before, this was a somewhat odd idea; but the monument was even odder. The proposal was to enclose the scientist's old house and observatory in a huge mausoleum. The house, which he occupied from 1710 till his death in 1727, was in St Martin's Street, Westminster. Surmounted by a globe, the stepped pyramid, 40 ft high, would have dominated the whole of the south side of Leicester Square.

The idea of building over a shrine appears to have been inspired by a similar treatment of the primitive Franciscan chapel at Assisi and the globe borrowed from E.-L. Boullée, whose tribute to Newton's genius consisted of a gargantuan sphere. By the next day Scharf had prepared two designs, and by July had completed his final drawing which he made into a lithograph (Plate 153) showing the house inside the pyramid.

Nothing further was heard of this plan to preserve for posterity Newton's house which Macaulay hoped would 'continue to be well known as long as our island retains any trace of civilisation'. In 1849 the brick façade was stuccoed; later the square observatory tower on the roof was removed; and the building was demolished in 1913. It is now the site of Westminster Central Reference Library.

A BATH FOR NORWOOD

154 Crescent for Beulah Spa, Upper Norwood, designed by a local architect, J. Atkinson

On the top of Beulah Hill in Upper Norwood flats command fine views over miles of Kent and Surrey. In their place there might well be a crescent of terraced houses as elegant as anything in Georgian Bath.

A plan to give south London a touch of architectural distinction arose in the 1830s when Beulah was found, like Bath, to have medicinal springs. The pure saline water attracted visitors to the sloping ground south of Beulah Hill. The pump room, rustic buildings, the layout of the valley and the still-surviving entrance lodge were designed by Decimus Burton.

Because of his close involvement with the Spa, Burton would have been the obvious person to design this crowning feature of 'the New Town of Beulah' as it was to be called, and to provide 'suitable residences for such as wish to render this beautiful spot a place of permanent abode'. But this rare engraving (Plate 154) was from the design of a lesser known local architect, J. Atkinson, who submitted his drawing to the Royal Academy in 1836.

Beulah Spa survived only twenty-four years. In 1855 the Spa closed, and ended any idea of building a gracious crescent. The opening of the Crystal Palace nearby in the previous year destroyed its popularity. Wooded slopes, rustic walks, and remnants of overgrown brickwork are now features of the neglected park, while a curved roadway, closed to traffic, indicates where the quadrant would have stood.

ALPINE PLEASURES FOR LAMBETH

155 Part of a prospectus of the New Theatre Company (1863) for a proposed rooftop pleasure-garden and leisure centre on the site of Astley's Theatre, Lambeth

Early in 1862 Members of Parliament were dismayed to hear that the dignity of their proud new Palace of Westminster was threatened by a bizarre rooftop pleasure garden to be built just across the river. It was a scheme by the Irish actor-manager, Dion Boucicault, and author of *London Assurance*, for converting Astley's Theatre into a grandiose leisure complex.

In the previous autumn Boucicault had converted the interior of the old theatre, and had 'rearranged the map of London' by grandly naming this Lambeth building the New Theatre Royal, Westminster.

Now he was planning to pull down eight houses adjoining the theatre to erect what looked like a very raffish and unorthodox place of entertainment. The prospectus shows a corner-site just across Westminster Bridge with two floors of intimate arbours where couples are eating and drinking (Plate 155). On a roof garden were more tables, a fountain, grottoes, cascades and a miniature Alpine village with fir trees and snow-covered mountains.

The announcement of this project coincided with a law case in which Boucicault, a great lady's man, was implicated in a scandal involving a young American actress, Emily Jordan. Noble patronage and finance was abruptly withdrawn. Before any work could start on his theatre pleasure garden, all his creditors sued. That summer he was declared bankrupt and the New Theatre Company was taken over. Parliament sighed with relief. Boucicault's unrepentant reaction was: 'Failures are still-born children that don't count.'

PLUMSTEAD GARDEN SUBURB

156 The proposed garden suburb for Plumstead (1866), designed by George Barnes Williams

London's earliest garden suburb was proposed on thirty-five acres of freehold land at Plumstead in 1866, and the Woolwich auctioneers, Messrs Hudson & Son, dangled a seductive scheme before the eyes of prospective speculators. Exercising his imagination, George Barnes Williams, an architect in Old Jewry, created a paradise of bijou villas in an open space between Shooters Hill and Plumstead Common. Winding paths lead to fountains, gazebos and rustic summer houses (Plate 156). The artist's north-westerly view from Shrewbury Hill commands a magnificent view up the Thames. The houses are on either side of a proposed road that meets Plum Lane at a T-junction.

Nothing vaguely resembling the splendid villas was built. This is a classic example of attempted aggrandisement misfiring. If the proposed road is the present Winstock Road, the area to the right never saw anything grander than very modest turn-of-the-century terraces. The ground on the left didn't sell at all. Today it is allotments.

ELEVATING TEMPLE BAR
Since the day Temple Bar was dismantled in 1878 its future has been the subject of continual controversy. For nearly ten years Wren's Strand gateway to the City lay in a thousand stone blocks before being rebuilt at Theobald's Park, Cheshunt. 'Bring back Temple Bar' has been – and still is – a frequent cry, and sites for its re-erection have been suggested for various parts of London.

157 Ernest Turner's suggestion for screw-jacking Temple Bar aloft and inserting a single-span arch beneath it. Two problems would be solved simultaneously: where to put the Bar, and how to deal with traffic congestion

It is less well known that the gateway's future was worrying Londoners even before the demolition. It had become shaky and a traffic bottleneck. 'The bone in the throat of Fleet Street' had to be moved, and there were proposals to re-erect it in the Temple Gardens, on the riverfront and in Guildhall Yard. The most radical solution came from Ernest Turner, a Bedford Row architect, who decided to elevate it above an arch with a wide span and provide a passage between the Temple and the Law Courts for lawyers. Turner's design (Plate 157) was exhibited at the Royal Academy in 1869.

WHITEHALL REBUILT

158 Whitehall (1873) conceived by Frederick Sang: the view south with the Houses of Parliament at the end of a great avenue

The most elaborate, detailed and realistic drawings for a new Whitehall were produced by an architect and interior decorator, Frederick Sang, in 1873. Sang (1846–84) delighted in the kind of exercise so elegantly displayed in his watercolour (Plate 158). This 'Concentration of Government Offices' has real dignity. Over the years he exhibited fifteen ideas ranging from a Royal Mint on the Embankment to Suggested Improvements for Trafalgar Square.

From his office in Sackville Street, Sang supplied a ground-plan explaining the layout of the offices grouped round a large square and a crescent facing Trafalgar Square and stretching south to the Houses of Parliament. There is a splendid spaciousness about his conception, though he will hardly escape whipping for demolishing Inigo Jones's Banqueting House.

The tall, towered building on the Embankment was to be a new Charing Cross Station. Sang also proposed joining the Embankment with the Mall through a tunnel under Charing Cross Station which, unlike most planners, he did not sweep away to the south side of the river.

An added charm is given to this drawing by the fact that apparently its creator had no axe to grind, was working to no commission, and had to persuade no competition assessors. He was simply letting his imagination run free for his own pleasure

THE SCOTLAND YARD OPERA HOUSE

159 The National Opera House (1875), showing Westminster Pier in the foreground

An opera house for London to rival La Scala, Milan, in size and grandeur should now be standing on the Embankment by Westminster Bridge. After an expenditure of about £103,000, the failure to raise a further £10,000 wanted for roofing meant that the Grand National Opera House was never completed.

The Embankment opera house (Plate 159) was the creation of Colonel J. H. Mapleson, the operatic impresario, previously associated with Her Majesty's (the Haymarket opera house burnt down in 1867) as well as Covent Garden and Drury Lane.

He was persuaded that the site by Westminster Bridge was ideal, but, after excavating 50 ft in 1875 for firm ground, water poured in and fifteen pumps and an outlay of £33,000 for foundations were needed before building could even start.

Mapleson intended it to be nothing less than the leading opera house of the world. It was to have its own Underground station for the use of audiences on the District Railway. A subterranean passage was to run to the Houses of Parliament so that MPs 'after listening to beautiful music instead of dull debates might return to the House on hearing the division-bell'.

For the artists, recreation rooms were to be provided with billiard tables, two Turkish baths, and a surgery for doctors to deal with sore throats and indispositions. Tied up at Westminster pier was to be a small tug to tow a large houseboat on which the company could sail down river for rehearsal or recreation.

With the outside walls completed, but beaten for want of £10,000

207

Mapleson was forced to abandon his dream. 'For backing or laying against a horse, for starting a new sporting club or a new music-hall, the money could have been found in a few hours', he complained. Demolition, completed in 1888, alone cost £3,000, and Norman Shaw built New Scotland Yard on the site two years later. 'The site of what, with a little public spirit usefully applied, would have been the finest theatre in the world, is now to serve as a new police station,' wrote Mapleson, adding rather bitterly, 'With such solid foundations, the cells, if not comfortable, will at least be dry.'

PITE'S PEAK

160 *Design for a West End Club House, submitted by Arthur Beresford Pite for the RIBA's coveted Soane Medallion award in 1882. 'West End of where?' asked its critics. 'Colney Hatch? Bedlam Hospital?'*

The architectural world was plunged into acrimony by the announcement in March 1882 that the Royal Institute of British Architects had awarded the coveted Soane Medallion for 'A Design for a West-End Club-House'. The then unknown winner was Arthur Beresford Pite of Bloomsbury Square.

The drawing presented the astonished public with a view of a vast, turreted Gothic building, half-way between a chateau and a medieval cathedral (Plate 160). To anyone visualising a London clubhouse in terms of Pall Mall and St James's it was an outrage.

'Too bewildering altogether for serious contemplation', decided the *Architect* which added that it must have been intended as 'a broad and farcical joke'. Another critic saw it as 'the lamented Viollet-le-Duc running amuck in the most blatant style of military fortification . . .'

When it was discovered that Pite was only twenty-one, fury increased. The RIBA Council was attacked for 'encouraging the production of such useless rubbish' (letter in the *Builder*). 'It has struck common sense dumb.'

Pite had achieved his object which was to shock and create personal publicity for his undeniably fine draughtsmanship. After this he settled down to a successful commercial career with conventional London churches and offices among his work, and later became a Professor of Architecture at the Royal College of Art.

HEXAGONAL LONDON

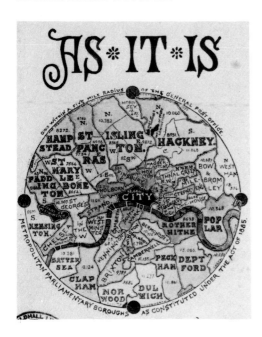

161 London's sprawling, differently shaped boroughs transformed into uniform hexagonals

Personal economy as a basis for national prosperity was so much a part of the creed of middle-class Victorians that there was even a campaign to prevent overcharging by cab-drivers. This involved a plan that would have changed the whole structure of the London boroughs. In the middle of the 19th century a slightly fanatical Fellow of the Society of Antiquaries published a scheme for an hexagonal London.

From an address in Ormonde Terrace, Primrose Hill, John Leighton suggested that the old borough boundaries should be altered to conform to a honeycomb pattern. Within a five-mile radius of the General Post Office all the sprawling, differently sized boroughs were to become hexagonal-shaped areas, each two miles across (Plate 161). There were nineteen altogether with the City in the centre of the honeycomb. Each hexagonal borough would be identified by a letter, and the letter as well as a number would be painted or cut out of tin-plate to be visible by day and night on lamp-posts at every street corner.

In the days before taximeters, cab-drivers charged according to distances published in a cumbersome handbook, and it was easy for them to cheat the unwary. Under the new system people would know exactly how far they had travelled because distances would be co-ordinated and readily calculated from the lamp-posts. That, anyway, was the theory.

The Society of Arts met to debate the virtues of dividing London up and the earliest idea was a square pattern with a fixed tariff for travelling from one to the next. But in 1867 Leighton advocated hexagonals rather than squares so that diagonal journeys could be assessed fairly. In his original letter to the *Journal of the Society of Arts* in February of that year he did not go beyond imposing a generalised honeycomb pattern on London; but sometime after 1885 he came out with his far more revolutionary map with each borough an interlocking hexagon of identical size.

NATIONAL THEATRES

From the time it was originally proposed, London had to wait nearly 130 years for a National Theatre. In 1848, a London publisher named Effingham Wilson published two pamphlets, both called *A House for Shakespeare: A Proposition for the Consideration of the Nation*, full of high-minded aspirations. These were met with favour but also pessimism by Charles Dickens and the actor Charles Kemble. Among many ardent supporters of the idea later in the century was Bernard Shaw.

The first practical move came in 1913 and then not for the present site on South Bank, but in Bloomsbury. An acre of land was bought on the corner of Gower Street and Keppel Street for a long, multi-gabled building with a Tudor flavour. This was to have been called the Shakespeare Memorial National Theatre, but never got any further than a wooden hut – the 'Shakespeare Hut' – in which wounded soldiers were entertained during the 1914–18 war.

The Bloomsbury site was resold in 1922 and after much searching (slums near the Waterloo Road were dismissed as too sordid) a small triangular plot was bought in the Cromwell Road opposite the Victoria and Albert Museum. Shaw was enthusiastic; others, dubious, thought it too small, and liable to lapse into the mummified apathy of museum-land. Sir Edwin Lutyens, an old-guard architect who had never previously designed a theatre, prepared a plan in solemn, civic style (Plate 162A), which had Shaw's approval. An inaugural ceremony was held in April 1938 on the site (Plate 162B) which was once a plague pit, became a post-war car park and is about to accommodate an Islamic centre.

The Second World War killed this scheme, as the Great War had killed the Bloomsbury plan. In 1951 a foundation stone was laid between the Festival Hall and the Shot Tower, but even this was not adopted and neither was the Portland stone design of Brian O'Rorke (the curved roof of which was likened

162 (A) *Bernard Shaw looking at the plans for the National Theatre with Sir Edwin Lutyens; (B) ceremonial dedication in April 1938 of the site in Cromwell Road, opposite the Victoria and Albert Museum*

by Sir Thomas Beecham to 'a baby's bum'). After endless controversy, heartburn and changes, Denys Lasdun's present building was started in 1969 and partially ready for a royal opening seven years later.

OXFORD STREET MAUSOLEUM

During the decade after the opening of Selfridge's in Oxford Street in 1909, the American department store king Gordon Selfridge asked an architect to design a monumental tower to surmount the building. A persistent publicist,

163 The monumental tower for Selfridge's department store, Oxford Street, designed by Philip Tilden in 1918

Selfridge had already made his store famous with a library, rest-rooms, roof garden and information centre. In about 1918 he wanted a tower that would make Selfridge's a landmark visible all over London.

The architect Philip Tilden (who had previously designed for him a grandiose private castle, never realised) produced something to challenge the Mausoleum at Halicarnassus – a classical tower on a high podium (Plate 163). Lions, reminiscent of those at Bodrum, guard the stairway to the entrance. A square upper temple has Ionic columns to match those on the main façade of the store. The immense tower, so heavy that the building would have bowed under the weight, is crowned by a circular Corinthian temple.

KING'S CROSS AIRPORT

A great wheel, each spoke a runway, to be built over the railway sidings just north of King's Cross and St Pancras, was suggested as a Central Airport for London in 1931. The idea was launched by the architect, Charles W. Glover, in an article in the *Illustrated London News* (Plate 164) and with a model at the Institution of Civil Engineers in June of that year.

Regular services would fly out of this 'Aerial King's Cross' and it was envisaged that businessmen would keep their own planes which would be 'garaged' there. The estimated cost was £5,000,000, and the northern sidings were chosen as the only suitable site for the development that the architects could find.

The approach down a new 'Aerial Way' would be from Pentonville Road leading up to the main concourse in front of the airport. Passengers would be carried up to the runways by lifts (as would the aircraft from hangars below), and the planes would taxi round the perimeter of the 'wheel' until clearance was given for them to go onto the concrete runways.

164 An overhead airport for King's Cross (1931), designed by Charles W. Glover. Though each spoke of the wheel provided a half-mile-long runway it was conceded that aircraft might need slotted wings and improved brakes

Chapter 18

Farewell to Follies

WE have reached a point early in 1982 when there appears to be a momentary lull in London's restless determination to tamper with its own image. So, even if there are no hopes for improvements, there are few apprehensions. The 'Green Giant' office block opposite Millbank which threatened to rise to a height of 500 ft – almost 200 ft higher than Big Ben – has been slain. After fidgeting us for so many years, Piccadilly Circus has settled for a tame compromise. If there are threats to our environment, they are hiding their intentions.

A tunnel, or tunnels, under the Thames are talked about – one just below Tower Bridge, another further down river connecting Poplar with Rotherhithe – but if they come about we are extremely unlikely to benefit from them before the end of the century. The one great imponderable is the conversion of London's dockland. A number of schemes already exist, but the problem, though extensive, is fairly self-contained.

In the lull we have a chance to decide if we are better off with the city we have or would prefer London changed by some of the proposals made during the last 400 years. We started out by saying that our streets were lined with unfulfilled good intentions, and we shed tears for architects and planners baulked by bureaucrats and unimaginative clients. The time has come to see if these misgivings are justified.

One thing is indisputable. From Wren to Abercrombie failure to adopt long-range plans has left us with a capital city that works only by the skin of its teeth and threatens to become a very uncomfortable place in which to live before we are much older. For this it is easy to accuse the city fathers of unduly conservative penny-pinching, but equally planners have often been high-handed and uncompromising. Decisions have frequently been affected by the public's aversion to change. People moan that nothing is done but cry havoc when change is suggested.

At every stage of London's history since the Great Fire there has been a disinclination to adopt radical proposals. Nash was the only man able to put his mark on the West End and really improve street plans. We have shown our gratitude by pulling down the colonnades which were the essential feature of his Regent Street quadrant and by turning his Piccadilly Circus into a garish funfair. We may admire Fifth Avenue in New York and the Haussmann boulevards in Paris, but would we really want such geometric regimentation in London? Progress has been hindered because nearly every nook and cranny, dark courtyard and twisting alley holds some historical and sentimental association. Wren's post-Fire plans would have given the City straighter and wider streets. John Gwynn's even more remarkable and extensive plans in the 18th century would undoubtedly have been splendid. Bressey's great elevated highway across London from north to south, proposed in 1938, would have been a boon to traffic. But as well as causing destruction, there was always the awful feeling that we should not like the result when we got it.

Unquestionably London is an architectural mess, but again that is because London likes it that way. Uniformity, whether Georgian or in the modern style of post-war London Wall, could be depressing. We have certainly got as much Victorian Gothic as we can stomach. When we look at William Bardwell's scheme for three great squares north of Victoria Street, and contrast them with the muddle of buildings that are there, the first reaction is to think that a great opportunity for town-planning was lamentably lost. But, pleasant though these Cubitt-style terraces look in the architect's drawings, it might have been monotonous for so large an extension of stuccoed and porticoed Belgravia to have taken up residence in Westminster.

This is true of so many grand conceptions, not excepting Colonel Trench's dazzling London Quay. They have been admired, considered and then rejected. We often feel angry that small-minded property-owners, such as those on the riverside, have blocked the creation of something that would have been so magnificent. But at the same time there is a sneaking feeling that the monumental would have been too formal. Timidity and obstruction may have been justified.

Perhaps, too, a great many of the brave and wonderful might-have-beens would, in reality, have been too much of a good thing. Dance's double London Bridge and the crescent-shaped approaches are breathtaking. The whole scheme seems irresistible. But then cold doubt sets in. It is *too* magnificent! The rest of dear drab old London would never have been able to stand up to such splendour. This is also probably true of all those Triumphal Bridges. They are splendid conceits. But actually *built* . . .? And with buses shaking their baroque splendour? Robbed of Italian sunshine, they would shiver pathetically under London's grey skies.

So many beguiling ideas would have struck snags as practical realities. Elevated railways running between houses down narrow streets look delightful in their sedate mid-Victorian context. But they would have been hell to live with — especially if your windows looked directly out on them and passengers were able to peer in. Paxton's Great Victorian Way girdling London inside a temperature-controlled glasshouse excites but at the same time confounds the imagination. An airport on top of King's Cross Station and Goodwin's vast south London cemetery with a chapel modelled on the Parthenon are equally transient mirages. As someone wrote of Seddon's towering Campo Santo at Westminster, there can be too much megalomania.

Timid to say so, but there is even a practical argument against building so fine a competition contender as Cockerell's Royal Exchange. This is far more decorative and attractive than the rather conventional classical Exchange actually built for us by Tite. But there is a necessity for buildings to blend in London. In practice, this is especially well seen in Trafalgar Square. The National Gallery we have (as opposed to Brodrick's multi-columned alternative) and Smirke's Royal College of Physicians (now Canada House) are both perfectly at ease with St Martin-in-the-Fields; and what is important is that Sir Herbert Baker's South Africa House, though not built until 1935, is able to live agreeably alongside all three because it, too, conforms to the classical 'Grand Manner'. By avoiding wilder excesses, seductive though they look on paper, London has retained a kind of harmony.

Timing as much as anything else has often been the deciding factor in whether a building or scheme comes into existence. Something acclaimed one moment is beyond the pale the next. For architects it can be a matter of luck. Inigo Jones or John Webb might easily have created a magnificent royal palace for Whitehall had Charles I shown more definite interest a few years earlier. But the moment – like the throne and the King's head – was lost. William Kent's Parliament House would almost certainly have been built but for the outbreak of war. Wars have killed many fine ideas simply because at the end of them there has been no money to spend. World War I prevented the eyesore of Hungerford Railway Bridge from being swept away. World War II finally killed Bressey's road plan, and lack of money and impetus in the aftermath meant death to the Abercrombie Plan. Bressey knew what he was talking about when he urged London to 'embark immediately on useful schemes' – even imperfect ones – rather than 'wait for some faultless ideal'. Delay, he said, will mean the scheme becomes unobtainable.

Plans, like tides in the affairs of men, have to be taken at the flood. It was Colonel Trench's tragedy that he always seemed to miss the tide. His Thames Quay got away to a tremendous start, but when his patrons died within a few years of each other his hopes died with them. In modern London, and for different reasons, timing has always been just wrong for Piccadilly Circus. People kept waiting too long become bored. After the Cotton fiasco had burnt itself out other good alternatives were suggested. But they were too late. Public interest had gone off the boil.

Follies have been among our most beguiling discoveries. Many have been splendidly outrageous. But it occurs to us that here and there a caprice such as Colonel Trench's two-mile boulevard from St Paul's to Hyde Park may have been treated a trifle over-seriously. We may have implied that their originators regarded them as more practical possibilities than they actually did. Poor Trench comes in for a lot of ridicule, some of which may be grossly unfair. He would probably argue that he never intended this or that idea to provide more than lively discussion at a fashionable dinner party.

Did Willson *really* think he was going to build that vast pyramid on Primrose Hill and imagine that London would be happy at the thought of five million corpses mouldering away in such a prominent mausoleum? The suddenness with which he dropped the whole idea makes his dedication a trifle suspect. A grotesque plan to drain the Thames and run a highway along the river bed is yet another fantasy that strains credulity. There has been a great deal of doodling.

With hand on heart, what changes can we say we believe unquestionably would have improved London? If planning, like diplomacy, is the art of the possible, the choice must lie with those rare schemes which combined inspiration with the least opposition and the most economical cost. Compromise seems a dull but necessary ingredient.

One idea that seems to us to answer all these requirements is the Palace of Fine Arts in Kensington Garden with its long avenue of approach from Hyde Park. Kensington Palace would have been pleasantly converted into a magnificent art gallery and the landscaping of the park would have been enormously enhanced. Crowded, ill-favoured Southwark could only have been improved by the circular park centred on St George's Circus – a fine amenity for a neglected area. A trifle fanciful (but somehow right in a melancholy way) would have been the canal approach to Kensal Green Cemetery. The idea of going to the grave in a floating hearse has its charms. Telford's single-span iron bridge would not only have been graceful but a fine monument to 19th-century technology.

The creation of a monumental approach and an open ambiance for St Paul's would have been an act of homage to Wren. Westminster Abbey, we think, would have been improved by the spire suggested by both Wren and Hawksmoor and for which the central, now topless, tower was clearly designed. To switch from a tower sacred to a tower profane, we would very much like to have seen the Eiffel Tower at Wembley. It would have added to the gaiety of London and done no one any harm. *Pax populo Wembliensi*!

Everyone will have his own preferences. Choice is a subjective question of taste. Of special appeal to us is the Georgian crescent on Beulah Hill, Norwood. Much of its charm lies in the total assurance with which the terrace sits above the trees that fringe the ridge of the park. Though obviously influenced by the Royal Crescent at Bath, little is known about this scheme. All that exists is one idealised prospect, the original drawing of which appears lost. The designer is not Decimus Burton, as would be seemly; but this is not really important. The combination of grandeur and simplicity, the building of something gracious for beauty's sake, is its own complete justification.

Beulah Crescent would have been an architectural enrichment to an area that could well do with it, and also be an adornment for London as a whole. How fine to have stepped out on a balcony with a view over several counties of southern England! How rewarding to call on one of the residents, or – even better – to be among those privileged to make this elegant terrace 'a place of permanent abode'! These vicarious pleasures may be incorrigibly romantic and shamefully antiquarian, but it is with this particular vision that we choose to say good-bye to the varied plans for London as it might have been.

Bibliography

The principal reference sources have been: *Catalogue of the Drawings of the Royal Institute of British Architects* (Farnborough: Gregg International, 1969–); *A Biographical Dictionary of British Architects, 1600–1840*, by Howard M. Colvin, 2nd edn. (London: John Murray, 1978); *History of the King's Works*, general editor Howard M. Colvin (London: HMSO, 1963–); *Victorian Architecture*, by James Stevens Curl (Newton Abbot: David & Charles, 1973); 'First Report from Select Committee on Metropolis Improvements', *Parliamentary Papers* (1839), vol. 13; *Catalogue of the Drawings Collection of the Royal Institute of British Architects: Inigo Jones and John Webb*, by John Harris (Farnborough: Gregg International, 1972); *Catalogue of the Drawings Collection of the Royal Institute of British Architects: the Wyatt Family*, Derek Linstrum (Farnborough: Gregg International, 1974); *The Architects of London*, by Alastair Service (London: Architectural Press, 1979); Sir John Summerson's *Architecture in Britain, 1530–1830* (London: Penguin, 1953) and *Georgian London*, 3rd edn. (London: Barrie & Jenkins, 1978); *A Short Dictionary of British Architects*, by Dora Ware (London: Allen & Unwin, 1967).

A great deal of information has also come from journals, chief among which are: the *Architect* (1869–1926); *Architectural History* (1958–); *Architectural Magazine* (1834–9); *Architectural Review* (1896–); *Art Union*, later *Art Journal* (1839–1912); *Athenaeum* (1828–1921); the *Builder* (1842–1966); *Building News* (1857–1926); *Engineering* (1866–); the *Graphic* (1869–1932); *Illustrated London News* (1842–); *John Bull* (1820–92); *London Journal* (1975–); *Nineteenth Century*, later *Twentieth Century* (1877–1950); *Punch* (1841–); *RIBA Journal* (1880–).

CHAPTER 2 : WHITEHALL PLEASURE-DOMES

HARRIS, John, ORGEL, Stephen, and STRONG, Roy, *The King's Arcadia: Inigo Jones and the Stuart Court* (London: Arts Council, 1973). Catalogue of exhibition at Banqueting House.

HARRIS, John, and TAIT, A. A., *Catalogue of the Drawings of Inigo Jones, John Webb, and Isaac de Caus at Worcester College, Oxford* (Oxford: Clarendon Press, 1979).

JONES, Inigo, *The Designs of Inigo Jones, Consisting of Plans and Elevations for Publick and Private Buildings; Published by William Kent with some Additional Designs* (London: W. Kent, 1727).

WHINNEY, Margaret D., 'John Webb's Drawings for Whitehall Palace', *The Thirty-first Volume of the Walpole Society* (London: Walpole Society, 1946).

WHINNEY, Margaret D., *Wren* (London: Thames & Hudson [1971]).

CHAPTER 3 : THE RELUCTANT PHOENIX

EVELYN, John, *London Revived: Considerations for its Rebuilding in 1666*, ed. by E. S. de Beer (Oxford: Clarendon Press, 1938).

REDDAWAY, T. F., *The Rebuilding of London after the Great Fire* (London: Edward Arnold, 1951).

REDDAWAY, T. F., 'The Rebuilding of London after the Great Fire: A Rediscovered Plan', *Town Planning Review*, July 1939.

THORPE, John, 'The Book of Architecture of John Thorpe in Sir John Soane's Museum', ed. by Sir John Summerson, *The Fortieth Volume of the Walpole Society* (London: Walpole Society, 1966).

WARD, John, *The Lives of the Professors of Gresham College . . .* (London: John Moore, 1740).

CHAPTER 4 : EXPERIMENTS TO THE GLORY OF GOD

DOWNES, John Kerry, *Christopher Wren* (London: Allen Lane [1971]).

DOWNES, John Kerry, *Hawksmoor* (London: Zwemmer, 1959).

HUNTING, Penelope, 'From Gothic to Red Brick: The Planning of Westminster Cathedral': *Country Life*, 28 February 1980.

MATTHEWS, W. R. (ed.), *A History of St Paul's Cathedral and the Men Associated with it* (London: Phoenix House, 1957).

PIERCE, S. Rowland, 'A Drawing of a New Spire for Old St Paul's, London', *Antiquaries Journal*, vol. 43 (1963), pp. 128–31.

WHINNEY, Margaret D., *Wren* (London: Thames & Hudson [1971]).

WIBIRAL, Norbert, and PEVSNER, Nikolaus, 'A Westminster Cathedral Episode', *Architectural History*, vol. 20 (1977), pp. 63–4.

WREN, Christopher, *Parentalia: or Memoirs of the Family of the Wrens . . .* (London: Osborn, 1750).

CHAPTER 5 : CROSSING THE RIVER

BENNOCH, Francis, *The Bridges of London: Are More Bridges Needed? Answered Affirmatively* (London: Effingham Wilson, 1853).

BOLTON, Arthur T., *The Portrait of Sir John Soane R.A.* (London: Sir John Soane's Museum [1927]).

BURNS, John, WEBB, Sir Aston, and BLOMFIELD, Reginald, 'The Charing Cross Improvement Scheme', *Observer*, 8, 15, and 22 October 1916.

Exhibition of Designs for a New Bridge at Charing Cross (London: London Society, 1923, Exhibition catalogue).

HARRIS, John, *Sir William Chambers* (London: Zwemmer, 1970).

HAWKSMOOR, Nicholas, *A Short Historical Account of London Bridge with a Proposition for a New Stone-Bridge at Westminster . . .* (London: J. Wilcox, 1736).

KEEN, Arthur, *Charing Cross Bridge* (London: Ernest Benn, 1930).

LANGLEY, Batty, *A Survey of Westminster Bridge as 'tis now Sinking into Ruin . . .* (London: Cooper, 1748).

'Report of Messrs Mott, Hay and Anderson, and Sir George H. Humphries on the Proposed Bridge at Charing Cross', *Parliamentary Papers* (1828–31), vol. 19.

'Report from the Select Committee on Metropolitan Bridges', *Parliamentary Papers*, (1854), vol. 14.

'Report on the Royal Commission on Cross-River Traffic in London', *Parliamentary Papers* (1926), vol. 13.

ROLT, L. T. C., *Thomas Telford* (London: Longmans [1938]).

SOANE, Sir John, *Designs for Public and Private Buildings* (London: Priestley & Weale, *et al* 1828).

The Story of Charing Cross Bridge: Past, Present and Future (London: London Society, 1929). Exhibition catalogue.

STROUD, Dorothy, 'Soane's Design for a Triumphal Bridge', *Architectural Review*, vol. 121 (1957), pp. 260–2.

SUMMERSON, Sir John, *Heavenly Mansions* (London: Cresset Press, 1949), chapter 5: 'The Vision of J. M. Gandy'.

SWINTON, George S. C., *London: Her Traffic, Her Improvement and Charing Cross Bridge* (London: John Murray, 1924).

WELCH, Charles, *History of Tower Bridge* (London: Smith, Elder & Co, 1894).

CHAPTER 6 : PALACES IN THE AIR

CROOK, J. Mordaunt, and PORT, Michael H., *History of the King's Works* vol. 6, 1782–1851 (London: HMSO, 1973).

DOWNES, John Kerry, *English Baroque Architecture* (London: Zwemmer, 1966).

GWYNN, John, *London and Westminster Improved . . .* (London: Author, 1766).

SMITH, H. Clifford, *Buckingham Palace, its Furniture, Decoration and History* (London: Country Life, 1931).

SOANE, Sir John, *Designs for Public and Private Buildings* (London: Priestley, 1828).

SUMMERSON, Sir John, *John Nash: Architect to George IV*, 2nd edn. (London: Allen & Unwin [1949]).

SUMMERSON, Sir John, *Sir John Soane, 1753–1837* (London: Art and Technics, 1952).

TRENCH, Sir Frederick William, *Royal Palaces* (London: Printed by T. Brettell, 1846).

CHAPTER 7 : MONUMENTS TO GENIUS

BEHNES, William, *The 'Nelson Testimonial'; A letter to the Committee Appointed to Select a Design . . .* (London: James Fraser [1839]).

BINDMAN, David, ed., *John Flaxman* (London: Thames & Hudson, 1979).

BRITTON, John, *The Autobiography of John Britton F.S.A.* (London: Author, 1850).

FLAXMAN, John, *A Letter to the Committee for Raising the Naval Pillar or Monument . . .* (London: T. Cadell *et al*, 1799).

HILLARY, Sir William, *Suggestions for the Improvement and Establishment of the Metropolis* (London: Simpkin & Marshall, 1825).

HODGSON, J. E., and EATON, F. A., *The Royal Academy and its Members, 1768–1830* (London: John Murray, 1905).

IRWIN, David, *John Flaxman, 1755–1826* (London: Studio Vista/Christie's, 1979).

[LONG, Charles, 1st Baron Farnborough] *Short Remarks and Suggestions upon Improvements now Carrying on or under Consideration* (London: Hatchard, 1826).

M., M., *Description of a Drawn Model (No. 113) Proposed for the Monument intended to be Erected in Trafalgar Square to the Memory of Lord Nelson* (London: Printed by C. Reynell, 1839).

MACE, Rodney, *Trafalgar Square* (London: Laurence & Wishart, 1976).

NOAKES, Aubrey, *Cleopatra's Needles* (London: Witherby, 1962).

PHYSICK, John, *Designs for English Sculpture, 1680–1860* (London: HMSO, 1969).

ROBINSON, John Martin, *The Wyatts: An Architectural Dynasty* (Oxford U.P., 1979).

WYATT, Lewis, *Prospectus of a Design for Various Improvements in the Metropolis . . . by an Architect* [i.e. Lewis Wyatt] (London: Printed by J. Barsfield, 1816).

CHAPTER 8 : THE THAMES QUAY

FEAVER, William A., *The Art of John Martin* (Oxford: Clarendon Press, 1975).

'First Report of the Royal Commission on Metropolis Improvements', *Parliamentary Papers* (1844), vol. 15.

GILKS, J. Spencer, 'Proposed Thames-Side Elevated Railway', *Railway Magazine*, July 1961.

GWYNN, John, *London and Westminster Improved . . .* (London: Author, 1766).

MARTIN, John, *A Plan for Abundantly Supplying the Metropolis with Pure Water* (London: 1834).

MARTIN, John, *Martin's Thames and Metropolis Improvement Plan: the Object Being to Supply the Metropolis with Pure Water . . . Preserve the Sewage [and] to Improve the Navigation . . .* (London: Ridgeway, 1842).

MARTIN, John, *Thames and Metropolis Improvement Plan* (London: Privately published 1846).

MARTIN, John, *Objections to the Tunnel Sewer Proposed by the Sewage Manure Company . . . together with an Alternative Plan . . .* (London: Author, 1847).

MARTIN, John, *Outline of a Comprehensive Plan for Diverting the Sewage of London and Westminster from the Thames and Applying it to Agricultural Purposes* (London: Wilson, 1850).

PERKS, Sydney, 'The Scheme for a Thames Embankment after the Great Fire of London', *RIBA Journal*, 3rd series, vol. 31 (1924), pp. 445–61.

Report of the Committee Appointed for the Purpose of Taking into Consideration Mr. Martin's Plan for Rescuing the River Thames from every Species of Pollution (London: 1836).

'Report of the Thames Bank Commissioners', *Parliamentary Papers*, (1861), vol. 31.

ROBINSON, John Martin, 'Sir Frederick Trench and London Improvements', *History Today*, May 1977, pp. 324–31.

ROBINSON, John Martin, *The Wyatts: An Architectural Dynasty* (Oxford U.P., 1979).

SMITH, William Henry, *London not as it is but as it should be . . .* (London: Waterlow, 1851).

TRENCH, Sir Frederick William, *A Lithographic Sketch of the North Bank of the Thames, from Westminster Bridge to London Bridge Showing the Proposed Quay and some Other Improvements . . .* (London: Hurst, 1825).

TRENCH, Sir Frederick William, *A Collection of Papers Relating to the Thames Quay; with Hints for some Further Improvements in the Metropolis . . .* (London: Carpenter, 1827).

TRENCH, Sir Frederick William, *Letters from Sir Frederick Trench to Viscount Duncannon, First Commissioner of Woods and Forests.* (London: J. Ollivier, 1841).

CHAPTER 9 : MANY HOUSES OF PARLIAMENT

BARRY, Revd. Alfred, *The Life and Works of Sir Charles Barry R.A., F.R.S.* (London: John Murray, 1867).

Catalogue of the Designs offered for the New Houses of Parliament now Exhibiting in the National Gallery. (London: W. Clowes & Sons, 1836).

COLVIN, Howard M., CROOK, J. Mordaunt, and DOWNES, J. Kerry, *History of the King's Works, vol. 5, 1660–1782* (London: HMSO, 1976).

HOPPER, Thomas, *Designs for the Houses of Parliament ...* (London: Printed for Author [1842?]).

METCALF, Priscilla, *James Knowles: Victorian Editor and Architect* (Oxford U.P., 1980).

'Minutes of Evidence before Select Committee on House of Commons' Buildings', *Parliamentary Papers* (1833) vol. 12.

PORT, Michael H. (ed.) *The Houses of Parliament* (Yale U.P., 1976).

SMIRKE, Sydney, *Suggestions for the Architectural Improvement of the Western Part of London* (London: Priestley & Weale, 1834).

SOANE, Sir John, *Designs for Public and Private Buildings* (London: Priestley, 1828).

THOMPSON, Peter, *Designs for the Proposed New Houses of Parliament* (London: Peter Thompson, 1836).

CHAPTER 10 : BATTLES OF THE GIANTS

CHANCELLOR, E. Beresford, 'The New Westminster: the Vision of Sir Charles Barry', *Architectural Review*, vol. 61 (1927), pp. 207–9.

HOPPER, Thomas, *A Letter to Lord Melbourne on the Rebuilding of the Royal Exchange* (London: John Weale, 1839).

LINSTRUM, Derek, 'Cuthbert Brodrick: An Interpretation of a Victorian Architect', *Journal of the Royal Society of Arts*, CXIX (1972), pp. 72–88.

PHYSICK, John, and DARBY, Michael, *Marble Halls* (London: Victoria and Albert Museum 1973). Exhibition catalogue.

PORT, Michael H., 'The New Law Courts Competition, 1866–67', *Architectural History*, vol. 11 (1978), pp. 75–93.

PORT, Michael H., 'Pride and Parsimony: Influences affecting the Development of the Whitehall Quarter in the 1850s', *London Journal*, vol. 2 (1976), pp. 171–99.

'Report from the Select Committee on Courts of Law and Equity together with the Minutes of Evidence', *Parliamentary Papers* (1842), vol. 10.

RÜNTZ, Ernest, *Suggested Design for London County Council Building, adapted to the vacant site of $2\frac{1}{3}$ acres at the Eastern End of the Victoria Embankment ...* (London: P. A. Gilbert Wood, 1890).

SCOTT, Sir George Gilbert, *Design for the New Law Courts* (London: Day [1867?]).

SCOTT, Sir George Gilbert, *Personal and Professional Recollections ...* ed. by his son, G. Gilbert Scott (London: Sampson Low, 1879).

SHEPPARD, F. H. W. (Gen. Ed.) *Survey of London, vol. 38: The Museums Area of South Kensington and Westminster.* (London: Athlone Press, 1975).

SUMMERSON, Sir John, *Victorian Architecture: Four Studies in Evaluation* (New York: Columbia U.P., 1970).

WATKIN, David, *The Life and Work of C. R. Cockerell* (London: Zwemmer, 1974).

CHAPTER 11 : RAILWAY MANIA

MITCHELL, Joseph, *Practical Suggestions for Relieving the Overcrowded Thoroughfares of London; securing Improved Means of Locomotion; Diverting the Sewage from the Thames, and Appropriating it to Agricultural Use ...* (London: Edward Stanford, 1857).

'Report from the Board of Trade on Schemes for facilitating the Approach to the Metropolis', *Parliamentary Papers* (1845), vol. 39.

'Report from the Select Committee on Metropolitan Communications', *Parliamentary Papers* (1854–5), vol. 10.

'Report from the Select Committee appointed to inquire into the matters of several Petitions, complaining of the Names of certain needy and indigent Persons having been inserted into the Subscription Lists of the Several Railways, and praying for inquiry into the case of the Westminster Bridge, Deptford and Greenwich Railway', *Parliamentary Papers* (1837), vol. 18, pt. 1.

'Report of the Commissioners appointed to investigate the various Projects for establishing Railway Termini within or in the immediate Vicinity of the Metropolis', *Parliamentary Papers* (1846), vol. 17.

SAMUEL, James, and HEPPEL, John M., *The Thames Viaduct Railway* (London: J. B. Nichols & Sons, 1863).

'Second Report from Select Committee on Railway Subscription Lists', *Parliamentary Papers* (1837), vol. 18.

THOMAS, R. H. G., *London's First Railway: The London and Greenwich* (London: Batsford, 1972).

CHAPTER 12 : PYRAMIDS, MAUSOLEUMS AND ANTI-VAMPIRE DEVICES

CURL, James Stevens, *The Victorian Celebration of Death* (Newton Abbot: David & Charles, 1972).

CURL, James Stevens, *The Celebration of Death* (London: Constable, 1980).

Extramural Burial: The Three Schemes: I – The London Clergy Plan; II – The Board of Health or Erith Plan; III – The Woking Necropolis Plan (London: Effingham Wilson, 1850).

Extra-Mural Sepulture: The Government, the Board of Health, and the London Necropolis and the National Mausoleum Company (London: Office of the Company [1851?]).

'Final Report on the Royal Commission Appointed to Inquire into the Present Want of Space for Monuments in Westminster Abbey', *Parliamentary Papers* (1890–1), vol. 44.

'First Report of the Royal Commission Appointed to Inquire into the present Want of Space for Monuments in Westminster Abbey ...', *Parliamentary Papers* (1890–1), vol. 44.

HYLAND, Anthony D. C., 'Imperial Valhalla', *Journal of the Society of Architectural Historians*, October 1962.

LEWIS, R. A., *Edwin Chadwick and the Public Health Movement, 1832–1854* (London: Longmans, 1952).

SMIRKE, Sydney, *Suggestions for the Architectural Improvement of the Western Part of London* (London: Priestley & Weale, 1834).

WALSH, David, 'A Scheme for a Great National Monument', *Strand Magazine*, April 1903.

CHAPTER 13 : THE EIFFEL TOWER AT WEMBLEY

LYNDE, Fred, C., *Descriptive Illustrated Catalogue of the Sixty-Eight Competition Designs for the Great Tower of London*. (London: *Industries*, 1890).

RICHARDS, J. M., 'A Tower for London', *Architectural Review*, vol. 88 (1940), pp. 141–4.

WILSON, Brian, and DAY, John R., 'A London Rival to the Eiffel Tower', *Country Life*, 19 May 1955.

CHAPTER 14 : STRANGE ROADS AND A WESTMINSTER SCANDAL

ACTON, Samuel, *Description of a Design for Improving the Public Ways of Holborn Bridge, Skinner Street, and Fleet Market, and for the Formation of a New Street thence into the High North Road* (London: Printed by Hansard, 1826).

[BARDWELL, William], *Westminster Improvements: A Brief Account of Ancient and Modern Westminster, with Observations on Former Plans of Improvement and on the Objects and Prospects of the Westminster Improvement Company ...* (London: Smith & Elder, 1839).

BLOMFIELD, Sir Reginald, *Richard Norman Shaw R.A.* (London: Batsford, 1940).

BRESSEY, Sir Charles, and LUTYENS, Sir Edwin, *Highway Development Survey 1937 (Greater London)* (London: Ministry of Transport, 1938).

'First Report from the Select Committee on Metropolis Improvements', *Parliamentary Papers* (1837–8), vol. 16.

GWYNN, John, *London and Westminster Improved ...* (London: Author, 1766).

MITCHELL, Joseph, *Practical Suggestions for Relieving the Overcrowded Thoroughfares of London ...* (London: Edward Stanford, 1857).

'Report from Select Committee on the Improvements of Westminster', *Parliamentary Papers* (1831–2), vol. 5.

SAINT, Andrew, *Richard Norman Shaw* (New Haven, Conn.: Paul Mellon Center of Studies in British Art, 1976).

'Second Report from Select Committee on Metropolis Improvement', *Parliamentary Papers* (1840), vol. 12.

STROUD, Dorothy, 'Hyde Park Corner', *Architectural Review*, vol. 106 (1945), pp. 397–9.

CHAPTER 15 : FRUSTRATED POST-WAR PLANS

ABERCROMBIE, Patrick, *Greater London Plan 1944* (London: HMSO, 1945).

Administrative County of London Plan (London County Council, 1955).

BARKER, Felix, *Riverside Highway: The* Evening News *Plan* (London: Associated Newspapers Publication, 1956).

FORSHAW, J. H., and ABERCROMBIE, Patrick, *County of London Plan* (London: Macmillan for LCC, 1943).

Greater London Development Plan (London: HMSO for Department of the Environment, 1973).

HOLFORD, Sir William, *Report to the Common Council of the Corporation of London on an Area South and West of St Paul's Cathedral ...* (London: Holford, 1968).

HOLFORD, Sir William, *Report to the Court of Common Council of the Corporation of the City of London on the Precincts of St Paul's* (London: Holford, 1956).

HUTCHINSON, David, and WILLIAMS, Stephanie, 'South Bank Saga', *Architectural Review*, September 1976.

LINDY, Kenneth J., and LEWIS, B. A. P. Winton, 'Sketch Plan for the City of London', *Parthenon*, April 1944.

London Replanned: The Royal Academy Planning Committee's Interim Report (London: Country Life, 1942).

RAWLINSON, Sir Joseph, and DAVIDGE, William Robert, *City of Westminster Plan* (Westminster City Council, 1946).

CHAPTER 16 : THE GREAT PICCADILLY CIRCUS RUMPUS

BUCHANAN, Sir Colin, *Development of the Monico Site at Piccadilly Circus: Report to the Minister of Housing and Local Government*. Stencilled typescript, n.d.

HOLFORD, Sir William, *Piccadilly Circus Future Development* (London County Council, 1962).

LEVIN, Bernard, 'The Monster of Piccadilly Circus', *Spectator*, 11 December, 1959.

1988 Olympic Games Feasibility Study (London: Greater London Council, 1979).

PADOVAN, Richard, 'The Vessel and the Empty Space', *International Architect*, vol. 1, no. 1 (1979) – for Hammersmith Centre.

CHAPTER 17 : THE AWKWARD SQUAD

DICKINSON, Henry Winram, and TITLEY, Arthur, *Richard Trevithick: The Engineer and the Man ...* (Cambridge U.P., 1934).

ELSOM, John and TOMLIN, Nicholas, *The History of the National Theatre* (London: Jonathan Cape, 1978).

FAWKES, Richard, *Dion Boucicault* (London: Quartet Books, 1979) – for 'Alpine Pleasures for Lambeth'.

PERKS, Sydney, *The History of the Mansion House* (Cambridge U.P., 1922).

PEVSNER, Nikolaus, 'John Bodt in England', *Architectural Review*, vol. 130 (1961), pp. 29–34 – for 'Les Invalides for Greenwich'.

ROSENTHAL, Harold, *The Mapleson Memoirs* (London: Putnam, 1966) – for 'Scotland Yard Opera House'.

TREVITHICK, Francis, *Life of Richard Trevithick, with an Account of his Inventions*. (London: Spon, 1872).

WARWICK, Alan R., *The Phoenix Suburb* (London: Blue Boar Press, 1972) – for 'A Bath for Norwood'.

Index

Sources of Illustrations

Plates 8, 24, 43A, 43B, 50, and 52 are reproduced by gracious permission of Her Majesty the Queen. The following individuals, firms and institutions are also thanked for permitting material in their collections to be used: Aerofilms Ltd, Boreham Wood, for the modern aerial photograph employed for Plate 6; All Souls College, Oxford, 9, 10, 15, 16, 18; Associated Newspapers Ltd, London, 143; BBC Hulton Picture Library, London, 162A, 162B; W. & F.C. Bonham & Sons Ltd, London, 1 (portrait photographed when in their sale room); British Architectural Library, RIBA, London, 34, 46, 51, 56A, 74, 87B, 87C, 89, 94, 95, 98, 113, 114, 116, 129, 158, 160, 163; British Library, Department of Manuscripts, 14; the Trustees of the British Museum, 54; the Calthrop/Boucicault Collection (see Richard Fawkes, *Dion Boucicault: A Biography)*, 155; the Trustees of the Chatsworth Settlement, 3; Christie's, 38 (portrait photographed when in their sale room; *Contract Journal*, 97; Corporation of London Record Office, 29 (Surveyors Bridges Plan 271), 30 (Surveyors Bridges Plan 281), 35 (I.3.a); Foster Associates Ltd, London, 147; Mr Fowke Mangeot, 86, 87A; the *Graphic* (1881), 80E; Greater London Council Prints Collection, 68, 88; Greenwich Local History Library, 57, 102, 156; Guildhall Library, City of London, 2, 11, 12, 13, 18, 20, 22, 23, 27, 28, 31, 32, 33, 37, 39, 44, 48, 58, 60, 64, 70, 72, 75, 76, 78, 79, 80B, 80C, 80F, 81, 83, 84, 85, 90, 92, 93, 99, 100, 101, 103, 104, 105A, 105B, 105C, 106, 108, 109, 111, 112, 117, 122, 131, 132, 133, 134, 135, 136, 137, 138A, 138B, 139, 141, 142, 149, 151, 152, 157, 159, 161, 164; Sir H.B. Huntington-Whitely, 65; Lady Lever Art Gallery, Port Sunlight, 62; Mary Evans Picture Library, London, 110; Museum of London, 130; National Portrait Gallery, London, 25A, 25C, 61, 63, 80D, 91, 140; Peter Jackson Collection, London, title-page illustration, 53, 55, 59, 66; Public Record Office, London, 73 (Works 29/47), 77 (Works 29/64); Dean and Chapter of St Paul's Cathedral, 17; Keeper of the Records of Scotland, Scottish Record Office, Edinburgh, 36 (RHP 13256/8); the Trustees of Sir John Soane's Museum, London, 26, 40, 41, 42, 71, 96, 128, 148, 150; Times Newspapers Ltd, London, 145; Victoria and Albert Museum, London 56B, 56C, 67, 69; Walker Art Gallery, Liverpool, 25B; Mrs Alan A. Warwick, 154; Wembley History Society, Grange Museum, 118, 119, 120, 121, 123, 124, 125, 126; the Dean and Chapter of Westminster, 19, 21; Archives Department, Westminster City Libraries, 45, 47, 49, 153; and Worcester College, Oxford, 4, 5.